DEAR CREATURE

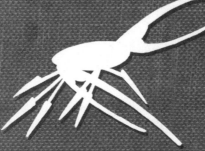

JONATHAN CASE

TOR®

A Tom Doherty Associates Book
New York

This is a work of fiction. All of the characters, organizations, and events portrayed in this graphic novel are either products of the author's imagination or are used fictitiously.

DEAR CREATURE

A Tor Book
Published by Tom Doherty Associates, LLC
175 Fifth Avenue
New York, NY 10010

www.tor-forge.com

ISBN 978-0-7653-3111-3

First Edition: October 2011

Printed in the United States of America

0 9 8 7 6 5 4 3 2 1

Table of Contents

Introduction by Steve Lieber

Eisner Award-winning artist of *Whiteout* and *Underground*

It's hard to imagine a more impressive comics debut than *Dear Creature* by Jonathan Case. He's come out of nowhere with one of the best original graphic novels anyone has seen in years, flooring everyone with his triple-threat abilities.

It's common for a new comic book creator to produce handsome drawings or have a fresh ear for dialogue. It's considerably less common for a cartoonist to arrive on the scene displaying fluency with the formal aspects of comic book storytelling. But that happens, too. All three? You just don't see debuts like that. Until now.

In his drawing, Jonathan deploys a palate of stark black and white. There's no crosshatching to make soft grays, just perfectly chosen lines and shapes. His technique is simple, but the result is never sterile, cold, or distancing. Every panel is bursting with graphic energy: dynamic compositions, expressive gestures, and thoroughly imagined and varied people, monsters, props, and environments.

The writing in *Dear Creature* is equally accomplished. There's such joy and variety in the cast's voices. If you black out the pictures and only read the balloons, the characters are still vivid and distinct: Grue's Elizabethan iambic pentameter; the crab chorus's Runyonesque wise-guy chatter; Zola's passionate, operatic English-as-a-second-language; Officer Craw's cowboy straight talk; Giulietta's fearful hesitation.

But in comics, it's impossible to separate the pictures from the writing. This isn't illustrated prose, with pictures included to decorate the text. This is comics; the pictures ARE the text. Every scene in *Dear Creature* turns on purely visual storytelling choices.

Comics is also a rhythmic art, and this story gets much of its impact from the way abstract visual elements are juxtaposed. In these pages, Case displays an unerring instinct for leading the eye around the page. He knows when to build pictures out of drifting horizontals or bursting diagonals. He designs cool areas of unmarked white or black and juxtaposes them with warm tracts of precisely rendered texture. He arranges forms in space to create calm or chaos, as appropriate. This is one of the most difficult things about making comics.

But all this would be empty technique if it wasn't in service of a great story. *Dear Creature* is a glorious mash-up of wildly disparate influences: Fellini, Frankenstein, Frankie and Annette, Shakespeare, Roy Orbison, and God only knows what else. There's humor, horror, adventure, compassion, lunatic spectacle, and a couple of unlikely romances. It's a big, risky story and it shouldn't work at all. But it does, unified by its compelling atmosphere, appealing characters, utterly sincere love story, and the considerable taste and talent of its creator.

ANTIPHOLUS of SYRACUSE:

Sweet mistress— what your name is else, I know not,
Nor by what wonder you do hit of mine—
Less in your knowledge and your grace you show not
Than our earth's wonder, more than earth divine.
Teach me, dear creature, how to think and speak;
Lay open to my earthy-gross conceit,
Smother'd in errors, feeble, shallow, weak,
The folded meaning of your words' deceit.

     —The Comedy of Errors, Act 3, Scene 2
     William Shakespeare

CHAPTER ONE
only the lonely

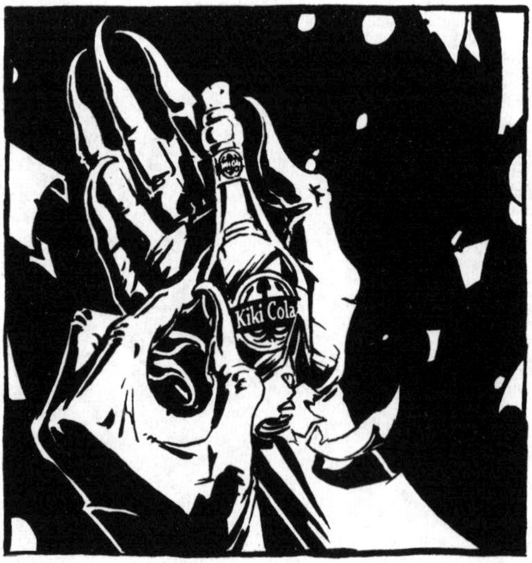
Kiki Cola

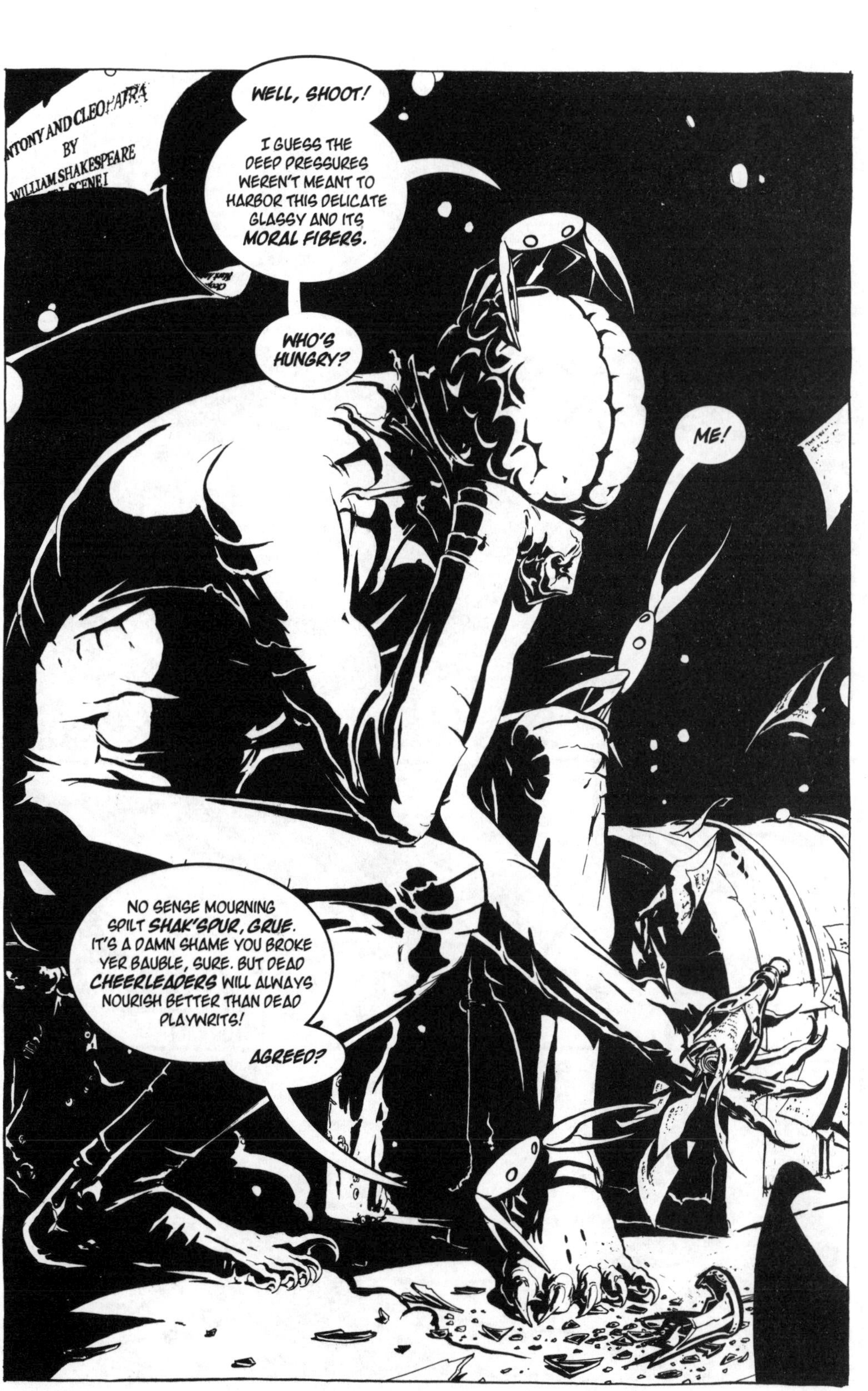
ANTONY AND CLEOPATRA
BY
WILLIAM SHAKESPEARE
WELL, SHOOT!
I GUESS THE DEEP PRESSURES WEREN'T MEANT TO HARBOR THIS DELICATE GLASSY AND ITS MORAL FIBERS.
WHO'S HUNGRY?
ME!
NO SENSE MOURNING SPILT SHAK'SPUR, GRUE. IT'S A DAMN SHAME YOU BROKE YER BAUBLE, SURE. BUT DEAD CHEERLEADERS WILL ALWAYS NOURISH BETTER THAN DEAD PLAYWRITS!
AGREED?

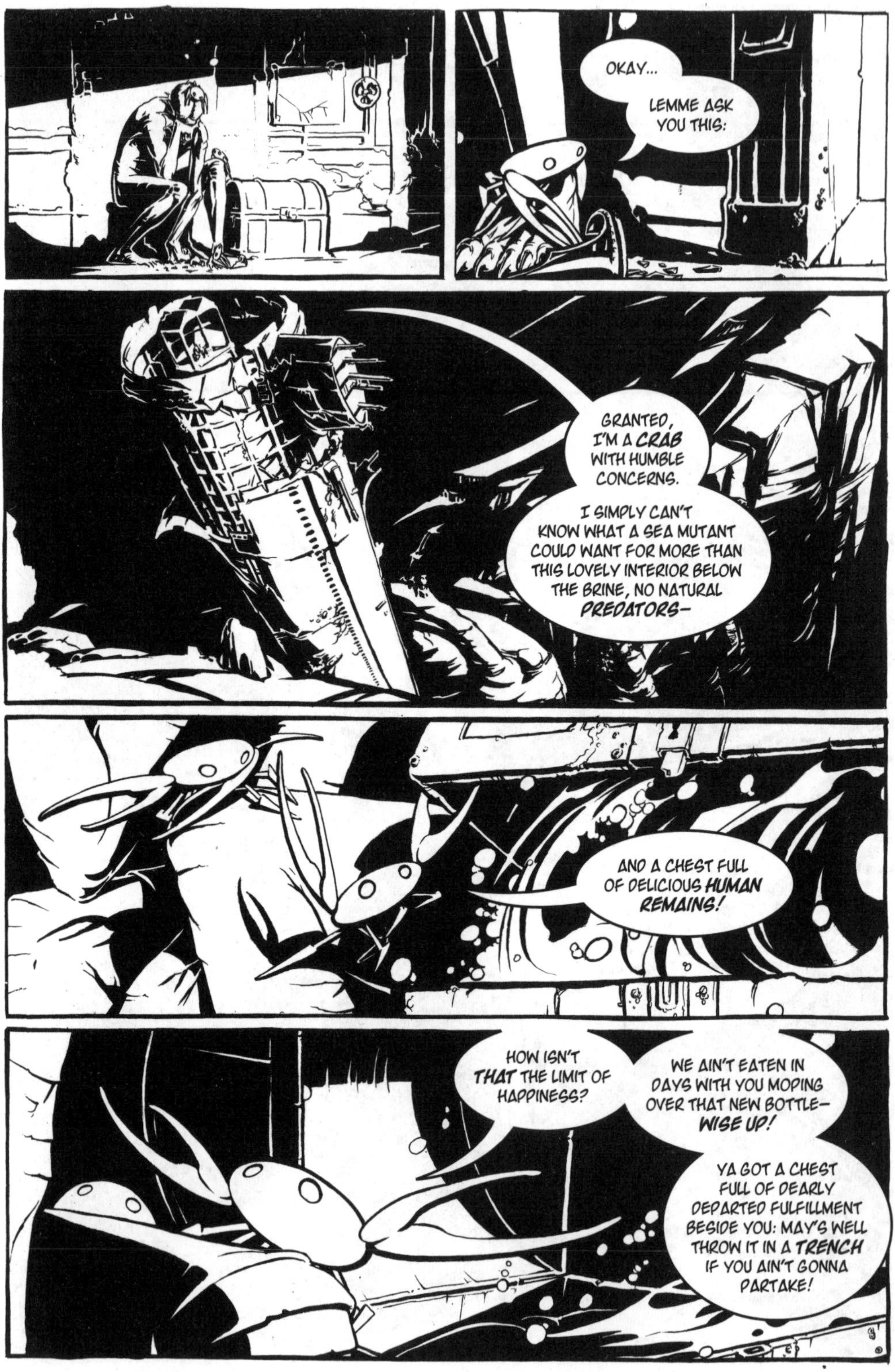
OKAY...
LEMME ASK YOU THIS:
GRANTED, I'M A CRAB WITH HUMBLE CONCERNS.
I SIMPLY CAN'T KNOW WHAT A SEA MUTANT COULD WANT FOR MORE THAN THIS LOVELY INTERIOR BELOW THE BRINE, NO NATURAL PREDATORS–
AND A CHEST FULL OF DELICIOUS HUMAN REMAINS!
HOW ISN'T THAT THE LIMIT OF HAPPINESS?
WE AIN'T EATEN IN DAYS WITH YOU MOPING OVER THAT NEW BOTTLE– WISE UP!
YA GOT A CHEST FULL OF DEARLY DEPARTED FULFILLMENT BESIDE YOU: MAY'S WELL THROW IT IN A TRENCH IF YOU AIN'T GONNA PARTAKE!

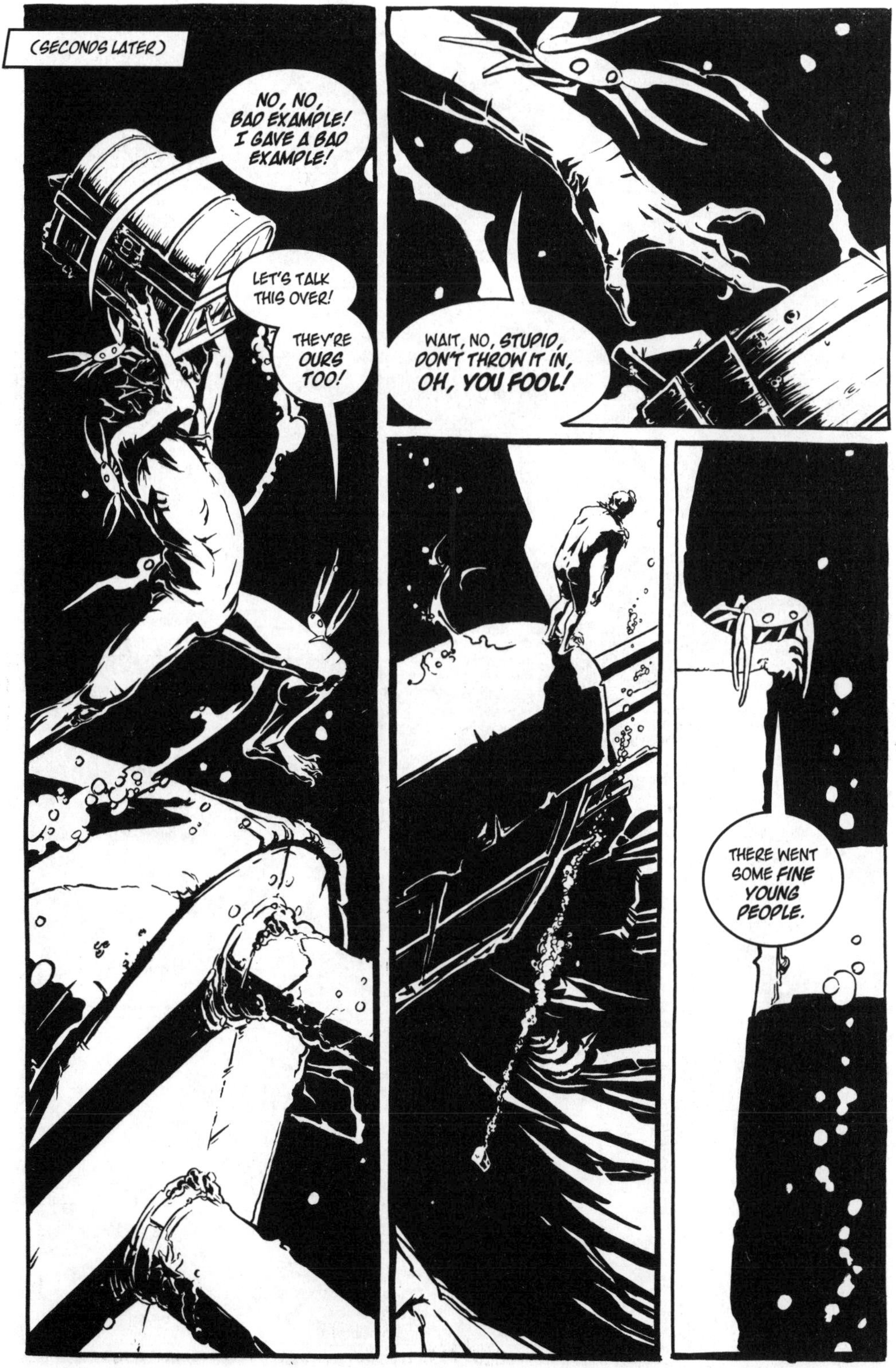
(SECONDS LATER)
NO, NO, BAD EXAMPLE! I GAVE A BAD EXAMPLE!
LET'S TALK THIS OVER!
THEY'RE OURS TOO!
WAIT, NO, STUPID, DON'T THROW IT IN, OH, YOU FOOL!
THERE WENT SOME FINE YOUNG PEOPLE.

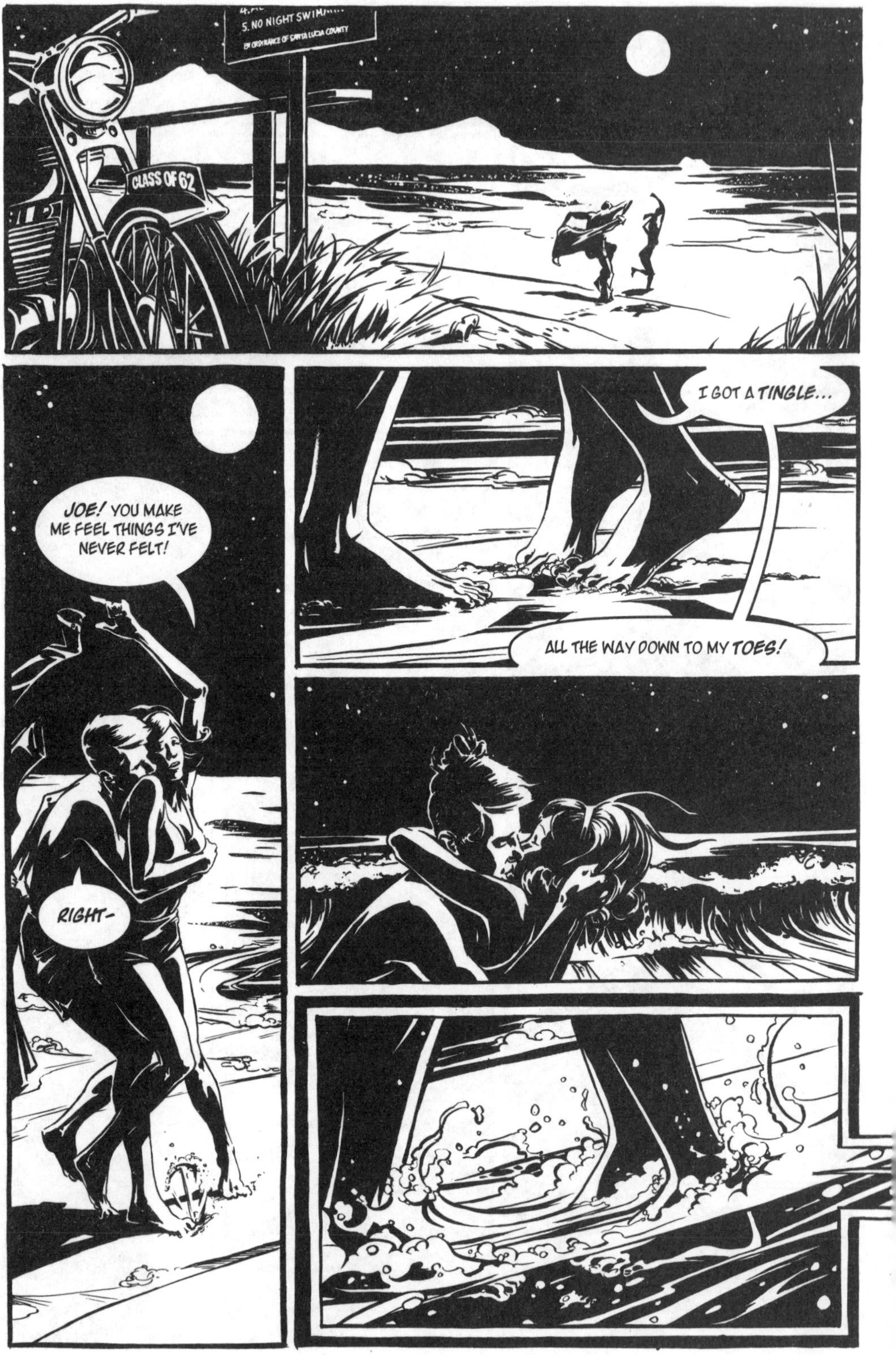
5. NO NIGHT SWIM
BY ORDINANCE OF SANTA LUCIA COUNTY
CLASS OF 62
JOE! YOU MAKE ME FEEL THINGS I'VE NEVER FELT!
RIGHT-
I GOT A TINGLE...
ALL THE WAY DOWN TO MY TOES!

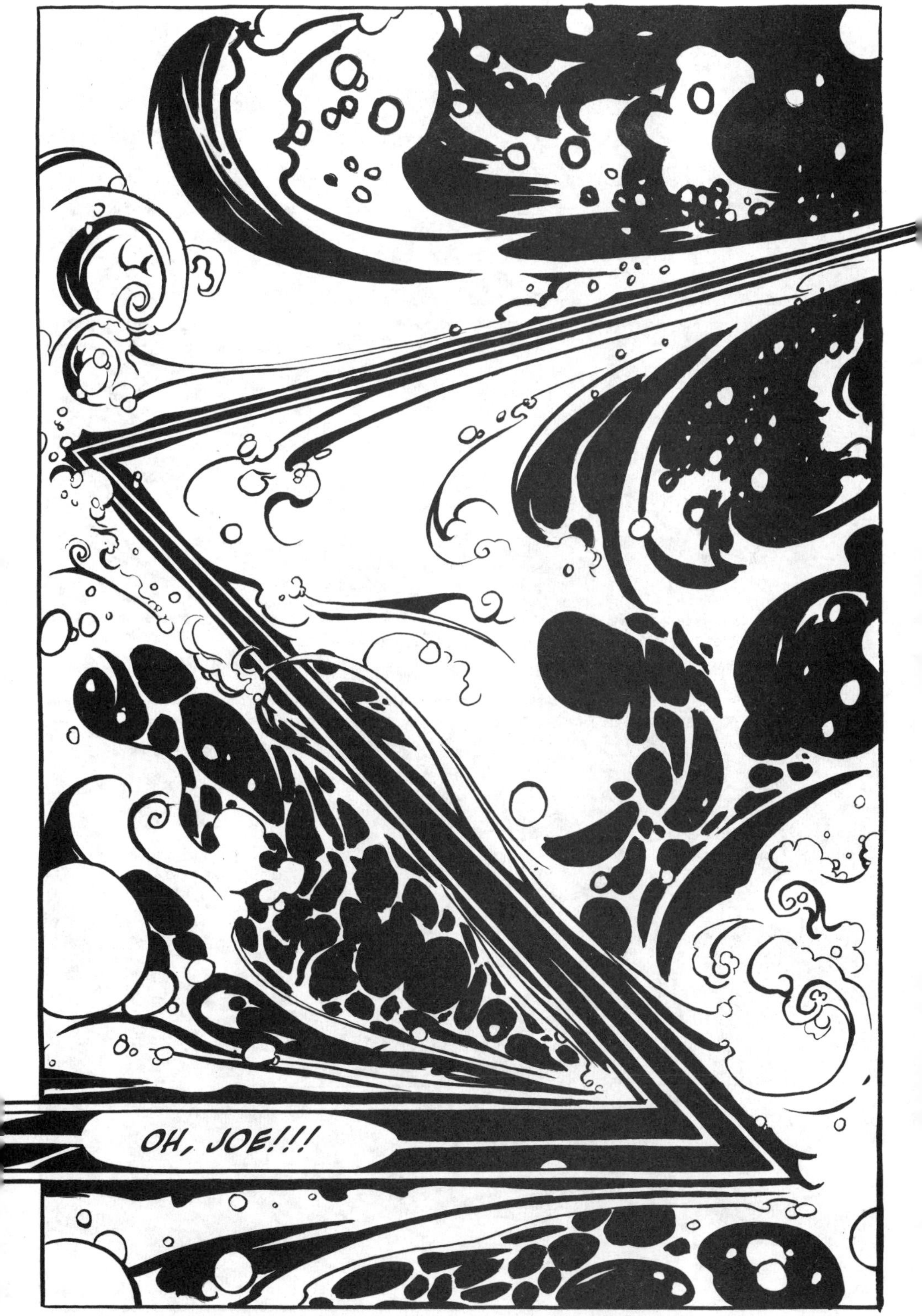
OH, JOE!!!

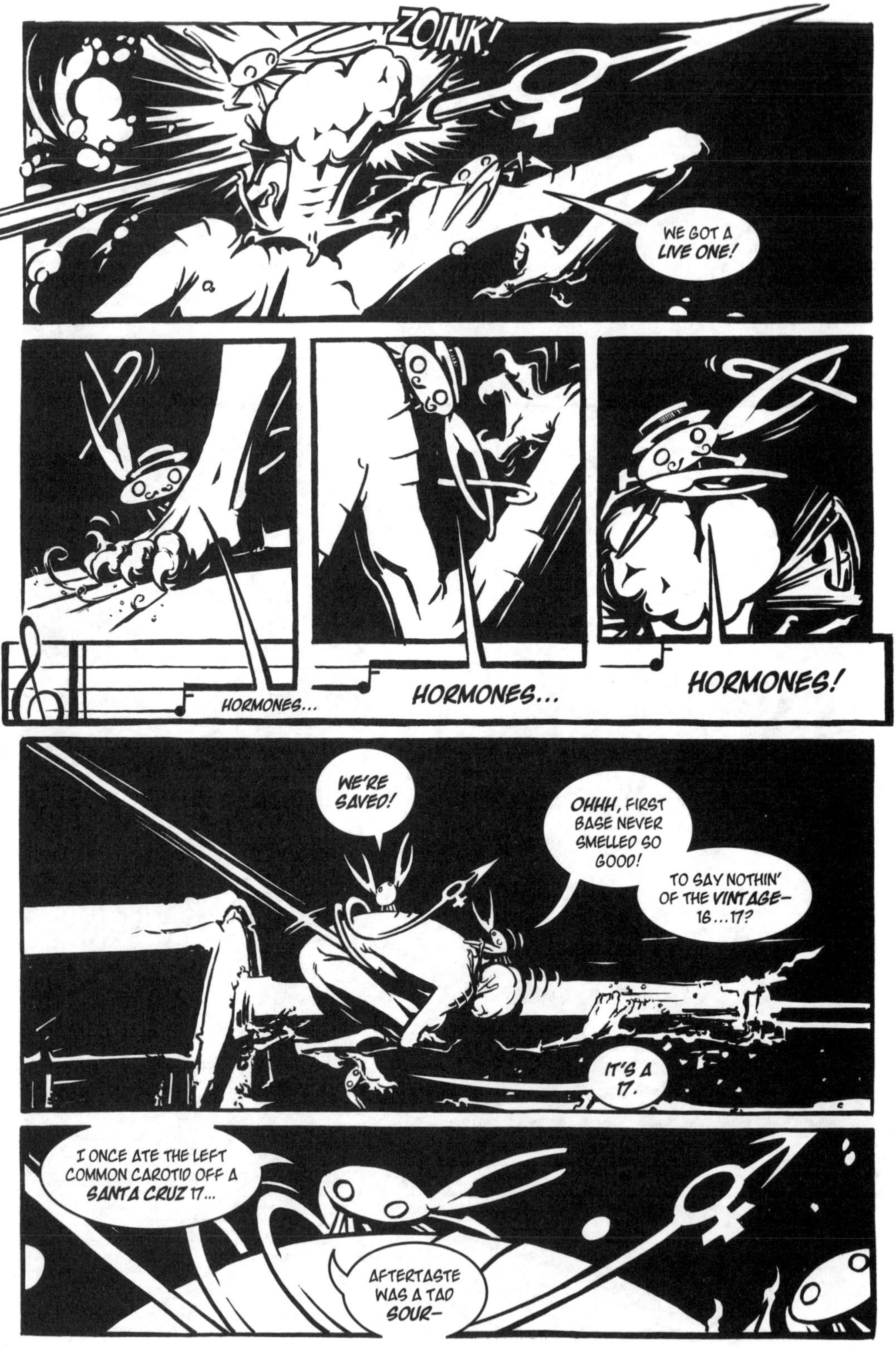
ZOINK!
WE GOT A LIVE ONE!
HORMONES...
HORMONES...
HORMONES!
WE'RE SAVED!
OHHH, FIRST BASE NEVER SMELLED SO GOOD!
TO SAY NOTHIN' OF THE VINTAGE- 16...17?
IT'S A 17.
I ONCE ATE THE LEFT COMMON CAROTID OFF A SANTA CRUZ 17...
AFTERTASTE WAS A TAD SOUR-

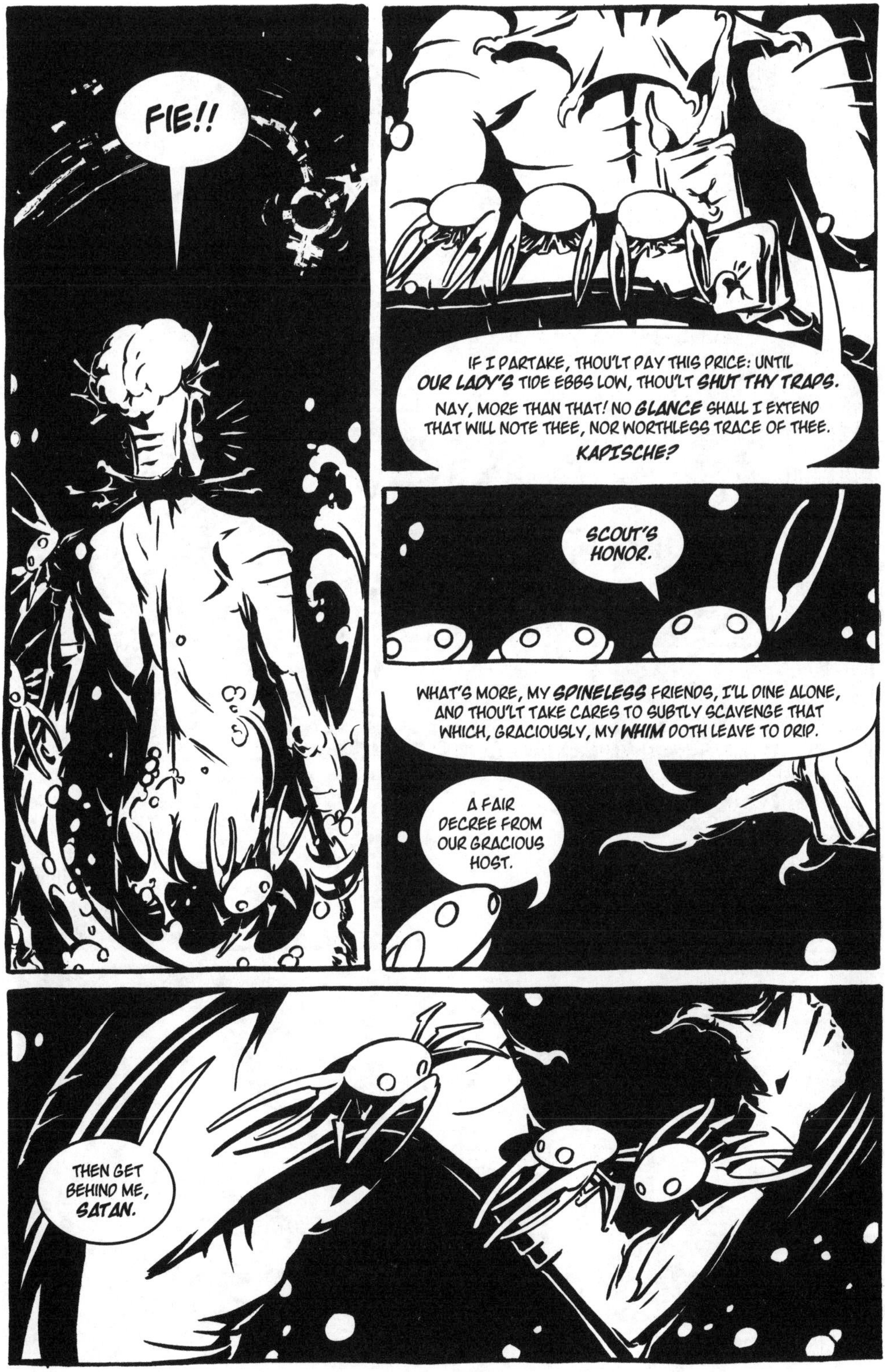
FIE!!
IF I PARTAKE, THOU'LT PAY THIS PRICE: UNTIL OUR LADY'S TIDE EBBS LOW, THOU'LT SHUT THY TRAPS.
NAY, MORE THAN THAT! NO GLANCE SHALL I EXTEND THAT WILL NOTE THEE, NOR WORTHLESS TRACE OF THEE.
KAPISCHE?
SCOUT'S HONOR.
WHAT'S MORE, MY SPINELESS FRIENDS, I'LL DINE ALONE, AND THOU'LT TAKE CARES TO SUBTLY SCAVENGE THAT WHICH, GRACIOUSLY, MY WHIM DOTH LEAVE TO DRIP.
A FAIR DECREE FROM OUR GRACIOUS HOST.
THEN GET BEHIND ME, SATAN.

The worm of conscience still begnaw thy soul!
...rest for traitors while thou liv...

SLAM

18

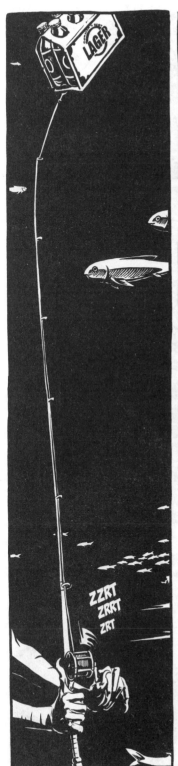

YOU'RE SO GOOD OH, *JOE!* ...TELL ME YOU LOVE ME!

TELL ME, *JOE!* THERE'S NOTHING I WANT MORE!

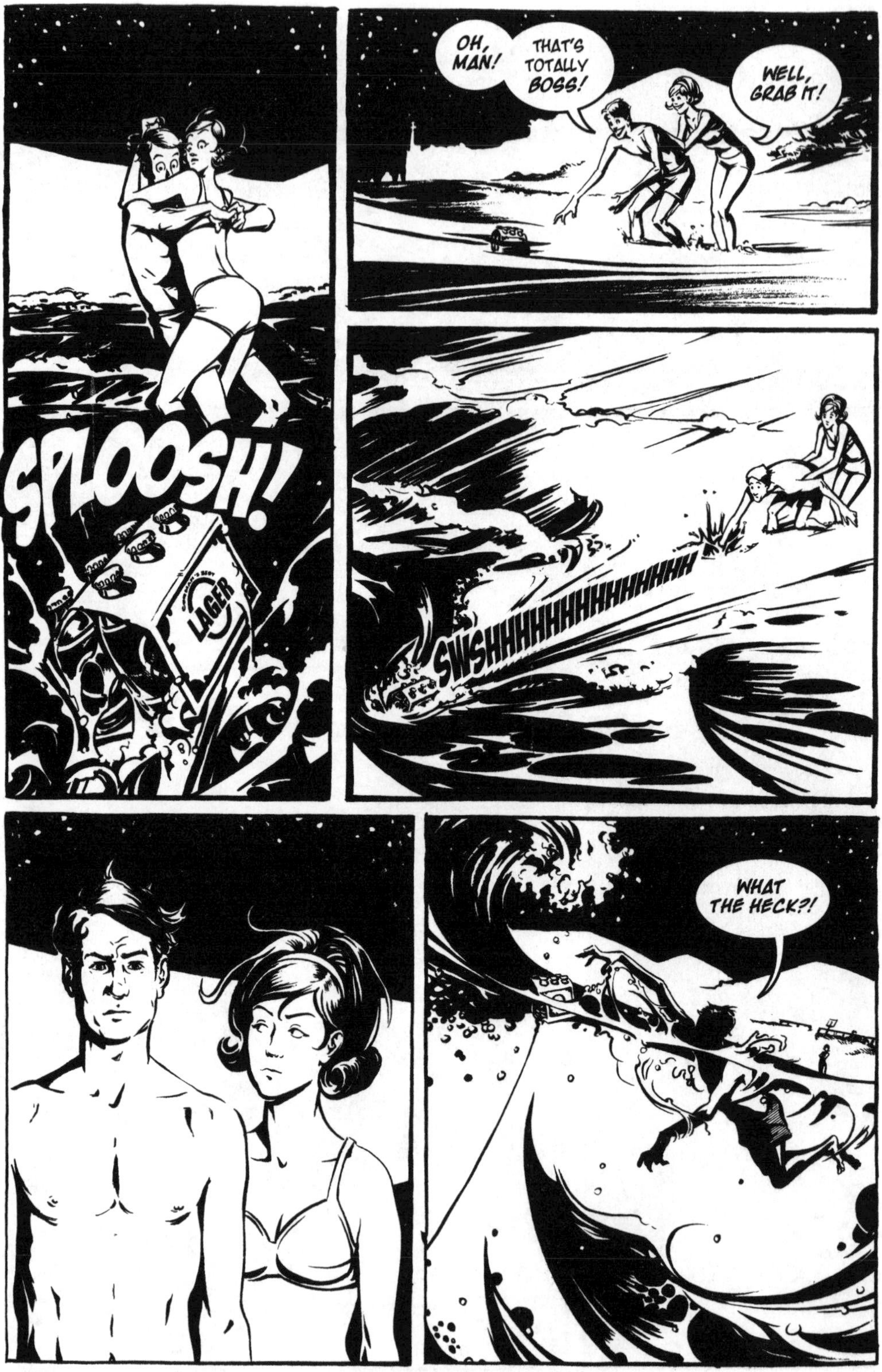
SPLOOSH!
LAGER
OH, MAN!
THAT'S TOTALLY BOSS!
WELL, GRAB IT!
SWSHHHHHHHHHHHHHHHHHH
WHAT THE HECK?!

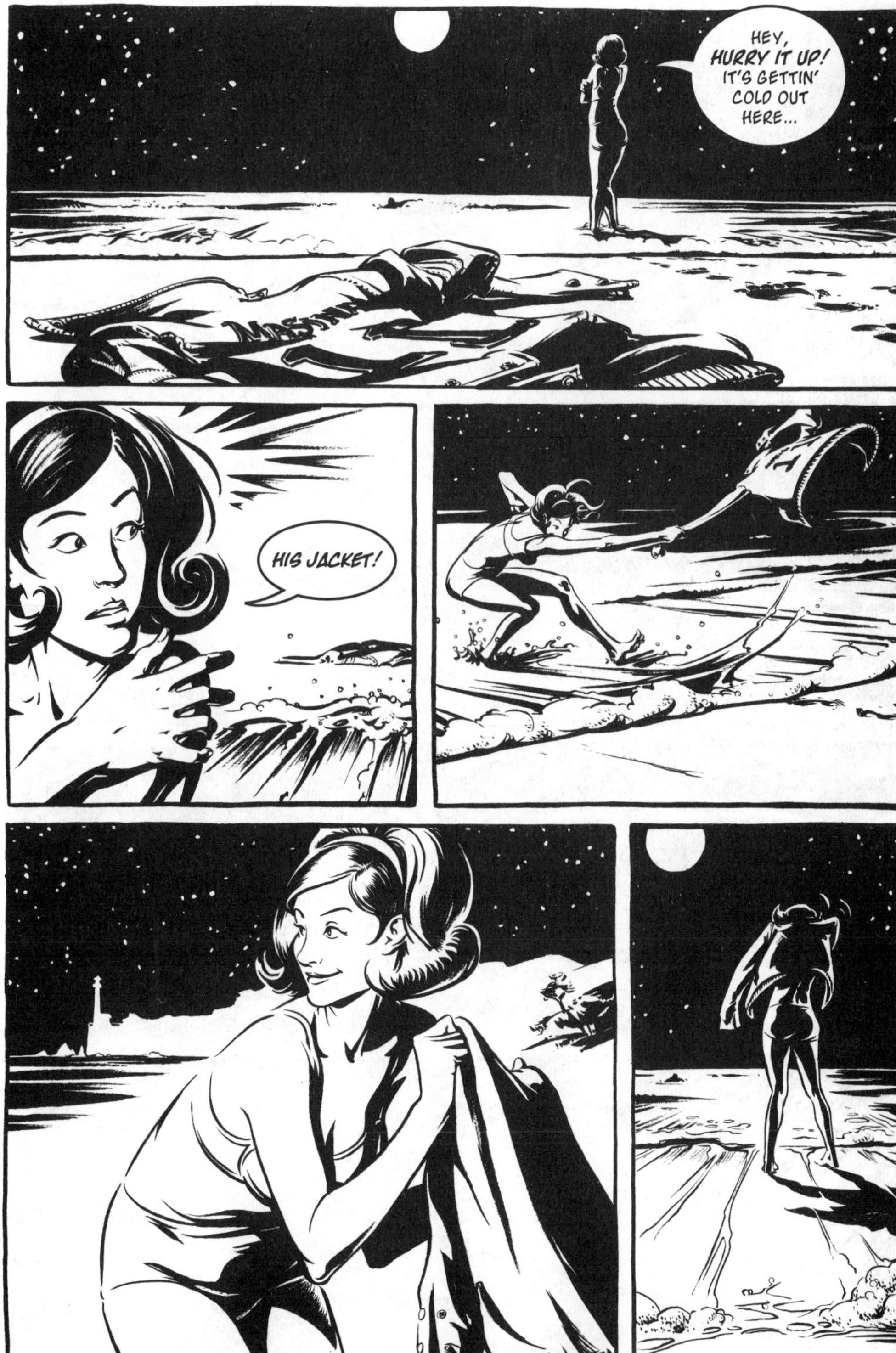
HEY, HURRY IT UP! IT'S GETTIN' COLD OUT HERE...
HIS JACKET!

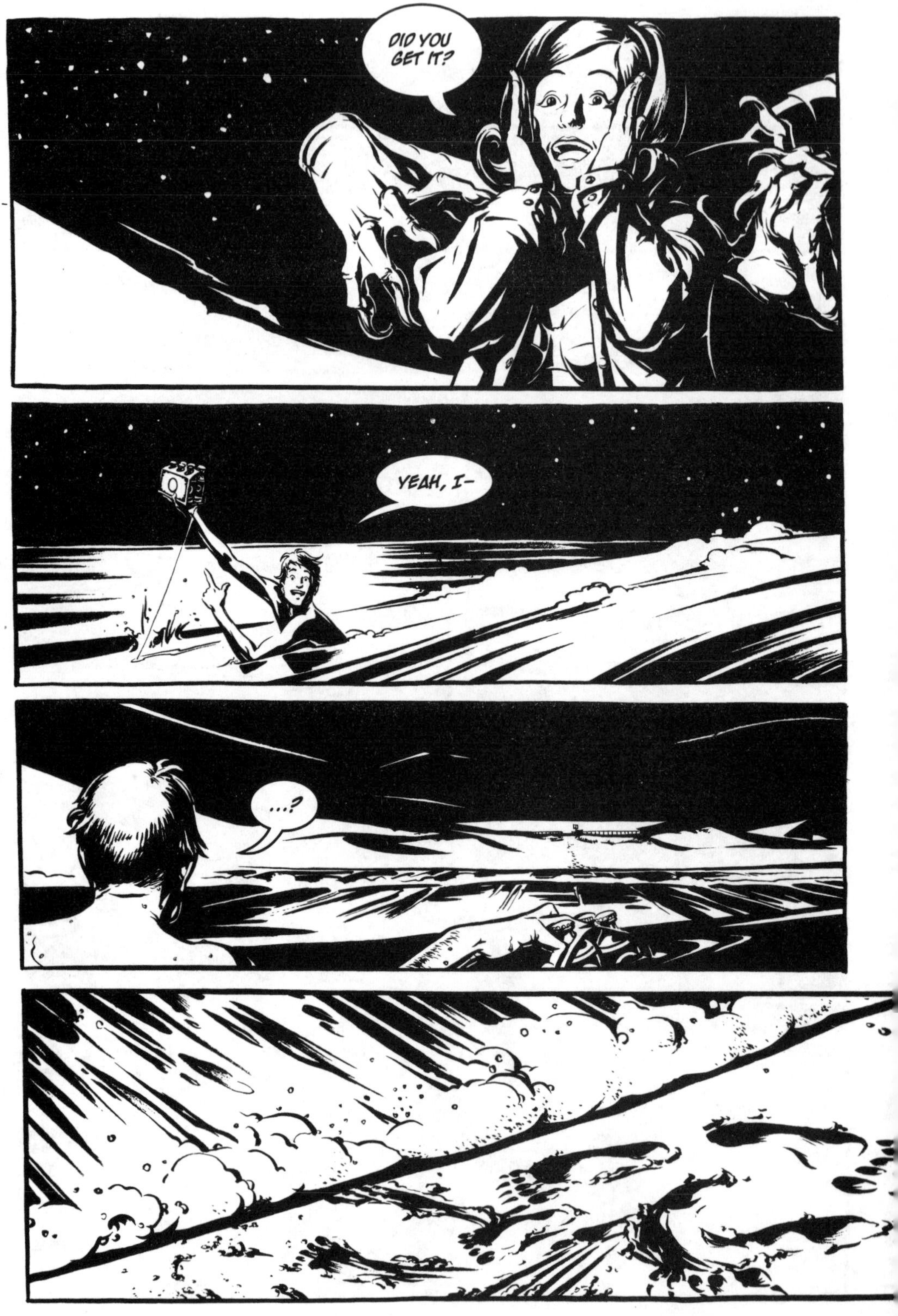
DID YOU GET IT?
YEAH, I-
...?

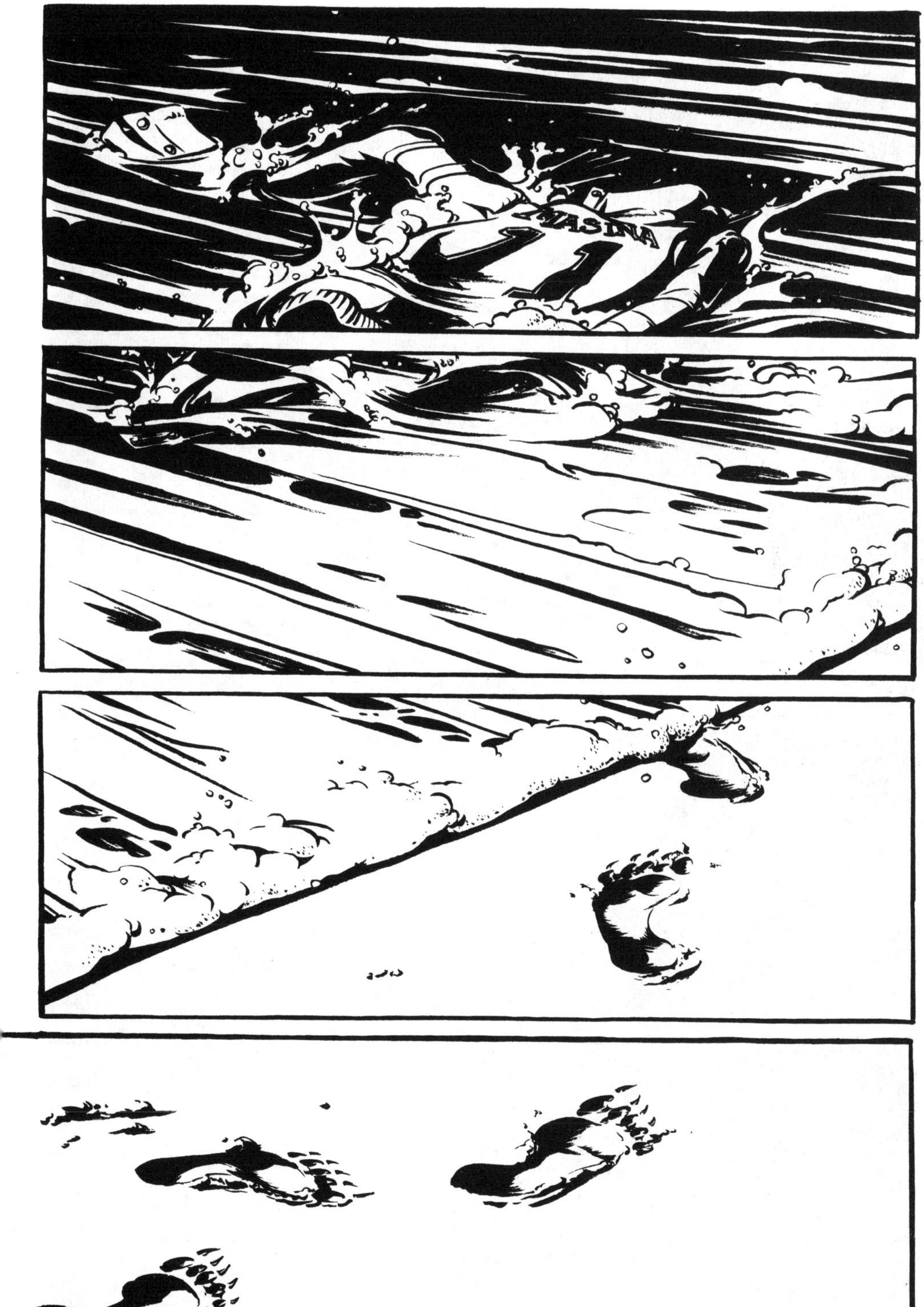
MASINA

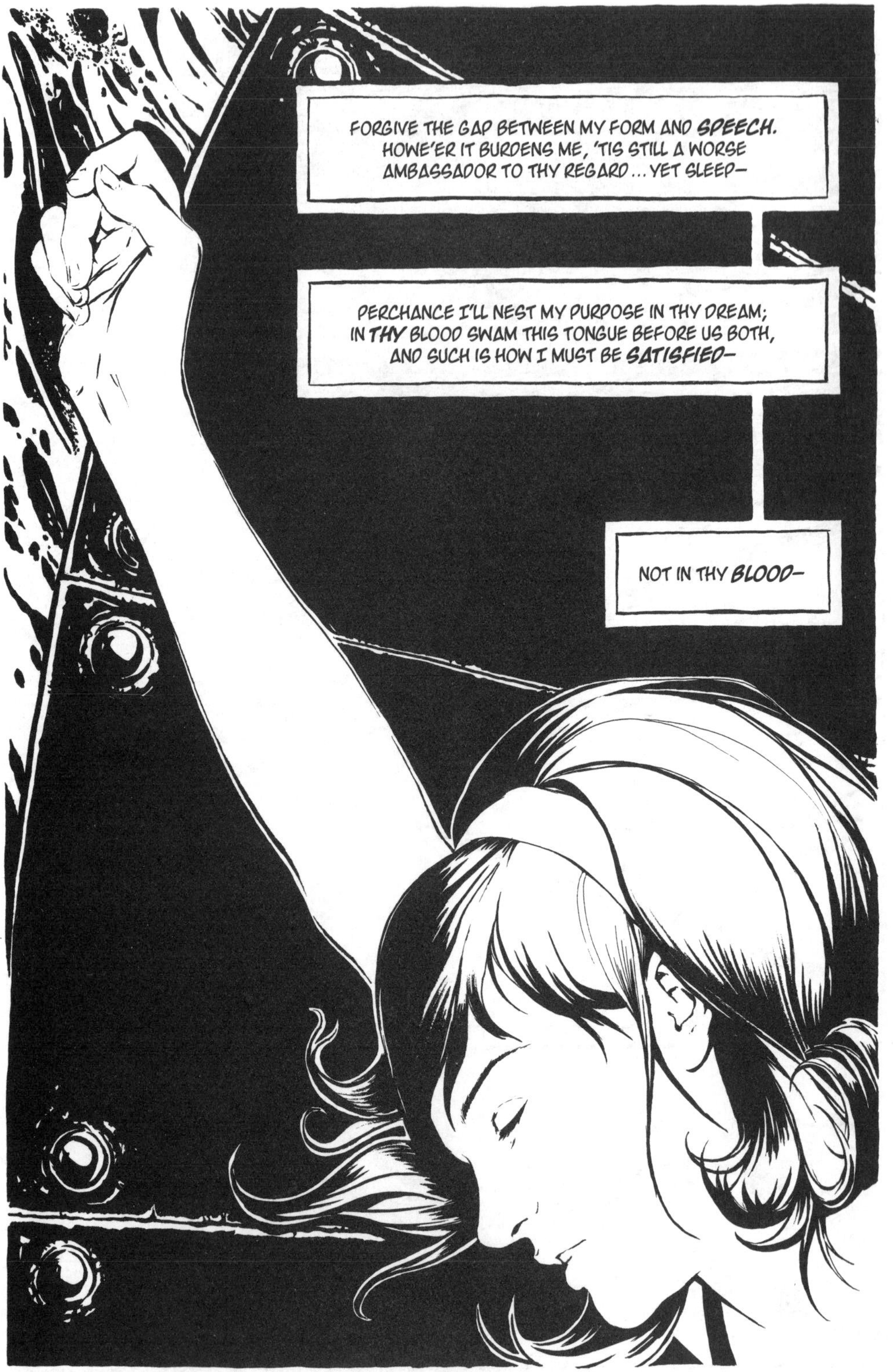
FORGIVE THE GAP BETWEEN MY FORM AND SPEECH. HOWE'ER IT BURDENS ME, 'TIS STILL A WORSE AMBASSADOR TO THY REGARD... YET SLEEP–
PERCHANCE I'LL NEST MY PURPOSE IN THY DREAM; IN THY BLOOD SWAM THIS TONGUE BEFORE US BOTH, AND SUCH IS HOW I MUST BE SATISFIED–
NOT IN THY BLOOD–

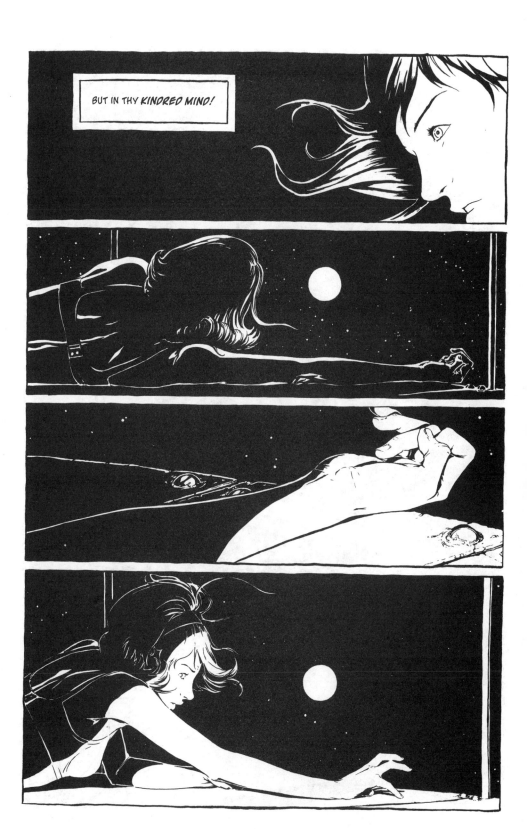

BUT IN THY *KINDRED MIND!*

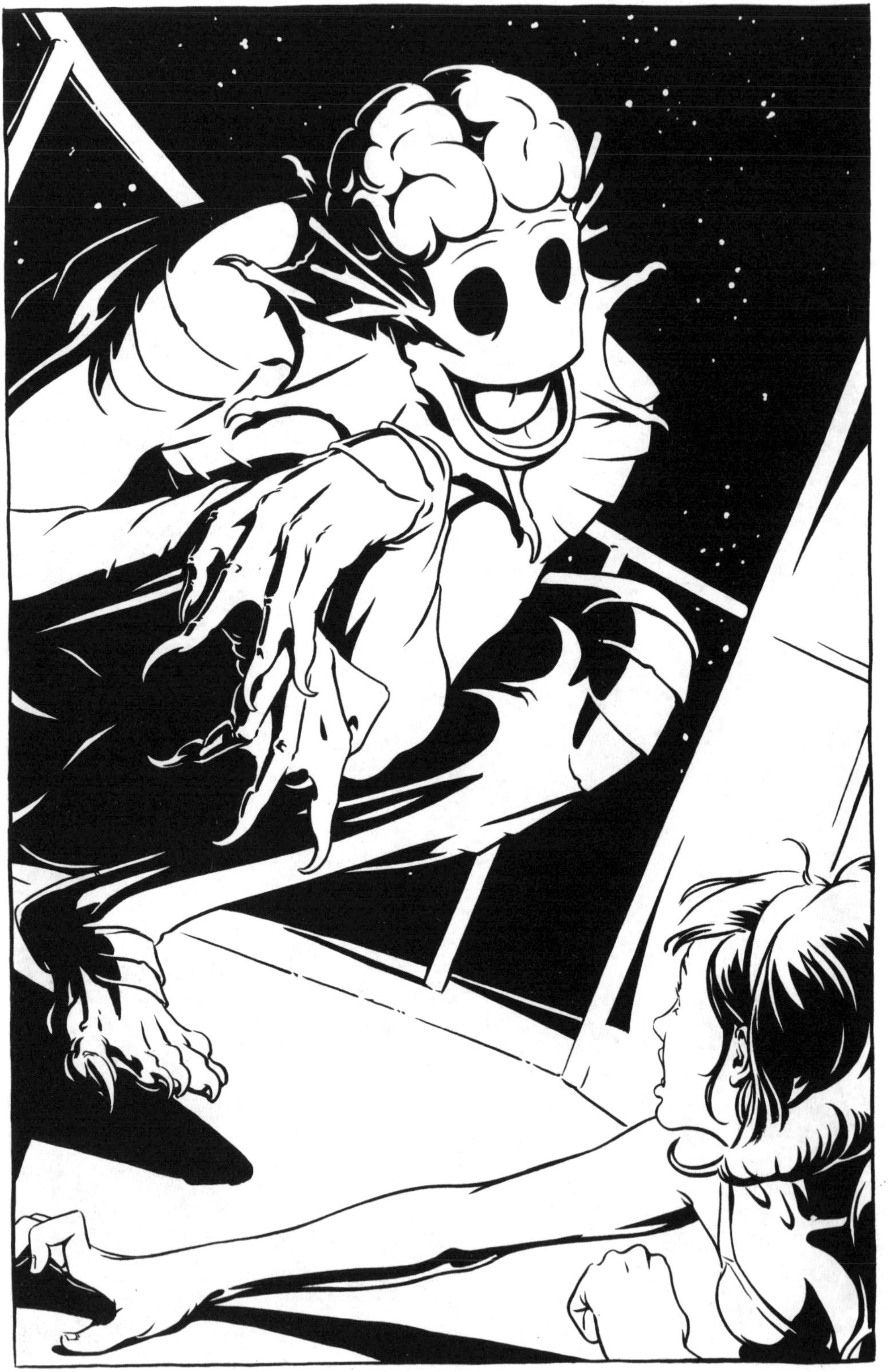

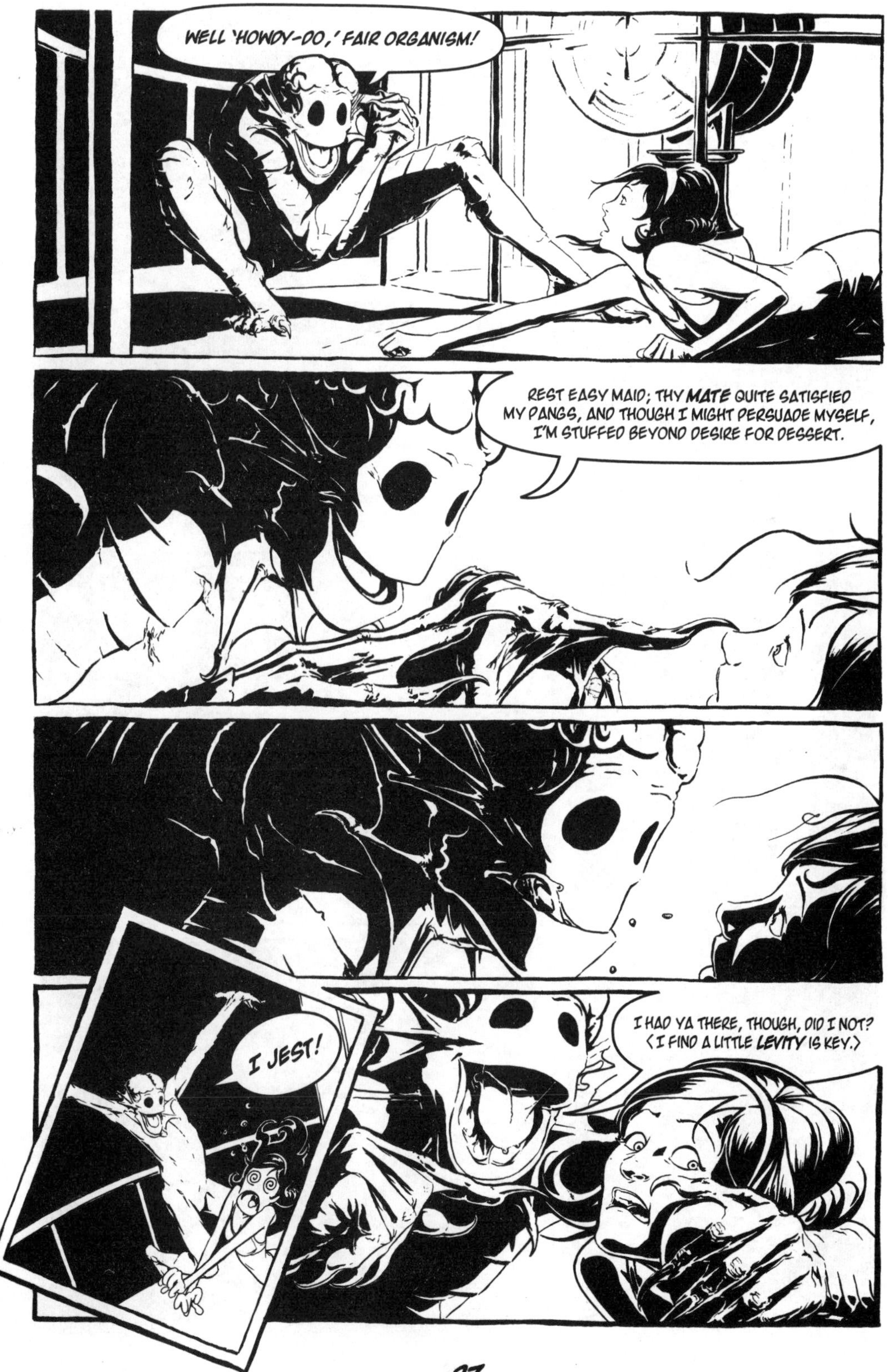
WELL 'HOWDY-DO,' FAIR ORGANISM!
REST EASY MAID; THY MATE QUITE SATISFIED MY PANGS, AND THOUGH I MIGHT PERSUADE MYSELF, I'M STUFFED BEYOND DESIRE FOR DESSERT.
I JEST!
I HAD YA THERE, THOUGH, DID I NOT? <I FIND A LITTLE LEVITY IS KEY.>

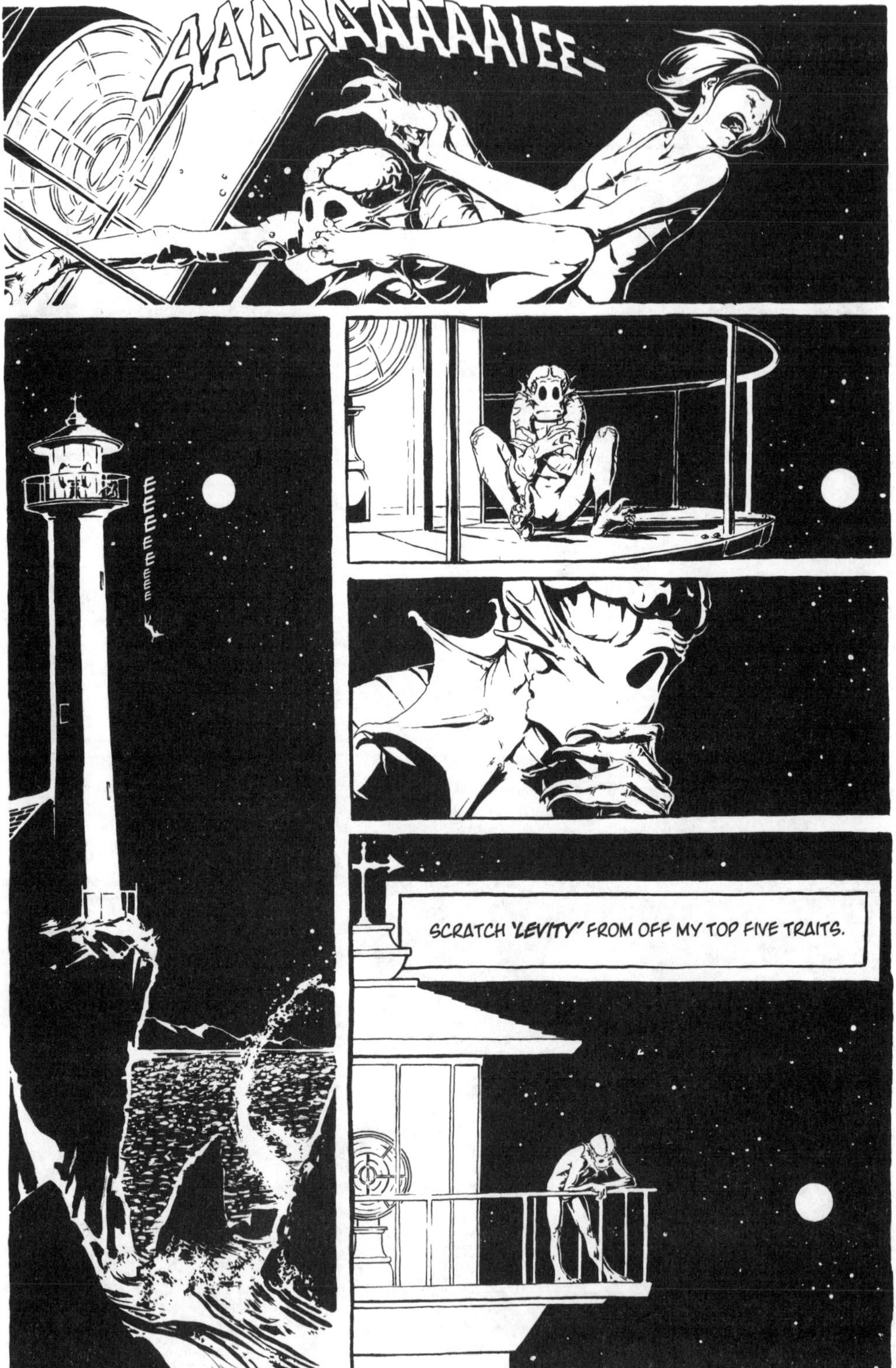
AAAAAAAAAAIEE-
EEEEEEEE
SCRATCH "LEVITY" FROM OFF MY TOP FIVE TRAITS.

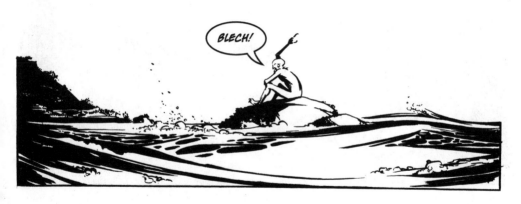

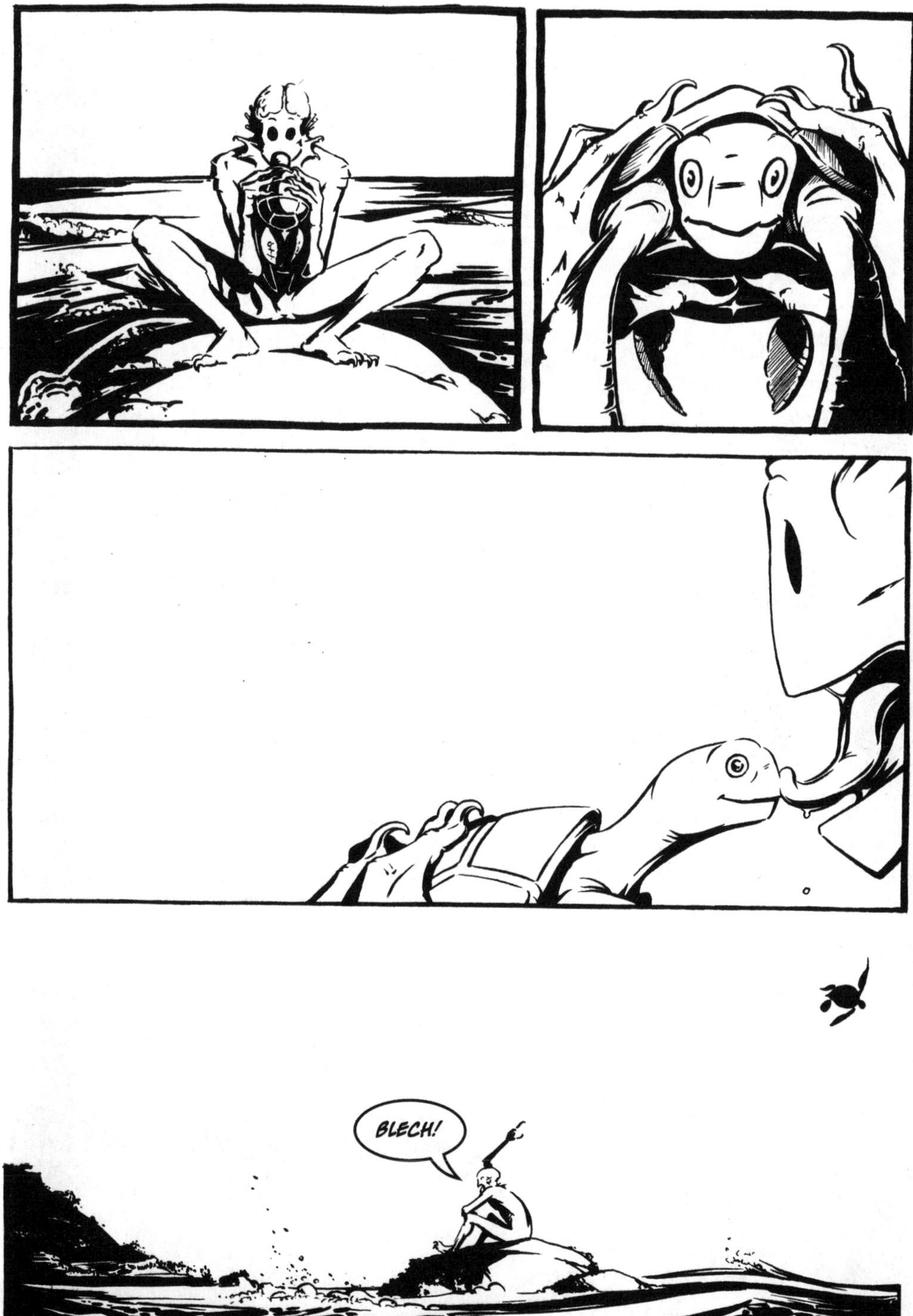
BLECH!

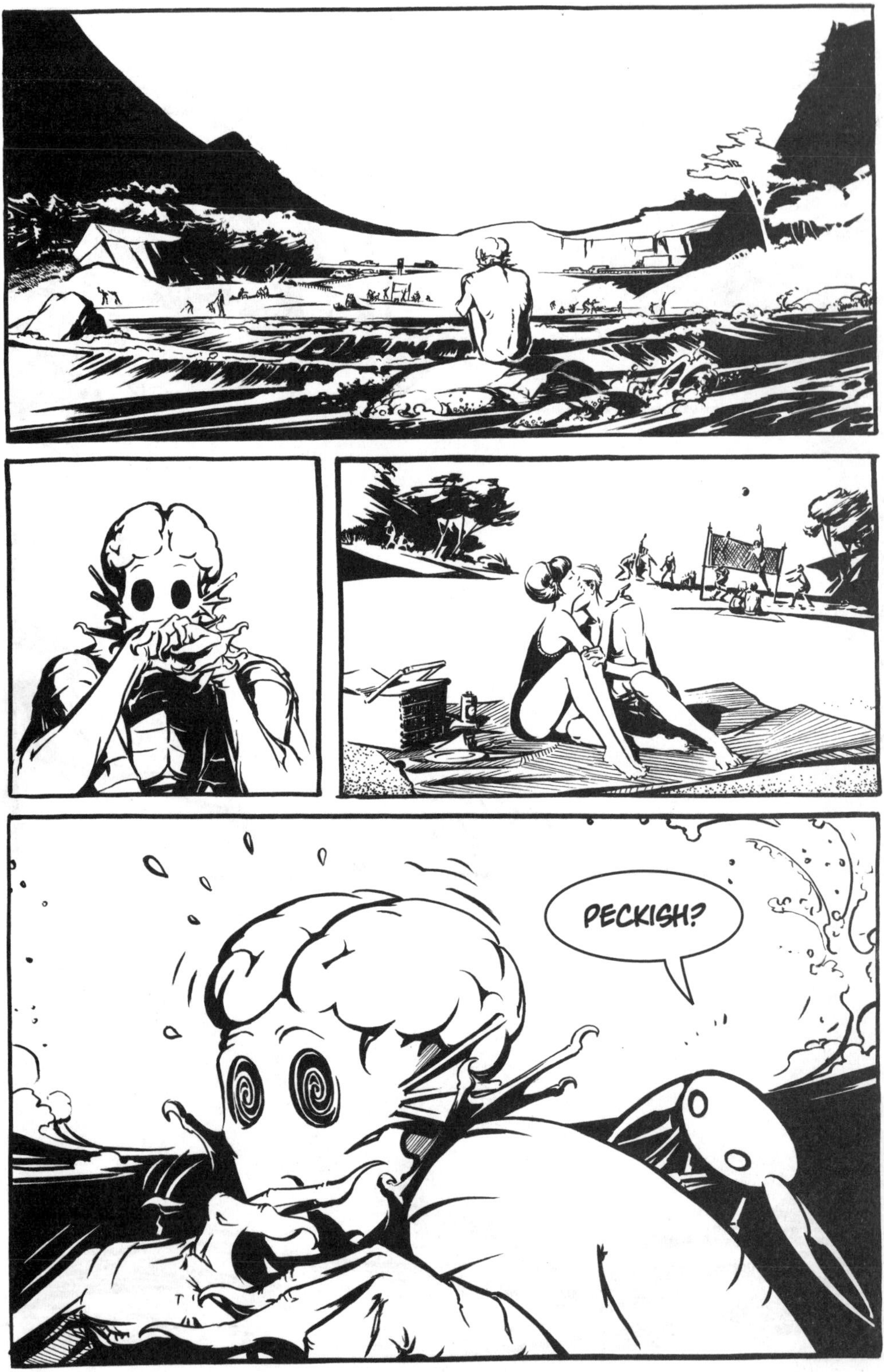
PECKISH?

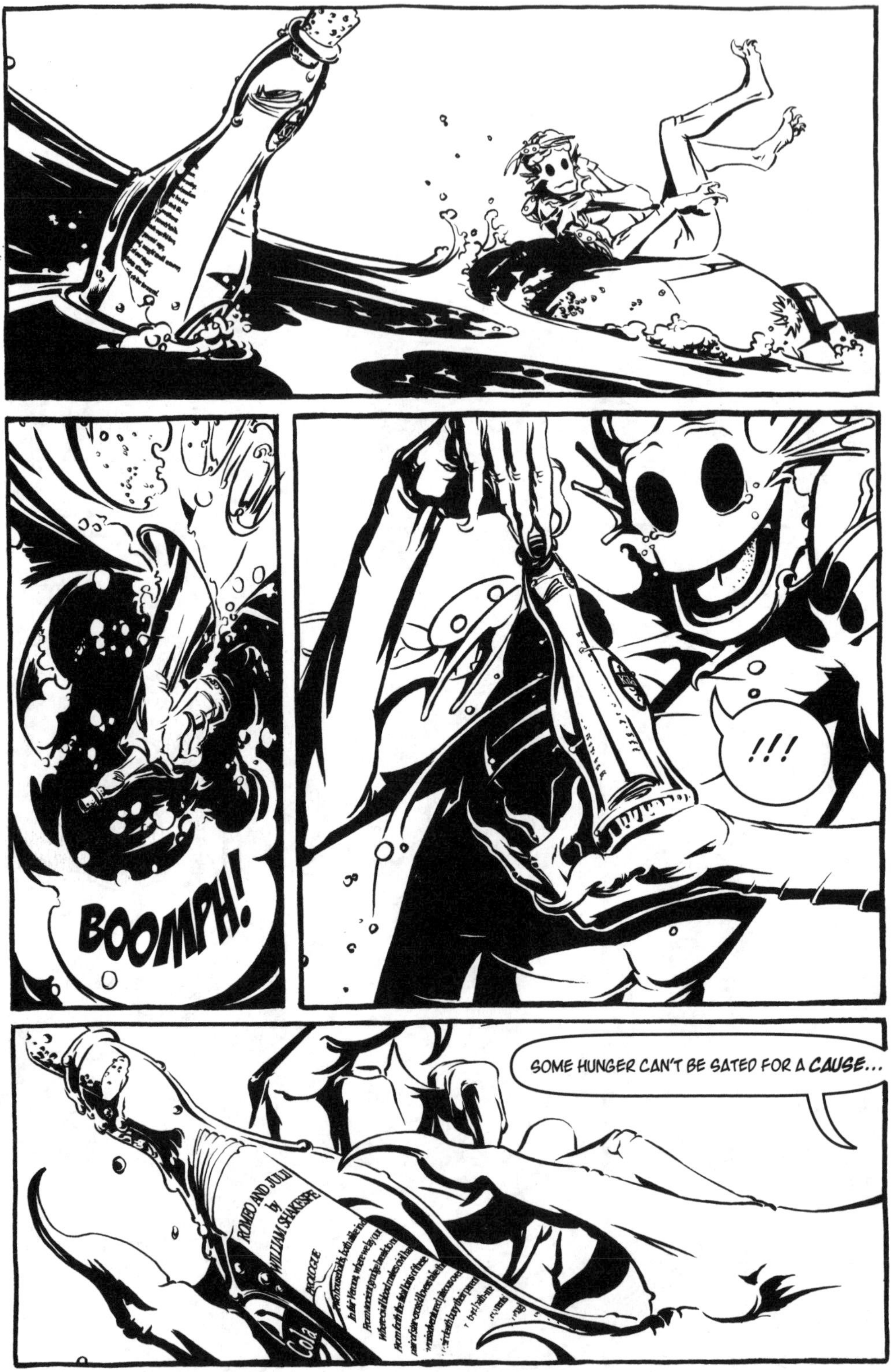
BOOMPH!
!!!
SOME HUNGER CAN'T BE SATED FOR A CAUSE...

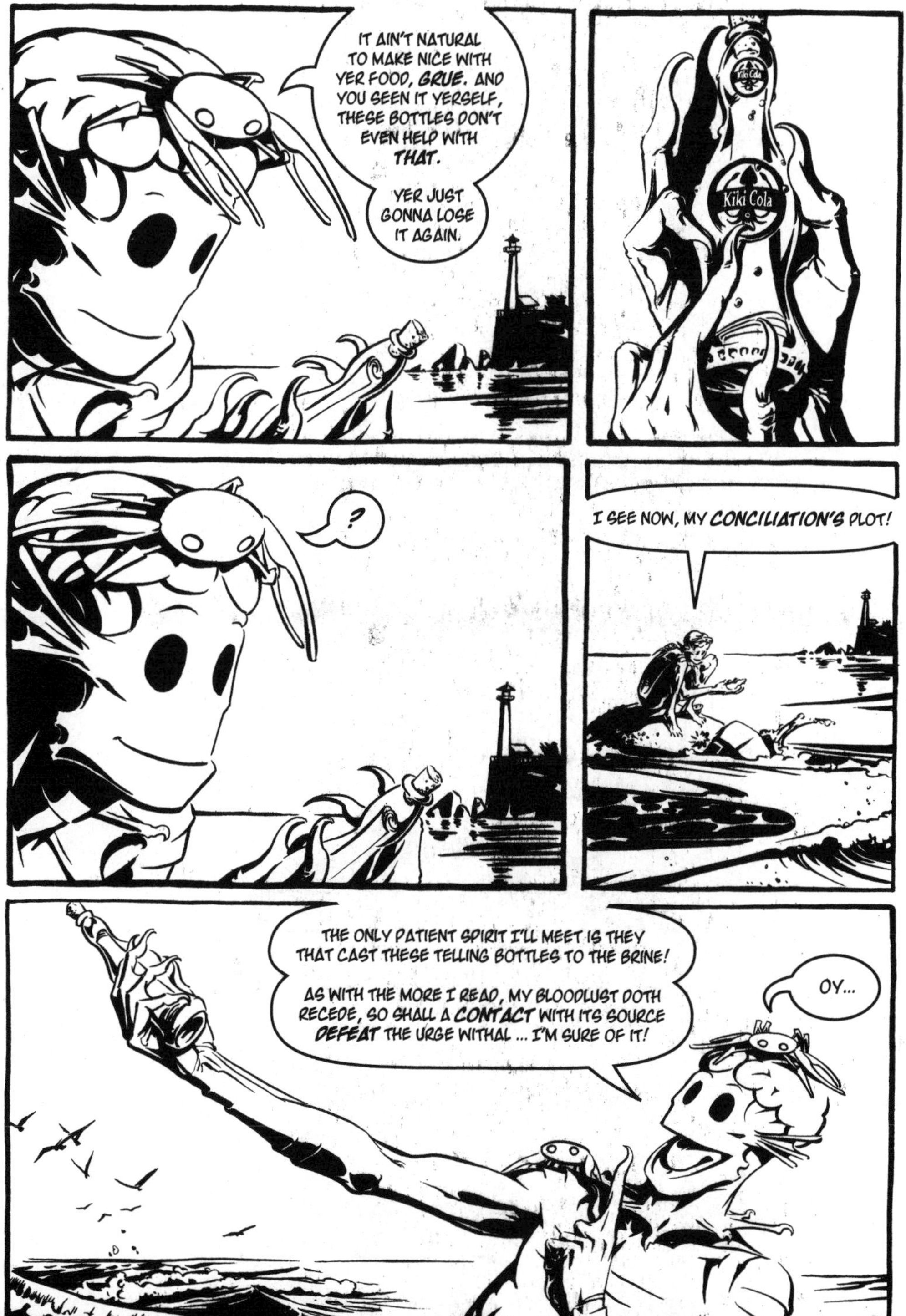
IT AIN'T NATURAL TO MAKE NICE WITH YER FOOD, GRUE. AND YOU SEEN IT YERSELF, THESE BOTTLES DON'T EVEN HELP WITH THAT.
YER JUST GONNA LOSE IT AGAIN.
Kiki Cola
?
I SEE NOW, MY CONCILIATION'S PLOT!
THE ONLY PATIENT SPIRIT I'LL MEET IS THEY THAT CAST THESE TELLING BOTTLES TO THE BRINE!
AS WITH THE MORE I READ, MY BLOODLUST DOTH RECEDE, SO SHALL A CONTACT WITH ITS SOURCE DEFEAT THE URGE WITHAL ... I'M SURE OF IT!
OY...

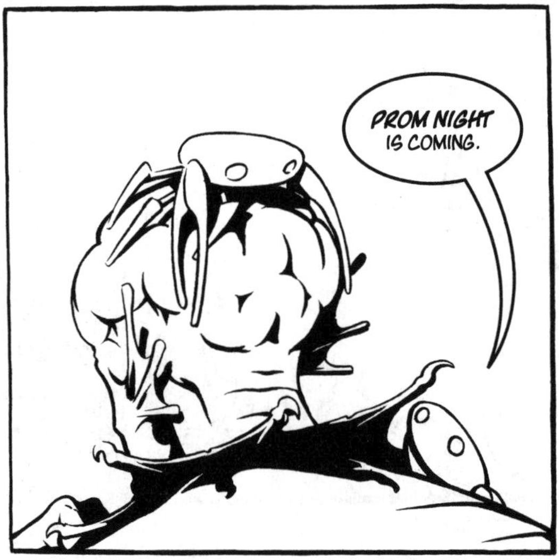
PROM NIGHT IS COMING.

CHAPTER TWO
ride away

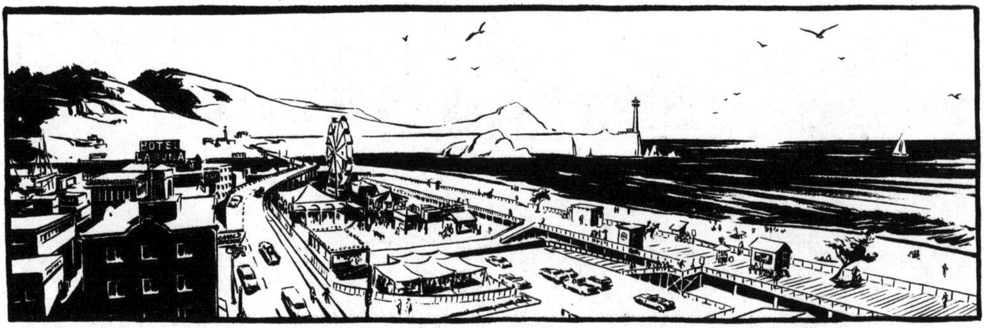
HOTEL LAGUNA

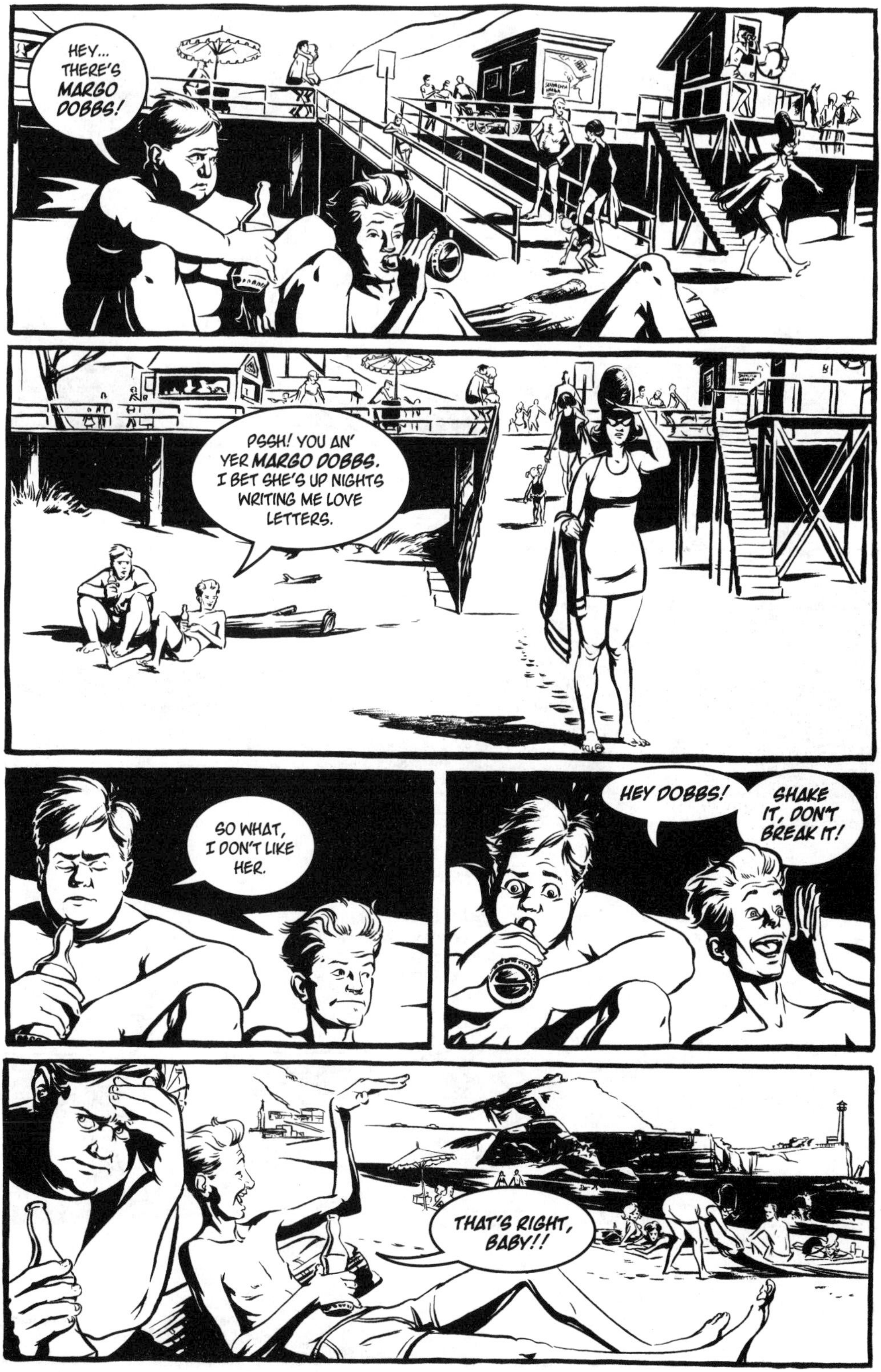
HEY... THERE'S MARGO DOBBS!
PSSH! YOU AN' YER MARGO DOBBS. I BET SHE'S UP NIGHTS WRITING ME LOVE LETTERS.
SO WHAT, I DON'T LIKE HER.
HEY DOBBS!
SHAKE IT, DON'T BREAK IT!
THAT'S RIGHT, BABY!!

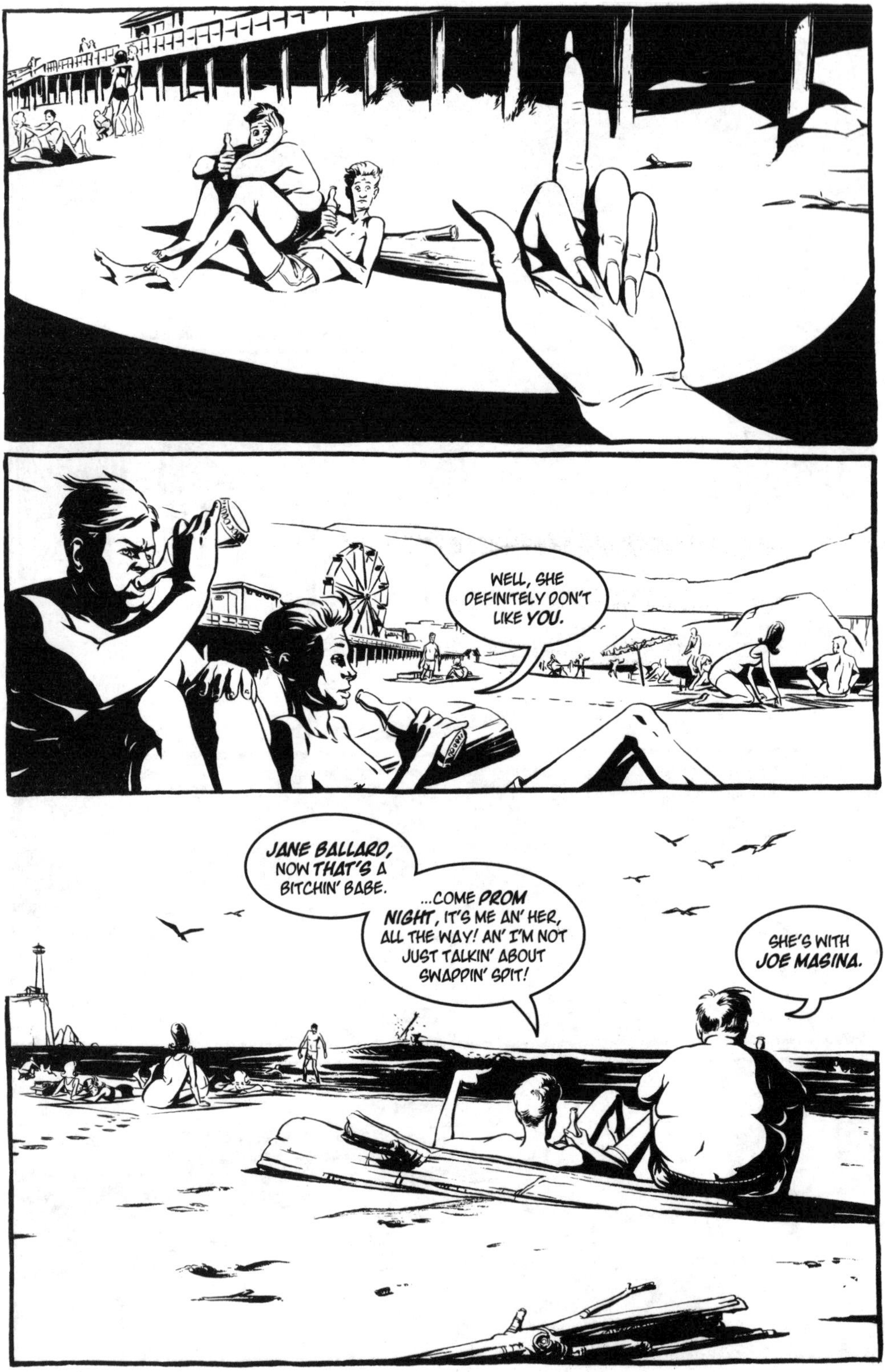
WELL, SHE DEFINITELY DON'T LIKE YOU.
JANE BALLARD, NOW THAT'S A BITCHIN' BABE.
...COME PROM NIGHT, IT'S ME AN' HER, ALL THE WAY! AN' I'M NOT JUST TALKIN' ABOUT SWAPPIN' SPIT!
SHE'S WITH JOE MASINA.

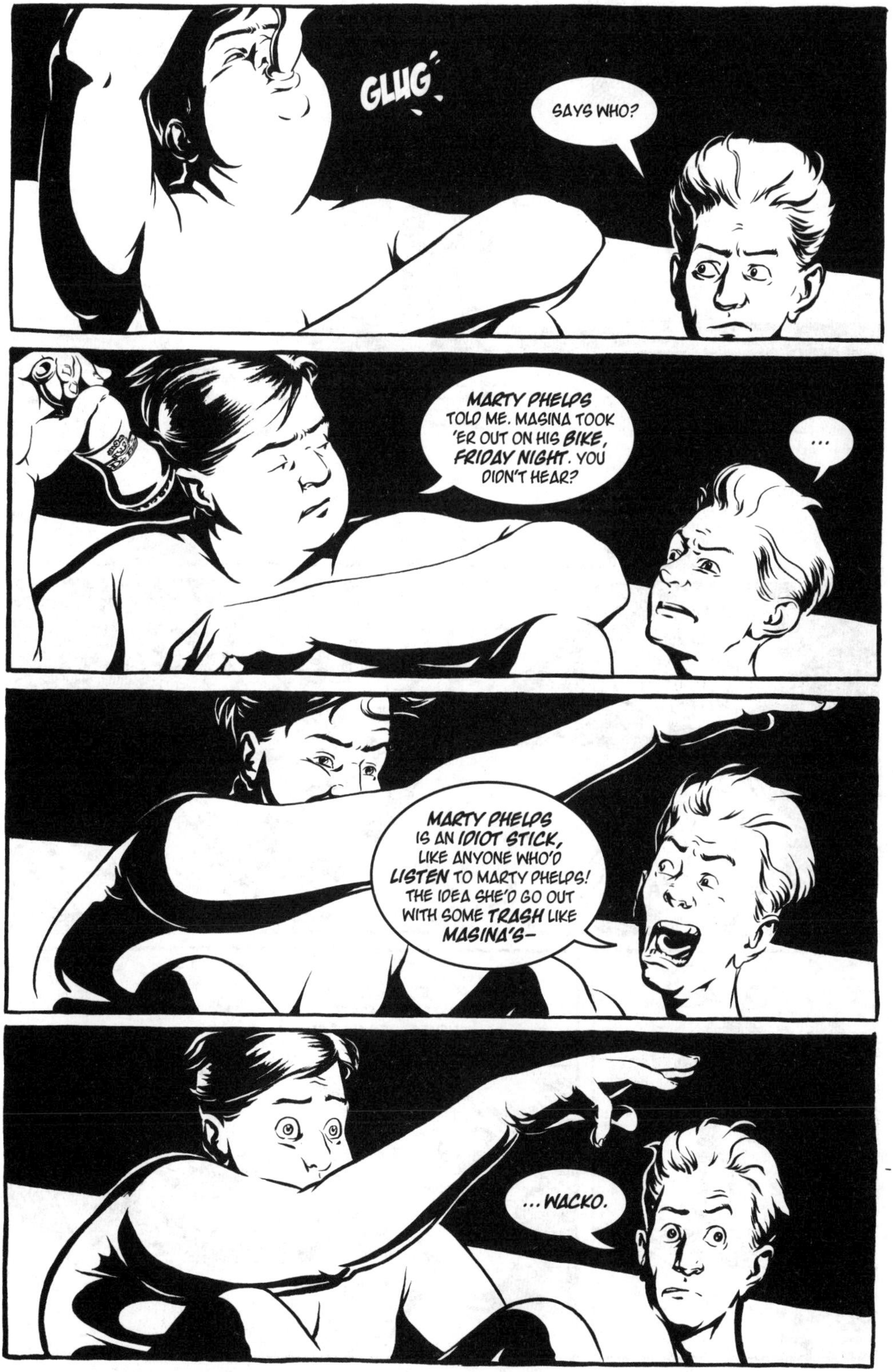
GLUG
SAYS WHO?
MARTY PHELPS TOLD ME. MASINA TOOK 'ER OUT ON HIS BIKE, FRIDAY NIGHT. YOU DIDN'T HEAR?
...
MARTY PHELPS IS AN IDIOT STICK, LIKE ANYONE WHO'D LISTEN TO MARTY PHELPS! THE IDEA SHE'D GO OUT WITH SOME TRASH LIKE MASINA'S–
...WACKO.

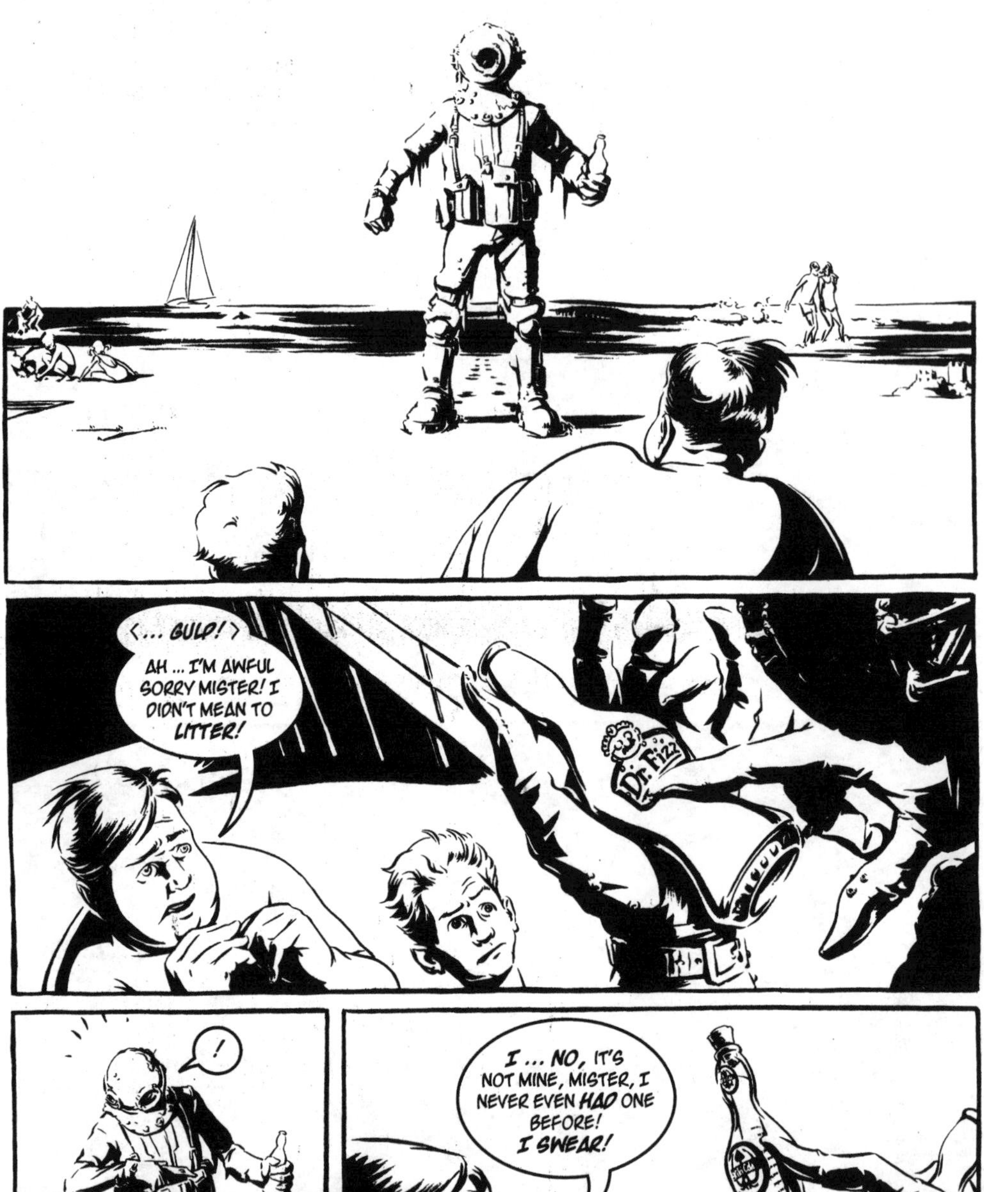
<... GULP! >
AH ... I'M AWFUL SORRY MISTER! I DIDN'T MEAN TO LITTER!
Dr. Fizz
!
I ... NO, IT'S NOT MINE, MISTER, I NEVER EVEN HAD ONE BEFORE! I SWEAR!

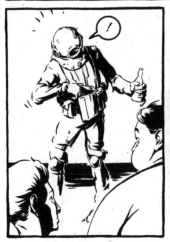

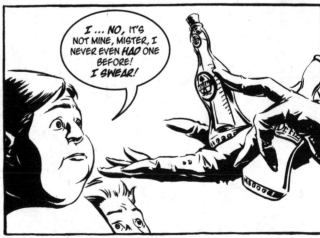

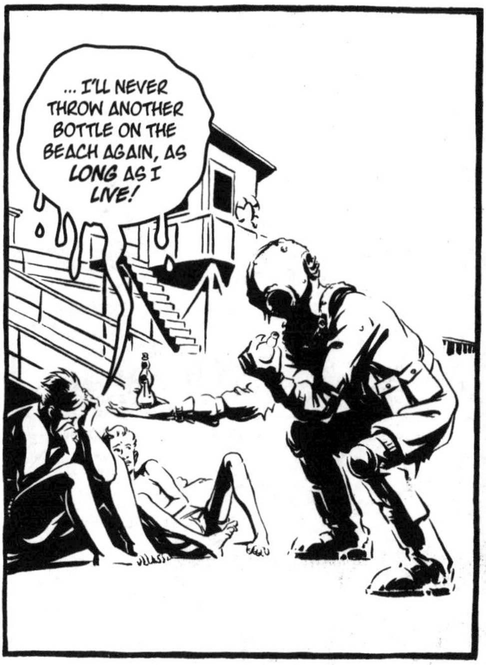
... I'LL NEVER THROW ANOTHER BOTTLE ON THE BEACH AGAIN, AS LONG AS I LIVE!

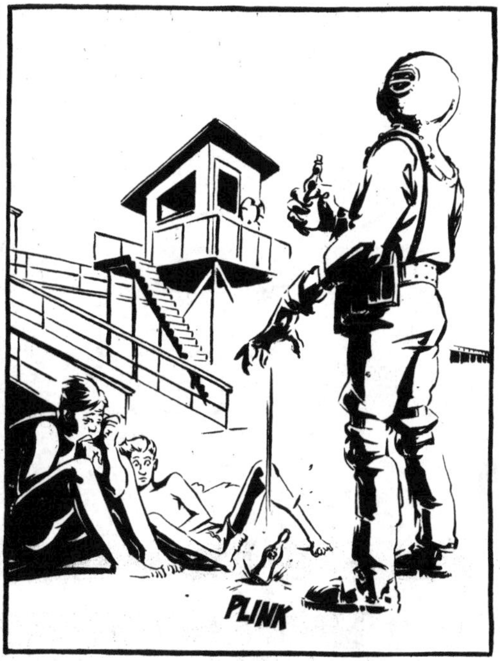
PLINK

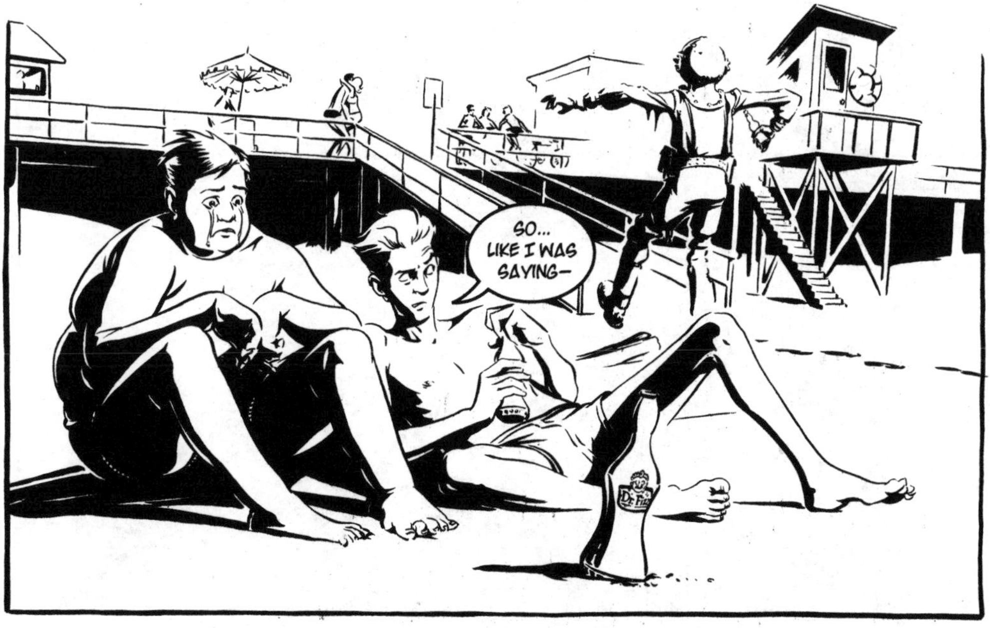
SO... LIKE I WAS SAYING—
Dr. Fizz

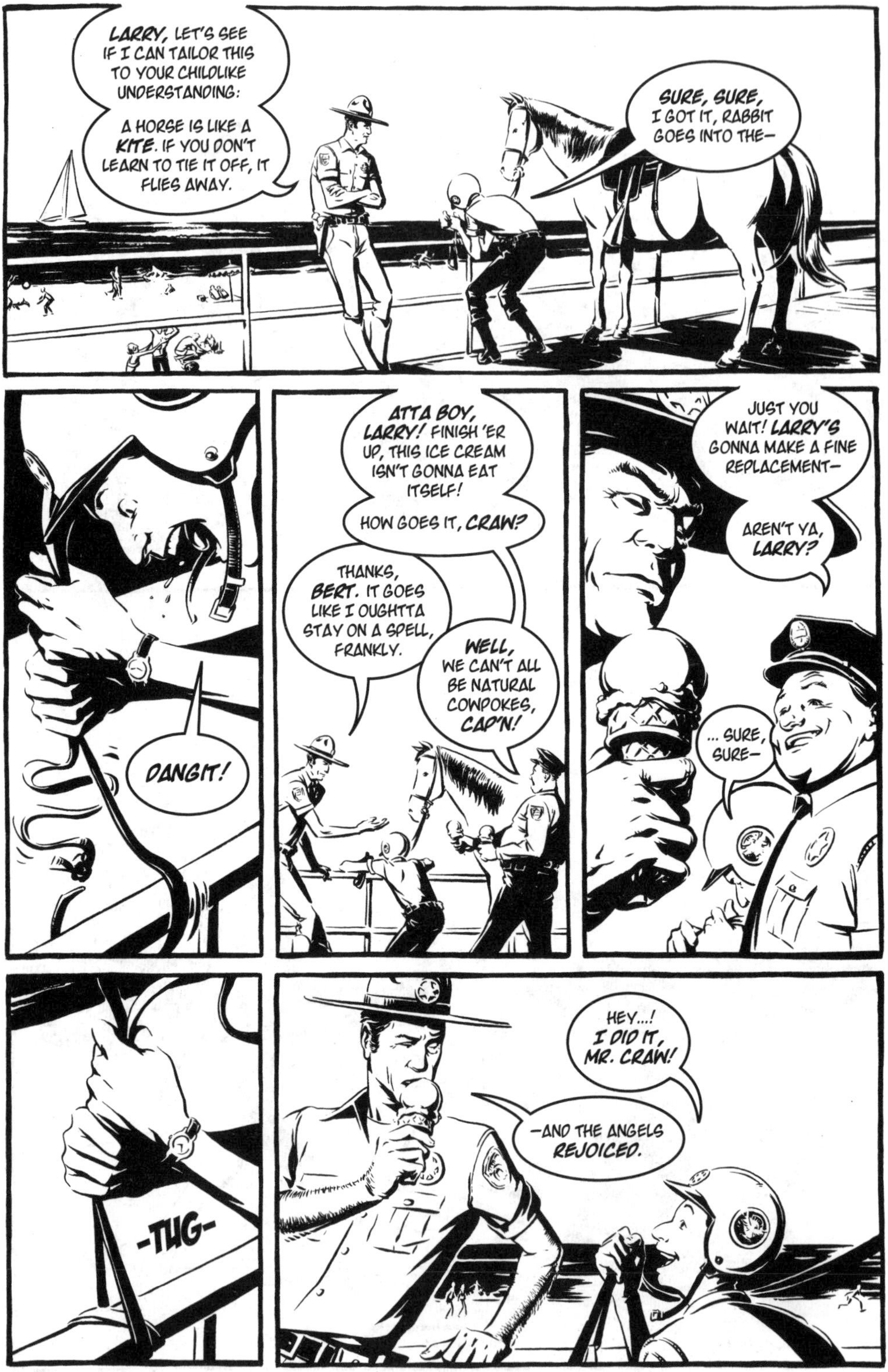
LARRY, LET'S SEE IF I CAN TAILOR THIS TO YOUR CHILDLIKE UNDERSTANDING:
A HORSE IS LIKE A KITE. IF YOU DON'T LEARN TO TIE IT OFF, IT FLIES AWAY.
SURE, SURE, I GOT IT, RABBIT GOES INTO THE–
DANGIT!
ATTA BOY, LARRY! FINISH 'ER UP, THIS ICE CREAM ISN'T GONNA EAT ITSELF!
HOW GOES IT, CRAW?
THANKS, BERT. IT GOES LIKE I OUGHTTA STAY ON A SPELL, FRANKLY.
WELL, WE CAN'T ALL BE NATURAL COWPOKES, CAP'N!
JUST YOU WAIT! LARRY'S GONNA MAKE A FINE REPLACEMENT–
AREN'T YA, LARRY?
... SURE, SURE–
-TUG-
HEY...! I DID IT, MR. CRAW!
–AND THE ANGELS REJOICED.

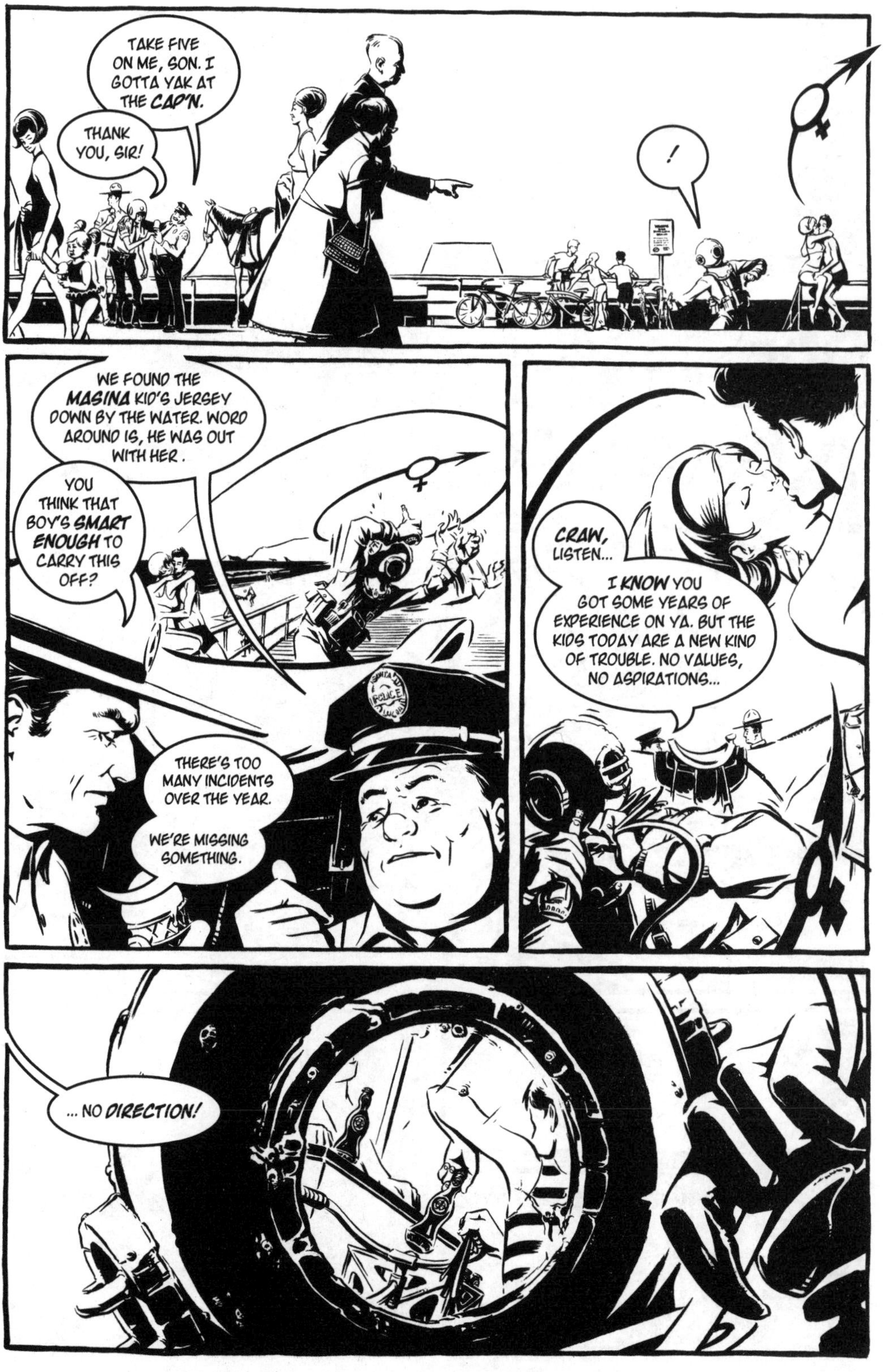
TAKE FIVE ON ME, SON. I GOTTA YAK AT THE CAP'N.
THANK YOU, SIR!
!
WE FOUND THE MASINA KID'S JERSEY DOWN BY THE WATER. WORD AROUND IS, HE WAS OUT WITH HER .
YOU THINK THAT BOY'S SMART ENOUGH TO CARRY THIS OFF?
THERE'S TOO MANY INCIDENTS OVER THE YEAR.
WE'RE MISSING SOMETHING.
CRAW, LISTEN...
I KNOW YOU GOT SOME YEARS OF EXPERIENCE ON YA. BUT THE KIDS TODAY ARE A NEW KIND OF TROUBLE. NO VALUES, NO ASPIRATIONS...
... NO DIRECTION!

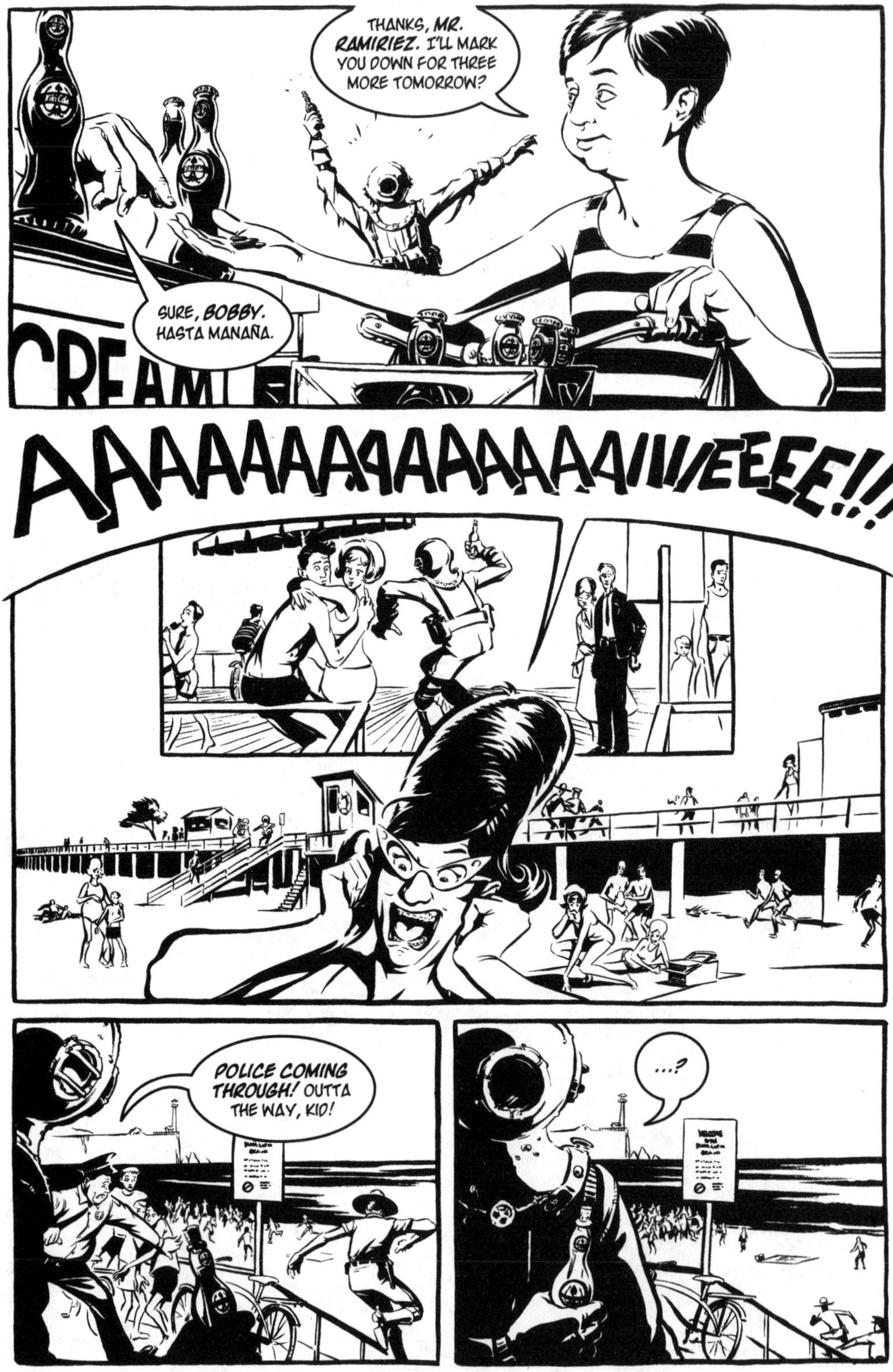
THANKS, MR. RAMIRIEZ. I'LL MARK YOU DOWN FOR THREE MORE TOMORROW?
SURE, BOBBY. HASTA MAÑAÑA.
CREAM
AAAAAAAAAAAAAAIIIIEEEE!!!
POLICE COMING THROUGH! OUTTA THE WAY, KID!
...?

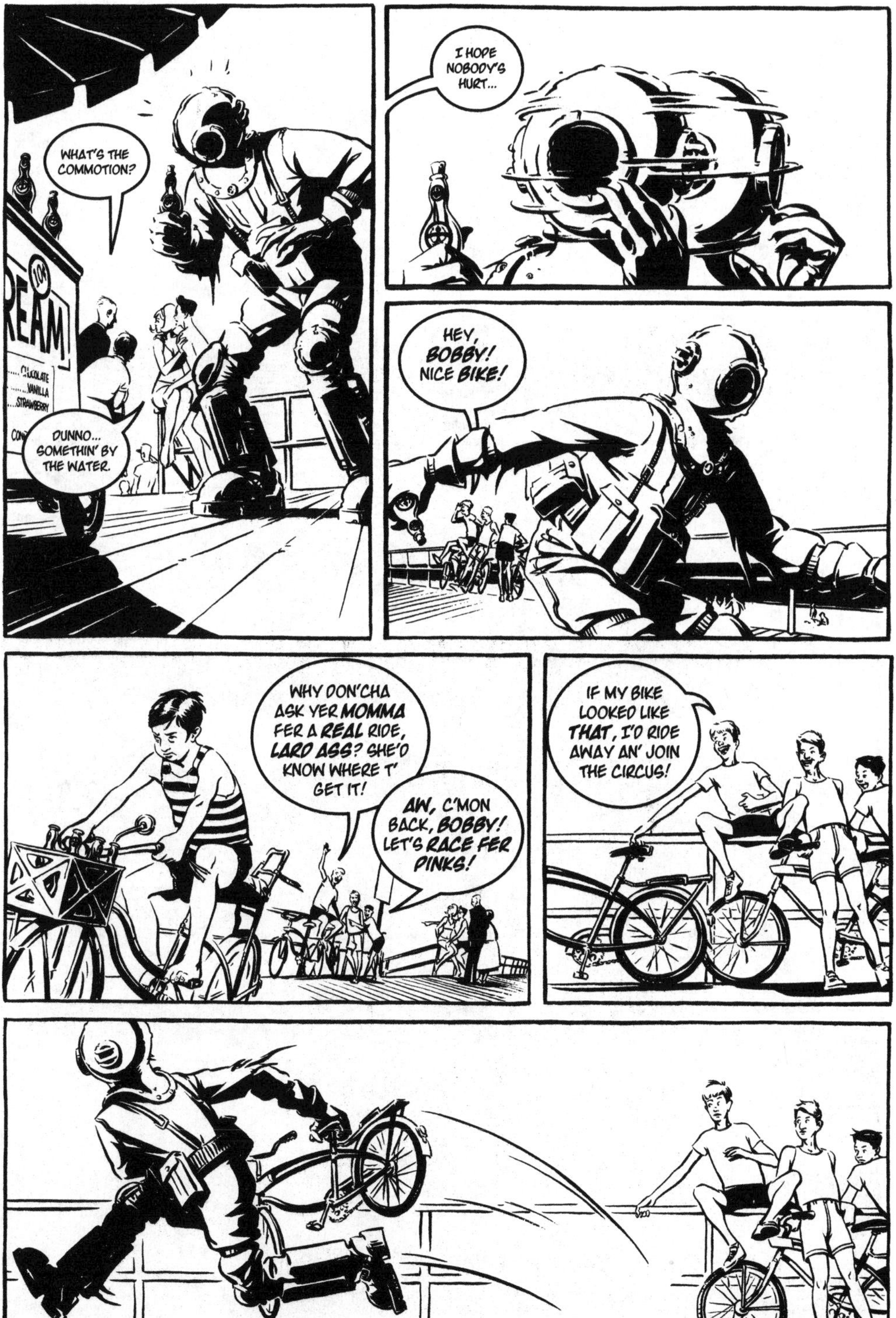
WHAT'S THE COMMOTION?
DUNNO... SOMETHIN' BY THE WATER.
I HOPE NOBODY'S HURT...
HEY, BOBBY! NICE BIKE!
WHY DON'CHA ASK YER MOMMA FER A REAL RIDE, LARD ASS? SHE'D KNOW WHERE T' GET IT!
AW, C'MON BACK, BOBBY! LET'S RACE FER PINKS!
IF MY BIKE LOOKED LIKE THAT, I'D RIDE AWAY AN' JOIN THE CIRCUS!

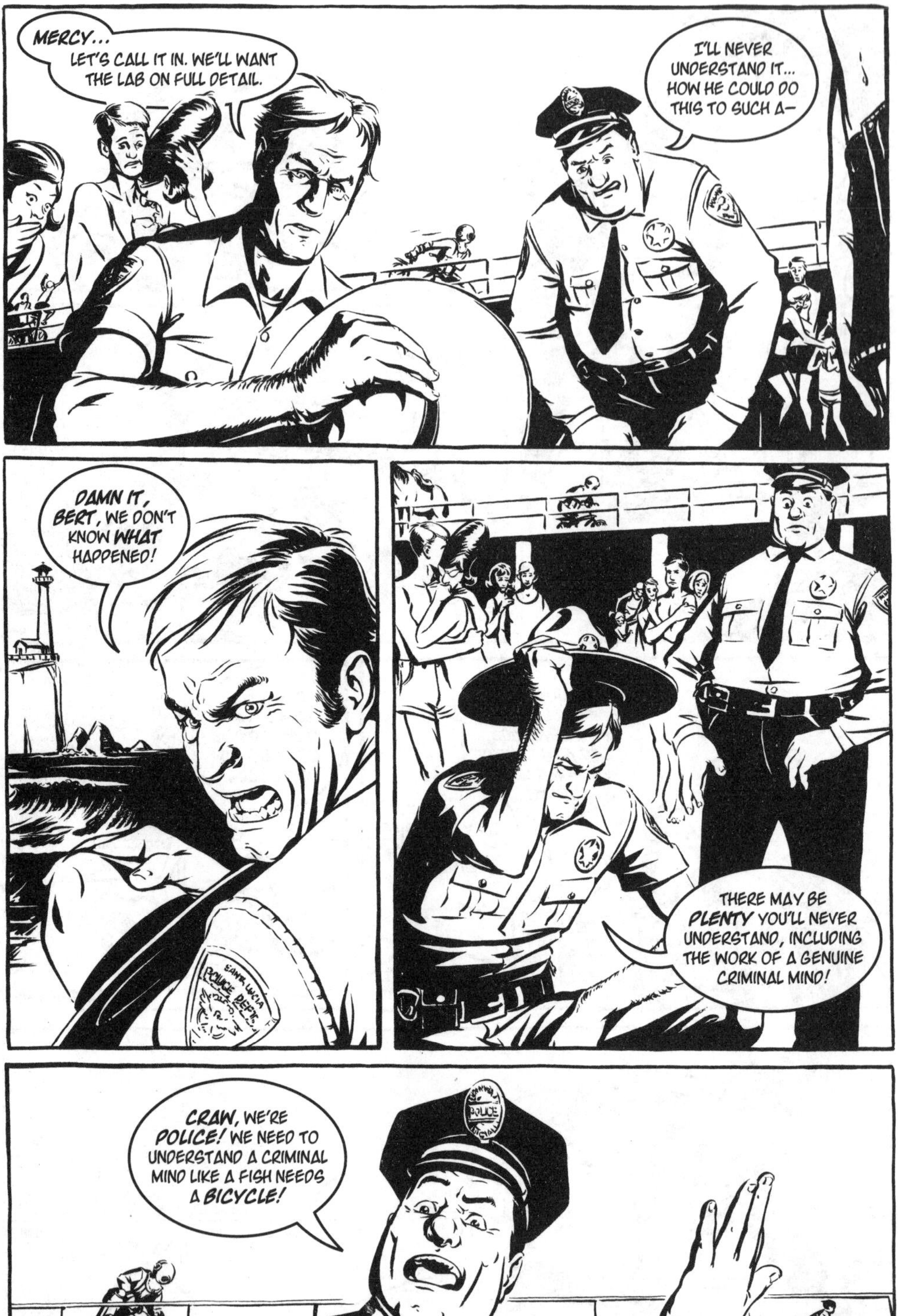
MERCY... LET'S CALL IT IN. WE'LL WANT THE LAB ON FULL DETAIL.
I'LL NEVER UNDERSTAND IT... HOW HE COULD DO THIS TO SUCH A-
DAMN IT, BERT, WE DON'T KNOW WHAT HAPPENED!
THERE MAY BE PLENTY YOU'LL NEVER UNDERSTAND, INCLUDING THE WORK OF A GENUINE CRIMINAL MIND!
CRAW, WE'RE POLICE! WE NEED TO UNDERSTAND A CRIMINAL MIND LIKE A FISH NEEDS A BICYCLE!

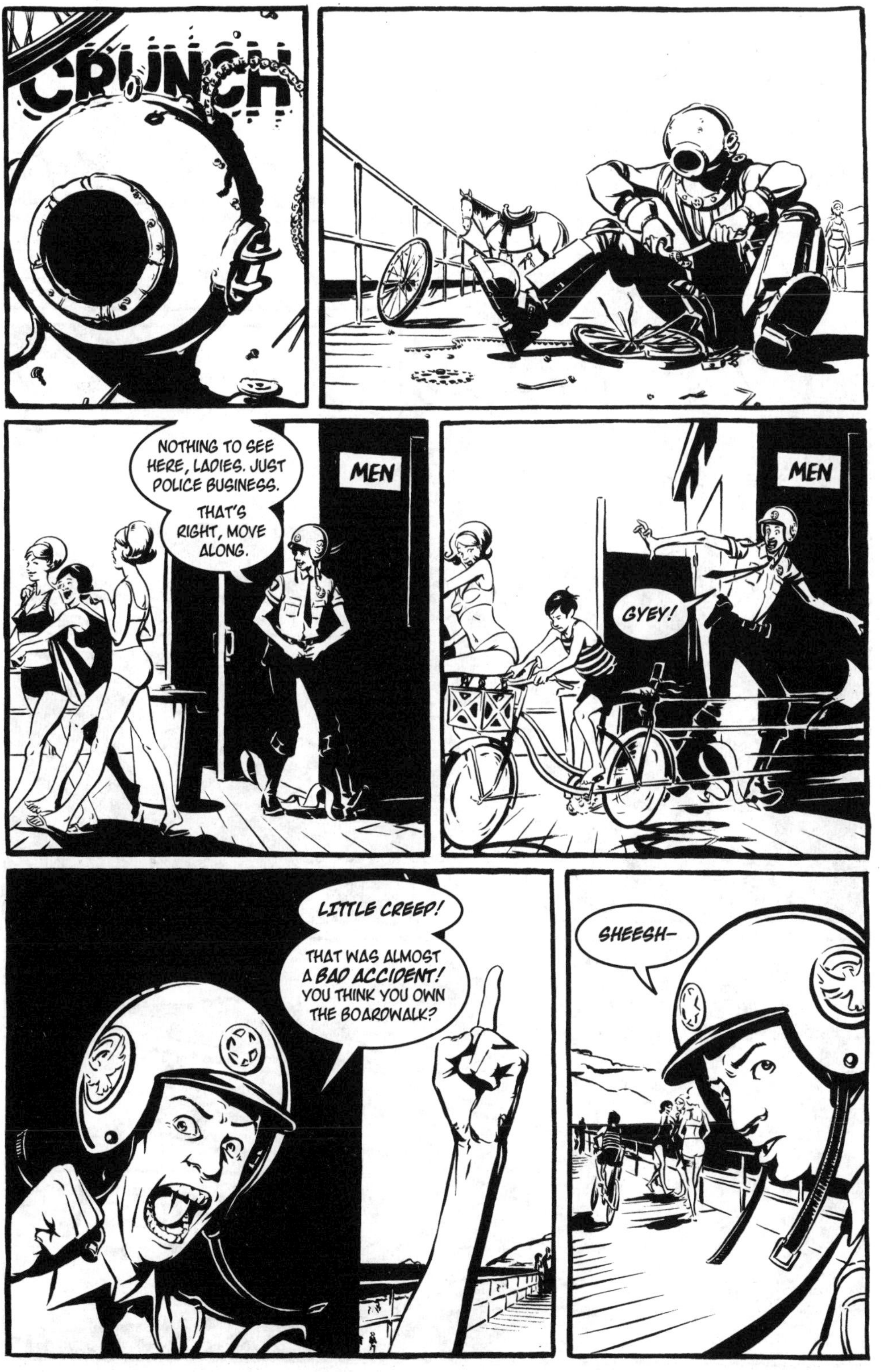
CRUNCH
NOTHING TO SEE HERE, LADIES. JUST POLICE BUSINESS.
THAT'S RIGHT, MOVE ALONG.
MEN
MEN
GYEY!
LITTLE CREEP!
THAT WAS ALMOST A BAD ACCIDENT! YOU THINK YOU OWN THE BOARDWALK?
SHEESH–

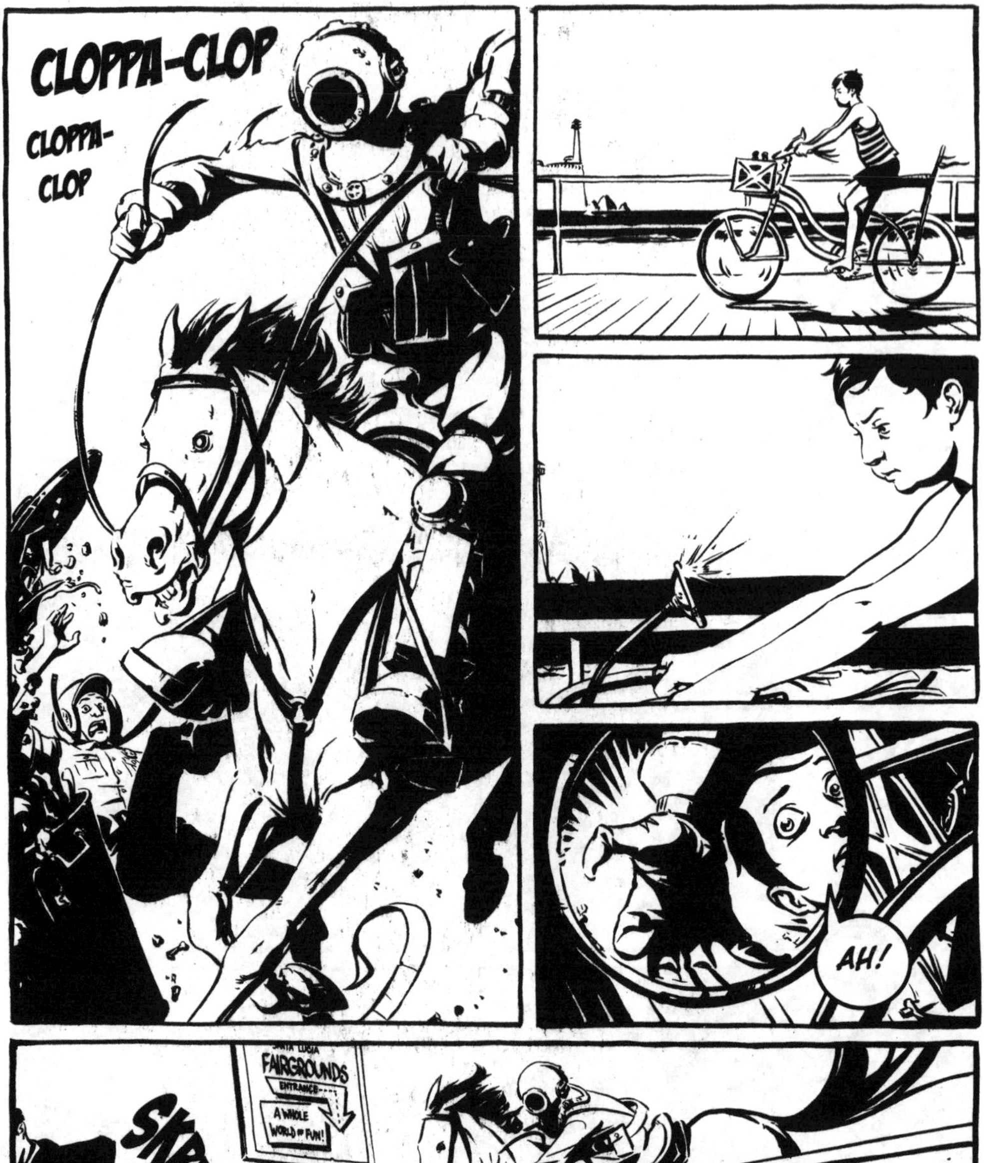
CLOPPA-CLOP
CLOPPA-CLOP
AH!
FAIRGROUNDS
ENTRANCE
A WHOLE WORLD OF FUN!
SKREEECH!
CLOPPA-CLOP

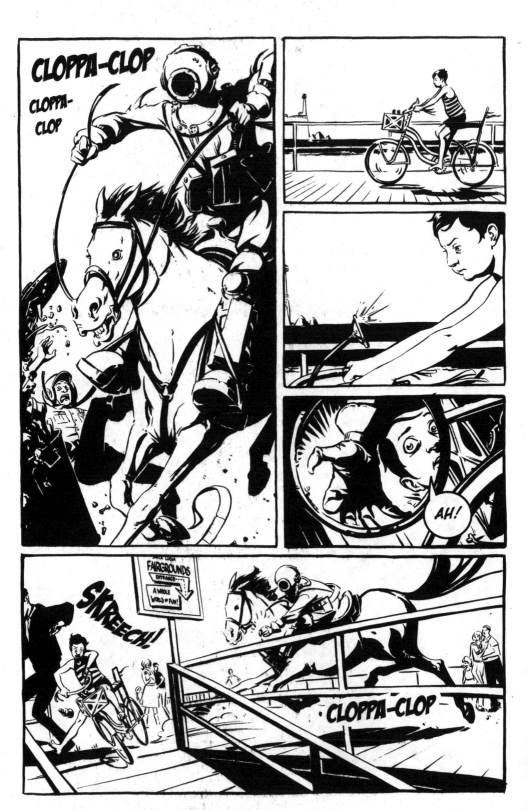

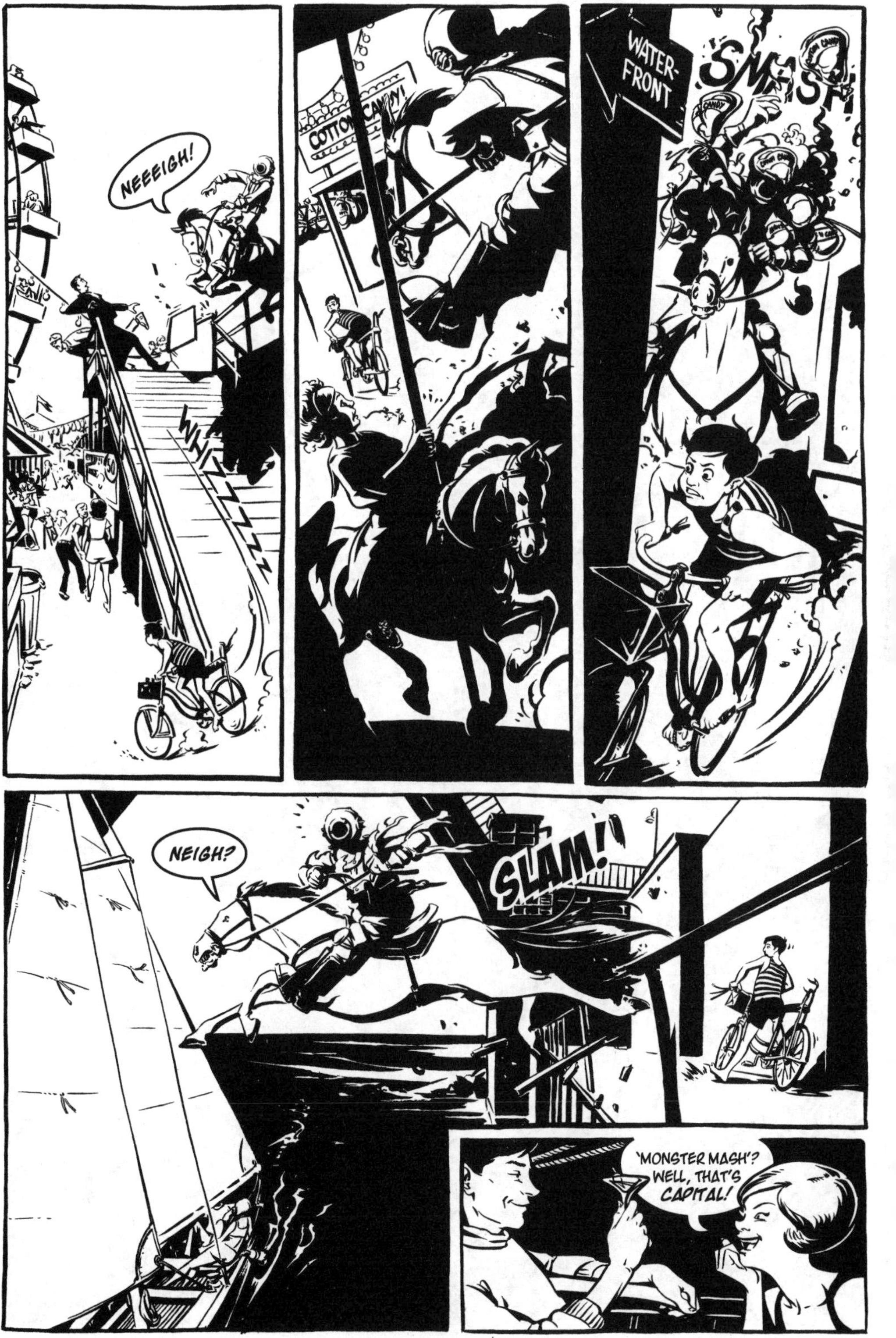
NEEEIGH!
COTTON CANDY!
WATER-FRONT
SMASH!
NEIGH?
SLAM!
'MONSTER MASH'? WELL, THAT'S CAPITAL!

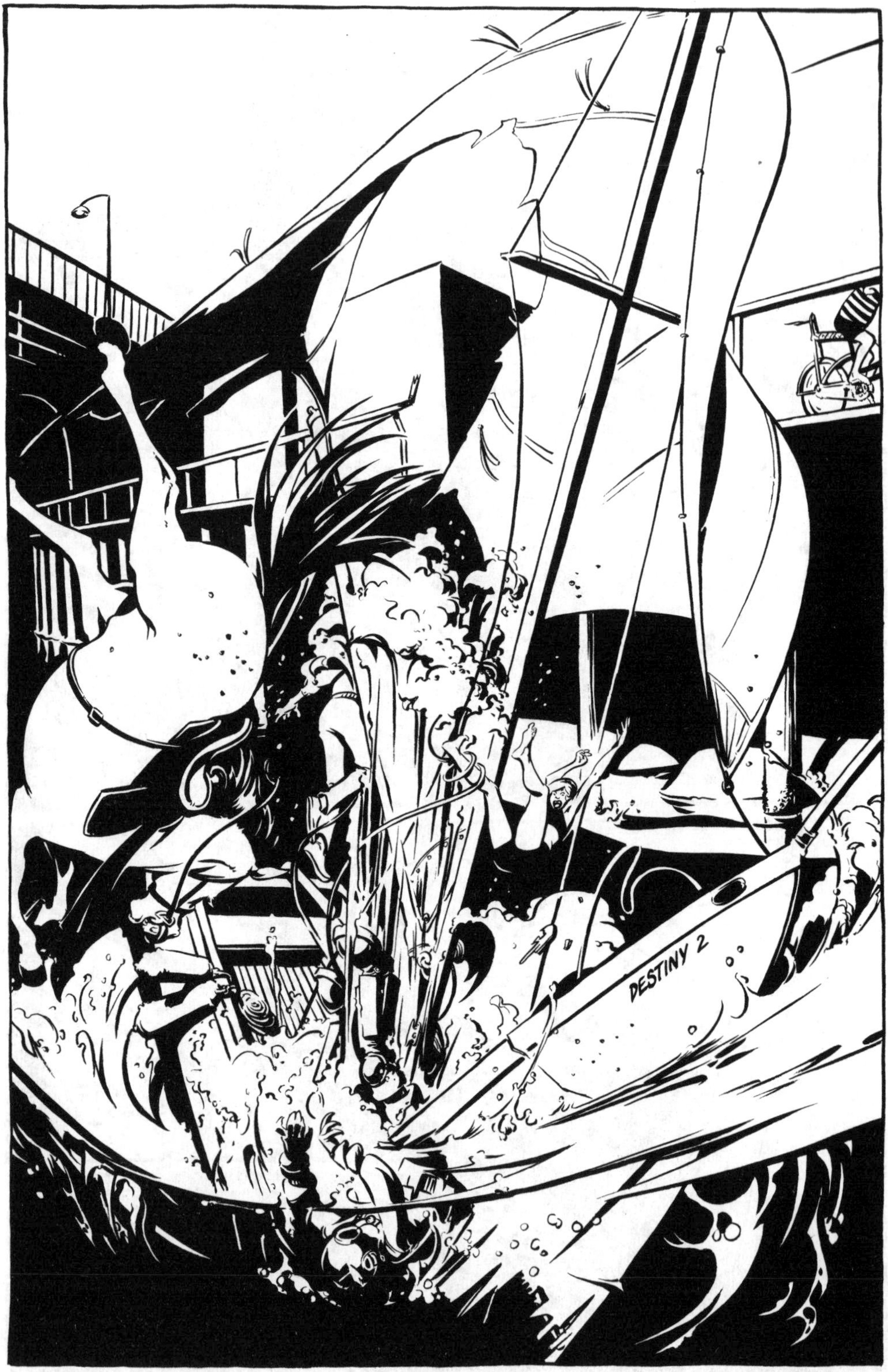
DESTINY 2

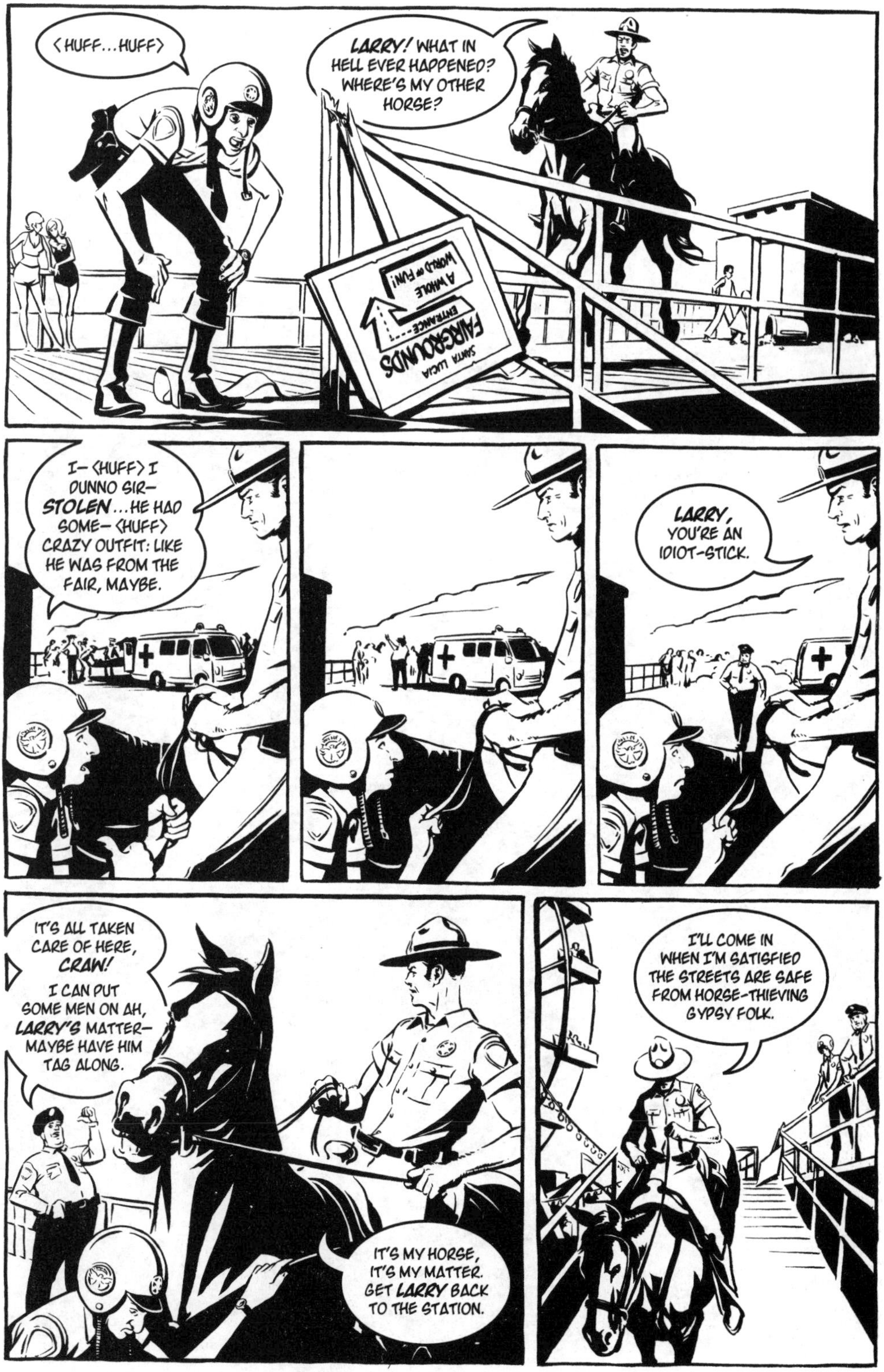
<HUFF...HUFF>
LARRY! WHAT IN HELL EVER HAPPENED? WHERE'S MY OTHER HORSE?
SANTA LUCIA FAIRGROUNDS ENTRANCE
A WHOLE WORLD of FUN!
I– <HUFF> I DUNNO SIR– STOLEN...HE HAD SOME– <HUFF> CRAZY OUTFIT: LIKE HE WAS FROM THE FAIR, MAYBE.
LARRY, YOU'RE AN IDIOT-STICK.
IT'S ALL TAKEN CARE OF HERE, CRAW! I CAN PUT SOME MEN ON AH, LARRY'S MATTER– MAYBE HAVE HIM TAG ALONG.
IT'S MY HORSE, IT'S MY MATTER. GET LARRY BACK TO THE STATION.
I'LL COME IN WHEN I'M SATISFIED THE STREETS ARE SAFE FROM HORSE-THIEVING GYPSY FOLK.

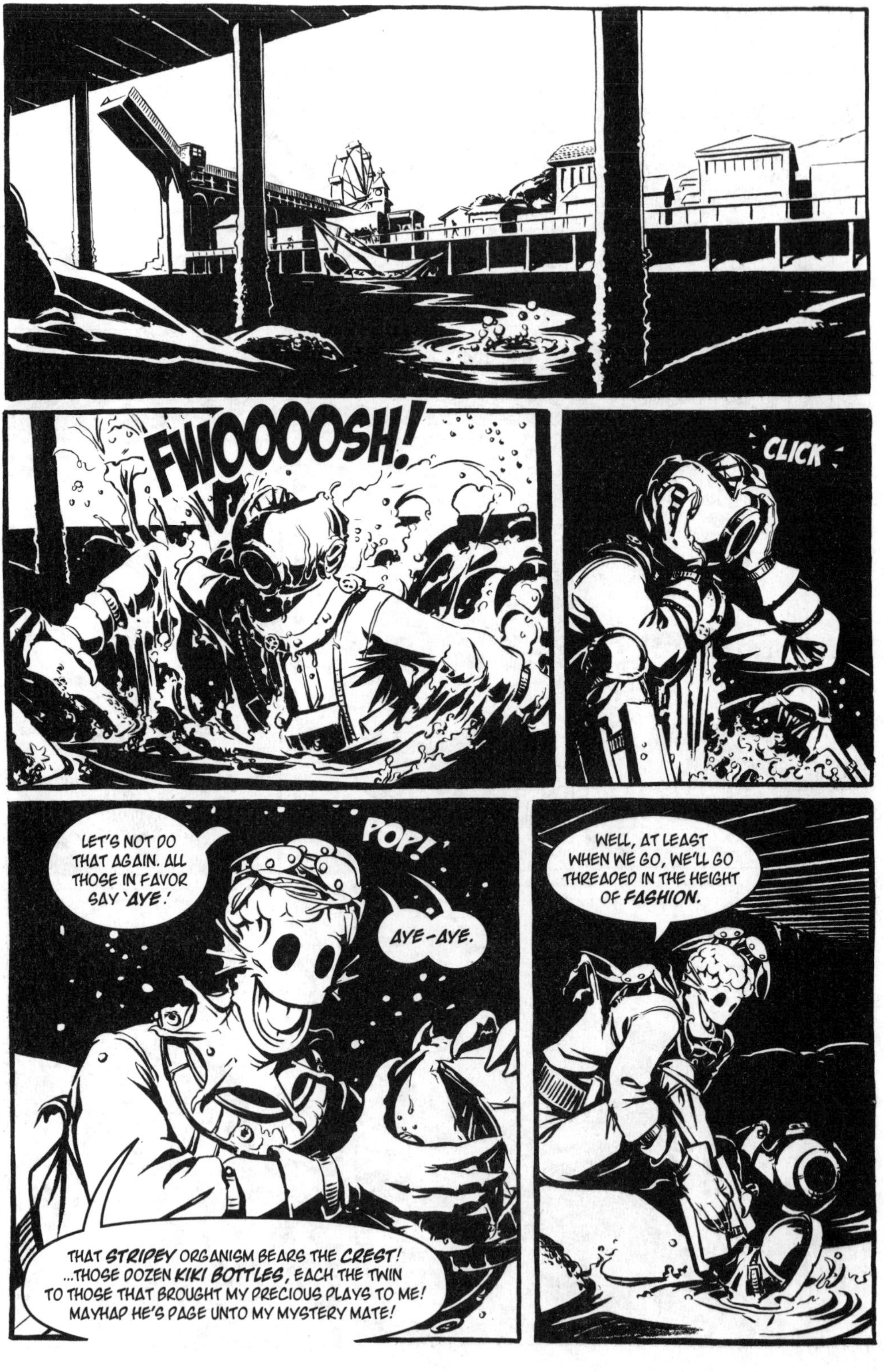
FWOOOOSH!
CLICK
LET'S NOT DO THAT AGAIN. ALL THOSE IN FAVOR SAY 'AYE.'
POP!
AYE-AYE.
THAT STRIPEY ORGANISM BEARS THE CREST! ...THOSE DOZEN KIKI BOTTLES, EACH THE TWIN TO THOSE THAT BROUGHT MY PRECIOUS PLAYS TO ME! MAYHAP HE'S PAGE UNTO MY MYSTERY MATE!
WELL, AT LEAST WHEN WE GO, WE'LL GO THREADED IN THE HEIGHT OF FASHION.

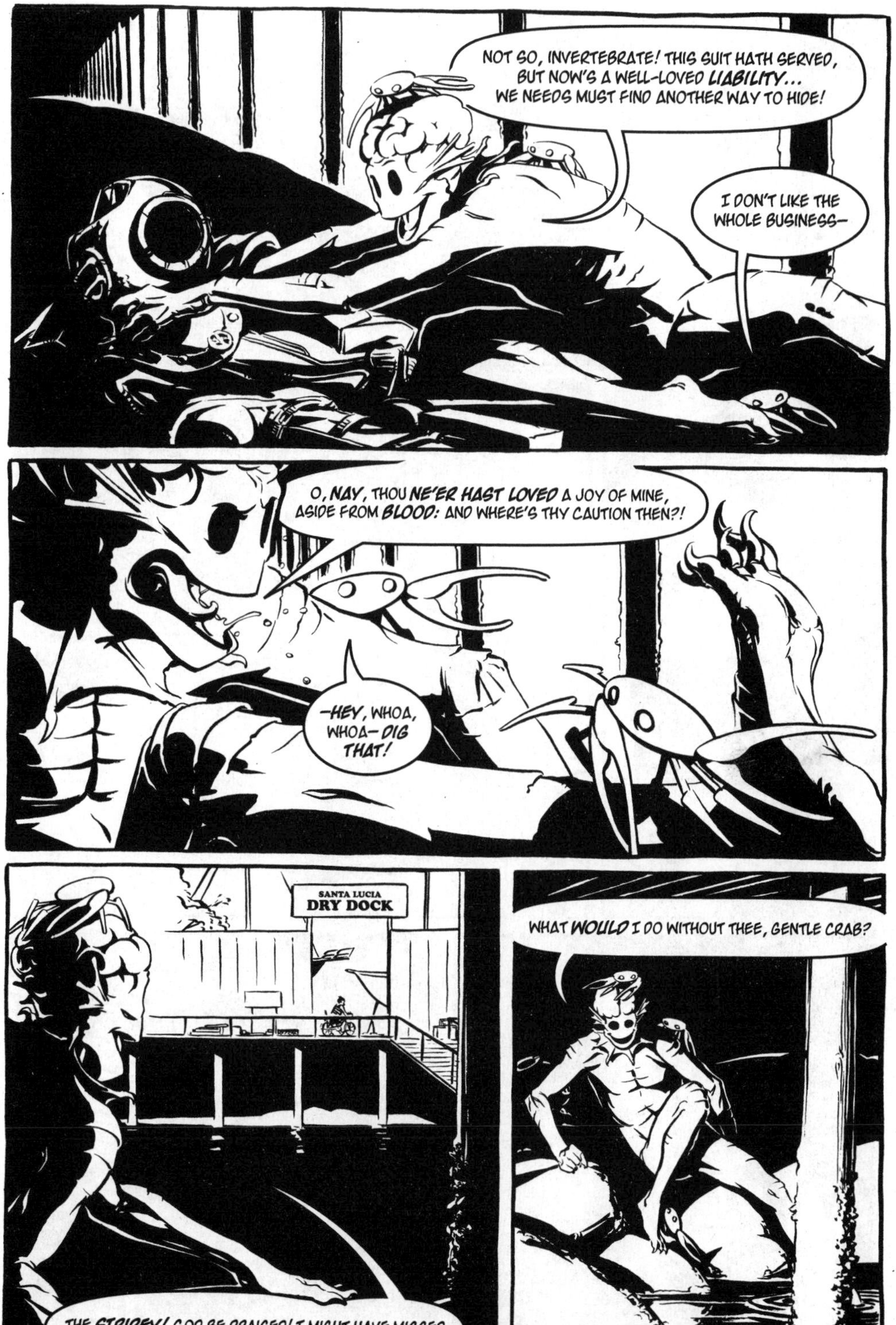
NOT SO, INVERTEBRATE! THIS SUIT HATH SERVED, BUT NOW'S A WELL-LOVED LIABILITY... WE NEEDS MUST FIND ANOTHER WAY TO HIDE!
I DON'T LIKE THE WHOLE BUSINESS—
O, NAY, THOU NE'ER HAST LOVED A JOY OF MINE, ASIDE FROM BLOOD: AND WHERE'S THY CAUTION THEN?!
—HEY, WHOA, WHOA—DIG THAT!
SANTA LUCIA DRY DOCK
THE STRIPEY! GOD BE PRAISED! I MIGHT HAVE MISSED THE CATCH FOR RAMBLING SO: NO MORE OF THAT!
WHAT WOULD I DO WITHOUT THEE, GENTLE CRAB?

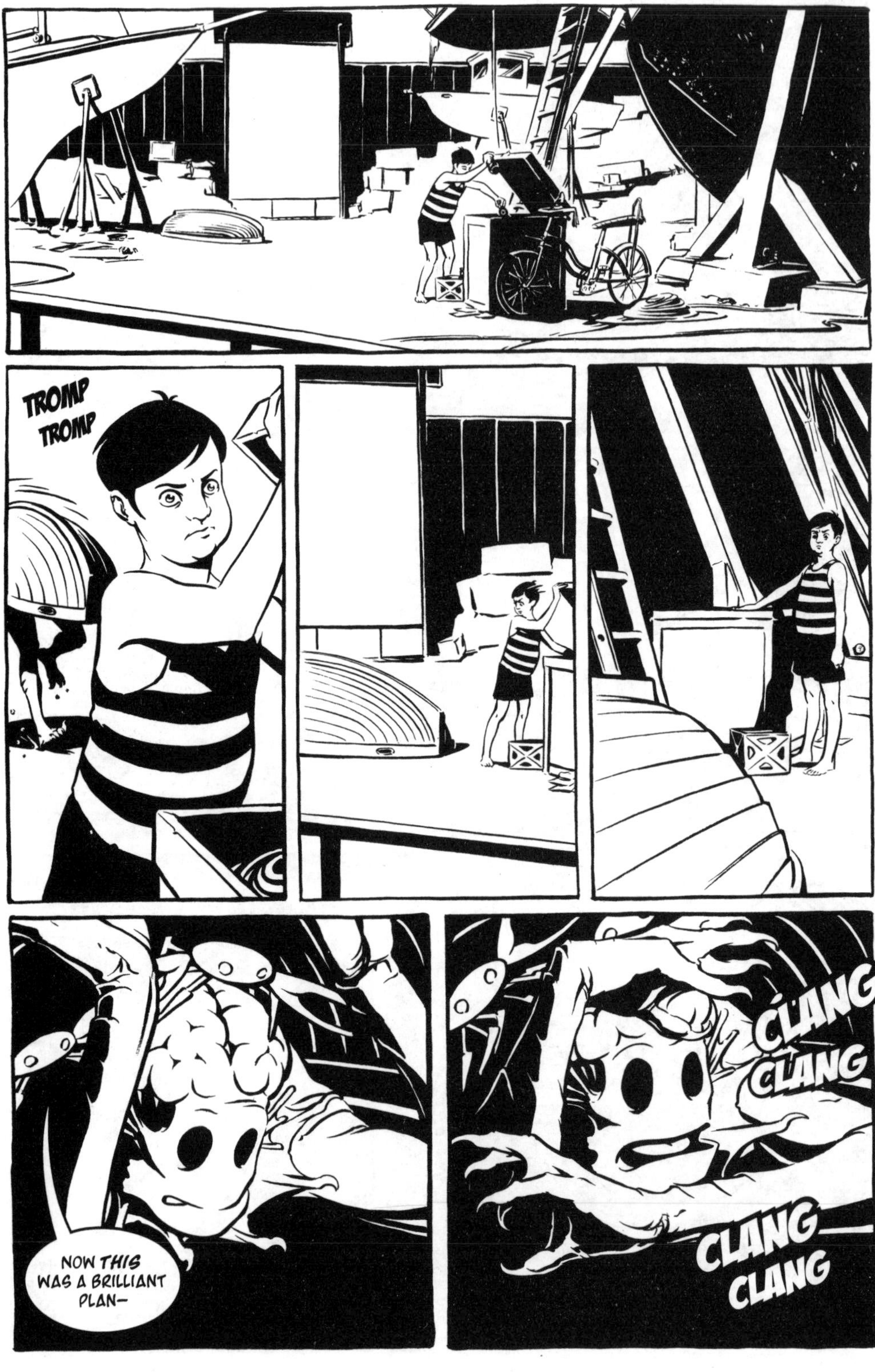
TROMP
TROMP
NOW THIS WAS A BRILLIANT PLAN—
CLANG
CLANG
CLANG—
CLANG

CLANG
CLANG

MARIETTA
NAPLES, ITALY
1905

LOOK WHERE THE *STRIPEY* CLIMBS! A MIGHTY SHIP!

CLANG

I DARE NOT GUESS WHAT *WONDERS* LIE WITHIN!

CLA-

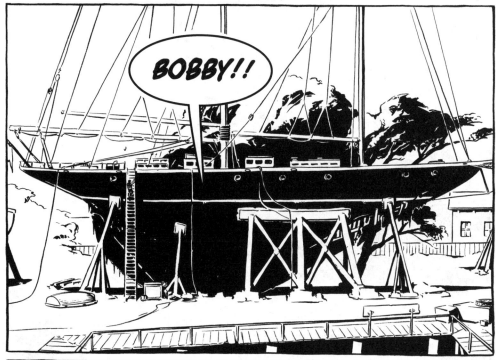

BOBBY!!

STOMP...
STOMP...
STOMP...
STOMP

UNHOLY ZEUS!

56

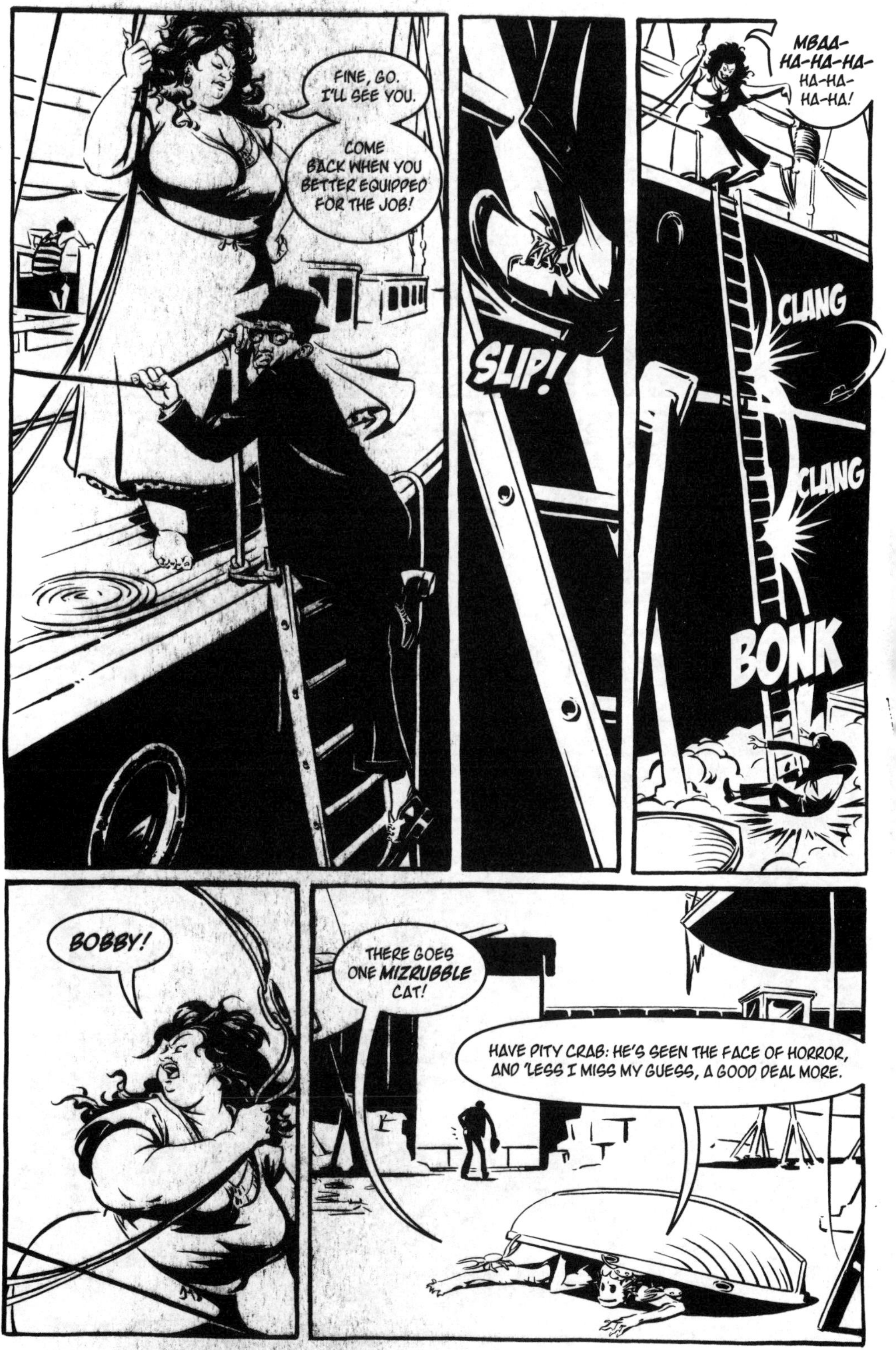
FINE, GO. I'LL SEE YOU.
COME BACK WHEN YOU BETTER EQUIPPED FOR THE JOB!
SLIP!
MBAA-HA-HA-HA-HA-HA-HA-HA!
CLANG
CLANG
BONK
BOBBY!
THERE GOES ONE MIZRUBBLE CAT!
HAVE PITY CRAB: HE'S SEEN THE FACE OF HORROR, AND 'LESS I MISS MY GUESS, A GOOD DEAL MORE.

STOMP

STOMP

YOU KNOW WHAT YOUR *FATHER* WILL DO WHEN HE COMES BACK? WHEN HE SEES I HAVEN'T HAD THE BOAT REPAIRED LIKE HE WANTED?

HE'LL LEAVE AGAIN, AND WE'LL BE STUCK HERE FOR GOOD. YOU NEED TO STAY OUT WHEN SOMEONE'S HERE TO HELP. UNDERSTAND?

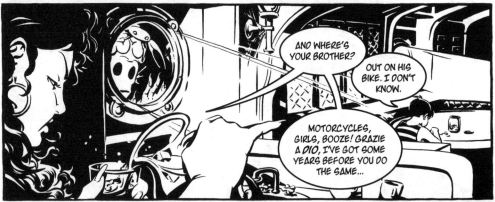

AND WHERE'S YOUR BROTHER?

OUT ON HIS BIKE. I DON'T KNOW.

MOTORCYCLES, GIRLS, BOOZE! GRAZIE A *DIO*, I'VE GOT SOME YEARS BEFORE YOU DO THE SAME...

HAVE YOU FED *GIULIETTA*?

NO...

YOU FINISH YOUR ROUTE, YOU FEED AUNT *GIULIETTA!* SHOW ME YOU CAN DO SOMETHING WORTHWHILE!

NO COMPRENDE, BIRDY?

YOU AIN'T ALONE.

BE SILENT, CRABS! THE *STRIPEY* RISES! LOOK...

THE *BOTTLE!*

58

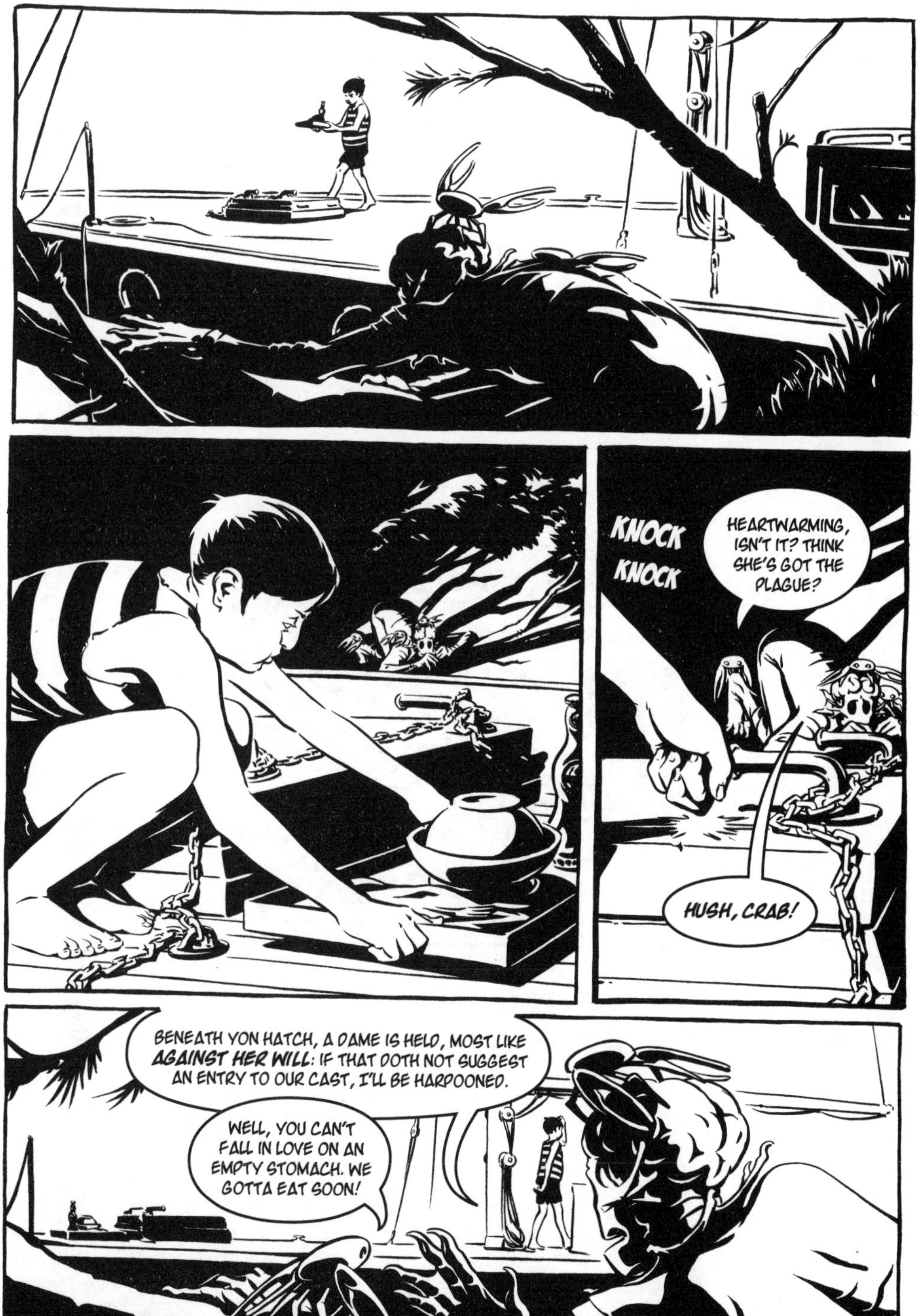
KNOCK
KNOCK
HEARTWARMING, ISN'T IT? THINK SHE'S GOT THE PLAGUE?
HUSH, CRAB!
BENEATH YON HATCH, A DAME IS HELD, MOST LIKE **AGAINST HER WILL**: IF THAT DOTH NOT SUGGEST AN ENTRY TO OUR CAST, I'LL BE HARPOONED.
WELL, YOU CAN'T FALL IN LOVE ON AN EMPTY STOMACH. WE GOTTA EAT SOON!
AND SO DOTH SHE . . . AS SUCH, SHE'LL SHORTLY RISE.

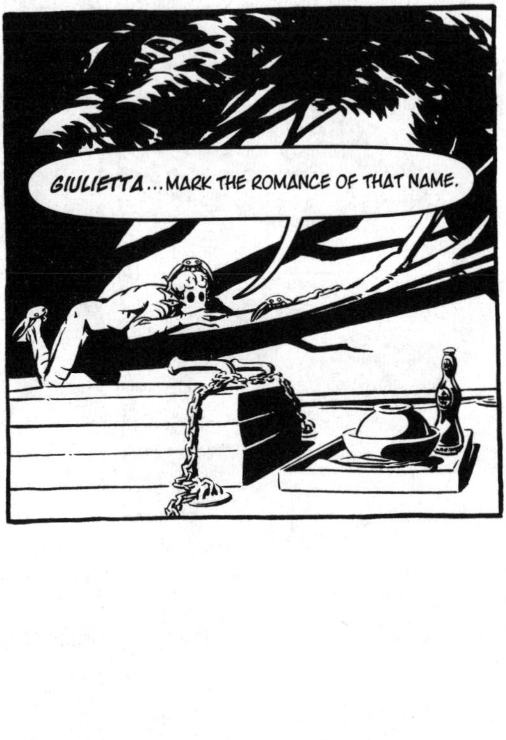
GIULIETTA...MARK THE ROMANCE OF THAT NAME.

CHAPTER THREE
in dreams

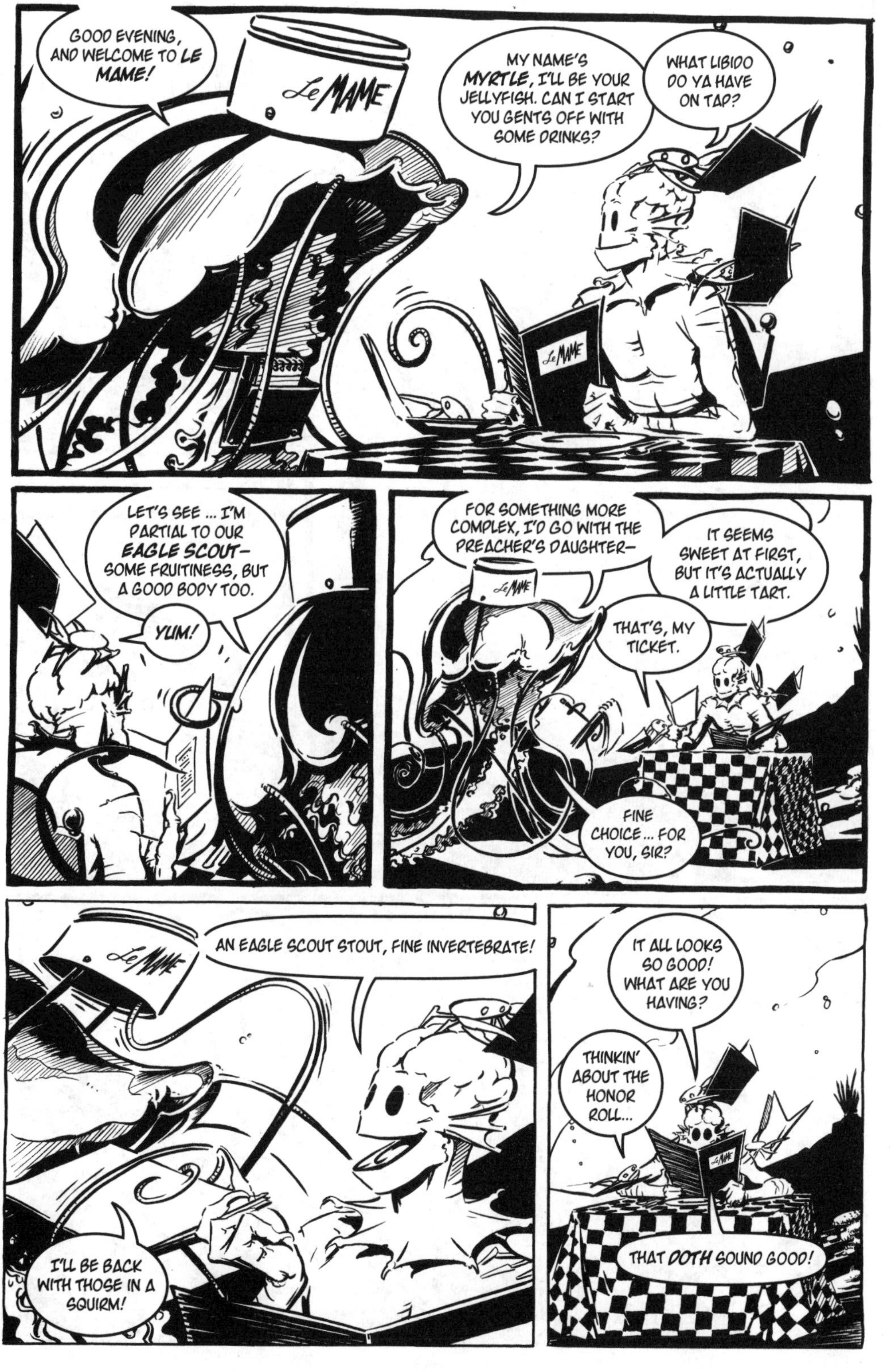
GOOD EVENING, AND WELCOME TO LE MAME!
Le MAME
MY NAME'S MYRTLE, I'LL BE YOUR JELLYFISH. CAN I START YOU GENTS OFF WITH SOME DRINKS?
WHAT LIBIDO DO YA HAVE ON TAP?
Le MAME
LET'S SEE ... I'M PARTIAL TO OUR EAGLE SCOUT— SOME FRUITINESS, BUT A GOOD BODY TOO.
YUM!
FOR SOMETHING MORE COMPLEX, I'D GO WITH THE PREACHER'S DAUGHTER—
Le MAME
IT SEEMS SWEET AT FIRST, BUT IT'S ACTUALLY A LITTLE TART.
THAT'S, MY TICKET.
FINE CHOICE ... FOR YOU, SIR?
Le MAME
AN EAGLE SCOUT STOUT, FINE INVERTEBRATE!
I'LL BE BACK WITH THOSE IN A SQUIRM!
IT ALL LOOKS SO GOOD! WHAT ARE YOU HAVING?
THINKIN' ABOUT THE HONOR ROLL...
Le MAME
THAT DOTH SOUND GOOD!

Panel 1:

HERE WE ARE! AND JUST TO LET YOU KNOW, OUR SPECIAL TONIGHT IS A PROM NIGHT COMBINATION PLATE: 'STOOD UP AND STAG' IN A SPIKED PUNCH SAUCE. THIS IS ALSO HAPPY HOUR, SO SPECIAL ED IS HALF PRICE 'TIL SIX.

DO THEY COME IN THE HELMETS?

NO SIR, WE SHELL THEM.

Panel 2:

YOU GENTS NEED ANY MORE TIME?

LET'S BOOGIE!

Panel 3:

DOES THE HONOR ROLL COME WITH A SPREAD OF SOME SORT?

CHEERLEADER. THAT OK?

PERFECT. ONE OF THOSE, PLEASE.

I'LL HAVE THE CHESS CLUB, OPENED FACES.

VERY GOOD... AND FOR THE SEA MUTANT?

Panel 4:

PRAY, HOW'S THE BEACH BUNNY SERVED?

Panel 5:

AH, MY FAVORITE DISH!

...THE SKIN'S LEFT ON, BRAISED IN COCONUT OIL AND SUN-CRISPED TO PERFECTION: CLASSIC!

64

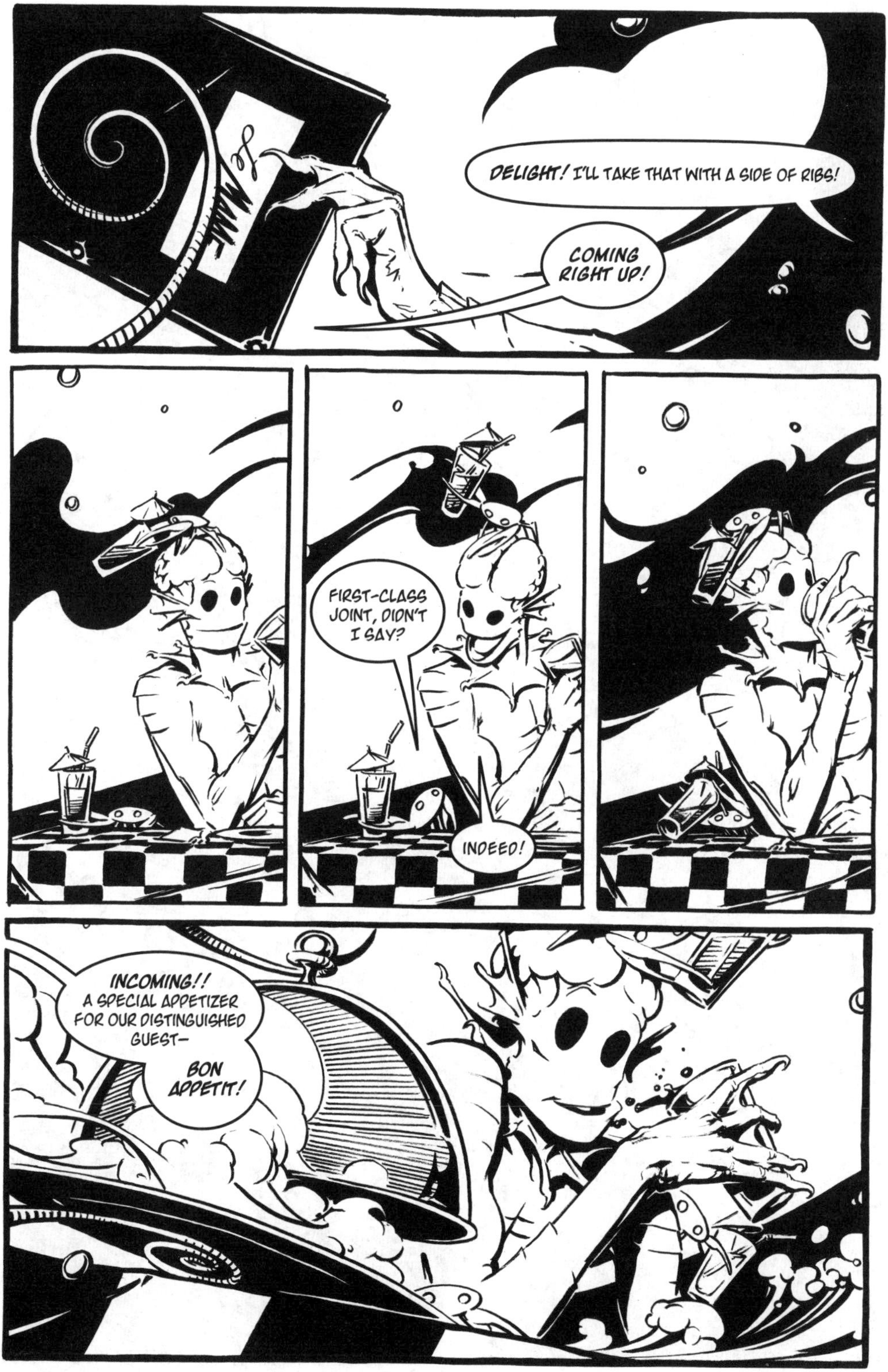
DELIGHT! I'LL TAKE THAT WITH A SIDE OF RIBS!
COMING RIGHT UP!
FIRST-CLASS JOINT, DIDN'T I SAY?
INDEED!
INCOMING!! A SPECIAL APPETIZER FOR OUR DISTINGUISHED GUEST—
BON APPETIT!

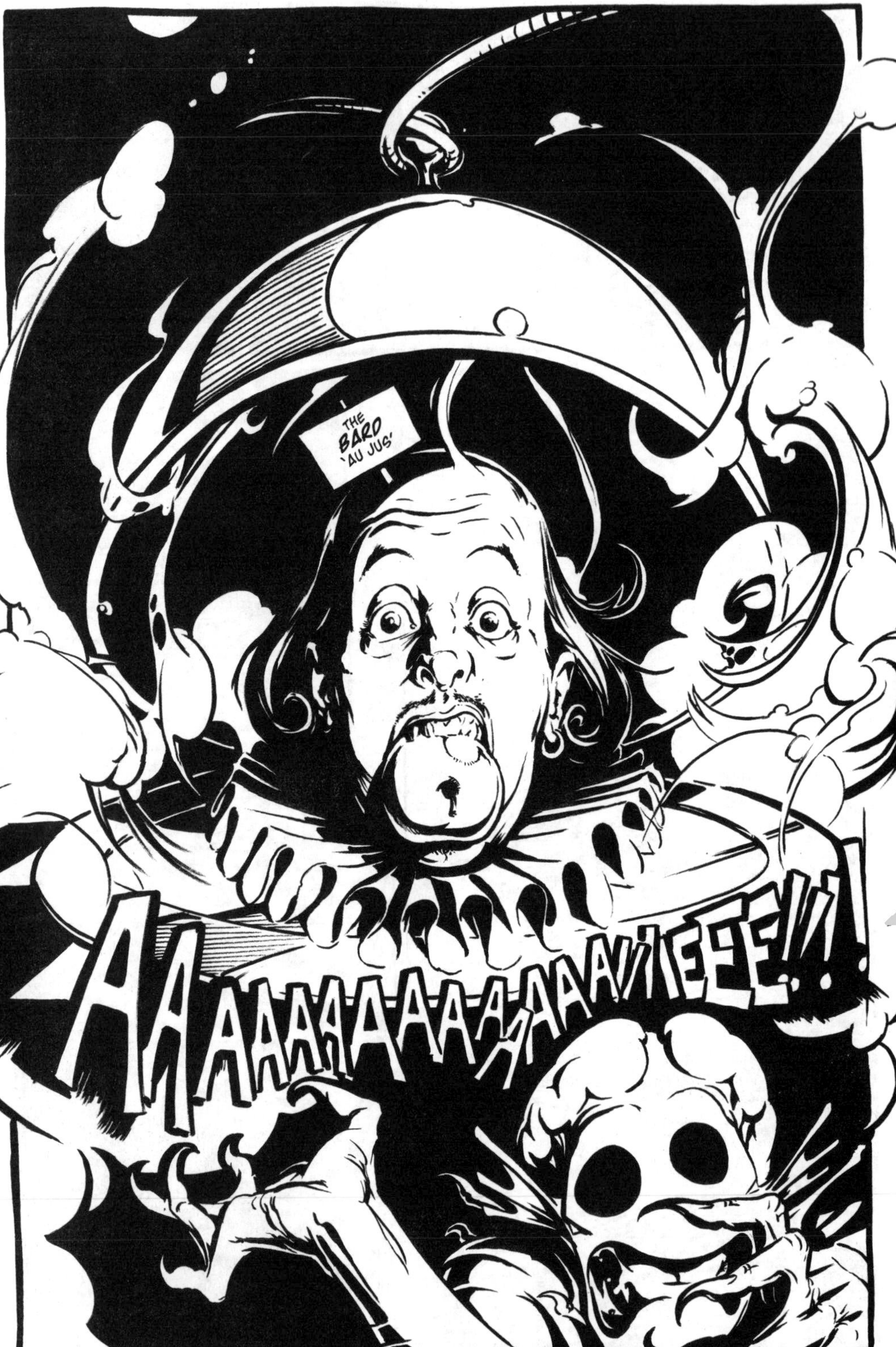
THE BARD `AU JUS'
AAAAAAAAAAAAAAAIEEEE!!!

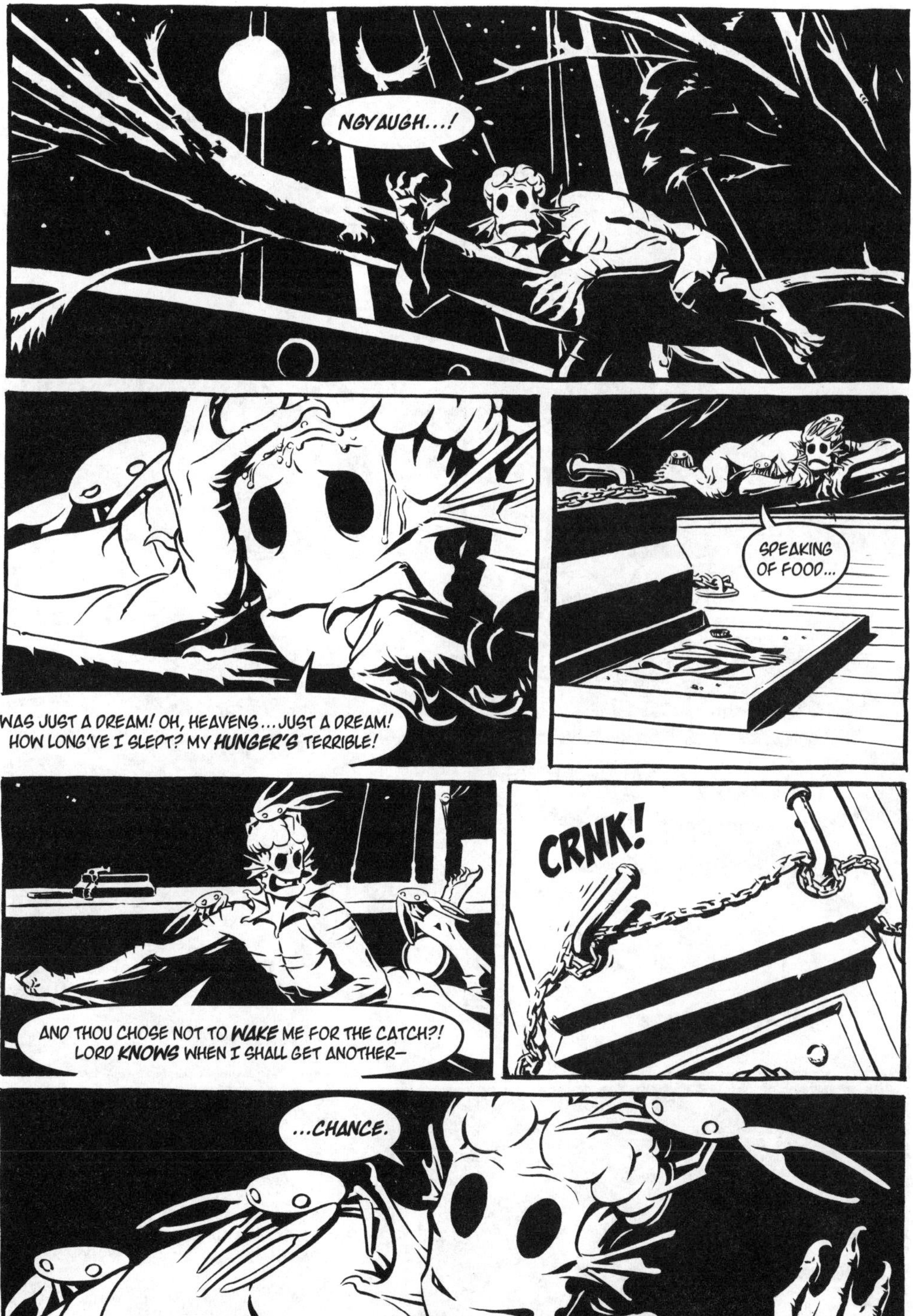
NGYAUGH...!
'TWAS JUST A DREAM! OH, HEAVENS... JUST A DREAM! HOW LONG'VE I SLEPT? MY HUNGER'S TERRIBLE!
SPEAKING OF FOOD...
AND THOU CHOSE NOT TO WAKE ME FOR THE CATCH?! LORD KNOWS WHEN I SHALL GET ANOTHER–
CRNK!
...CHANCE.

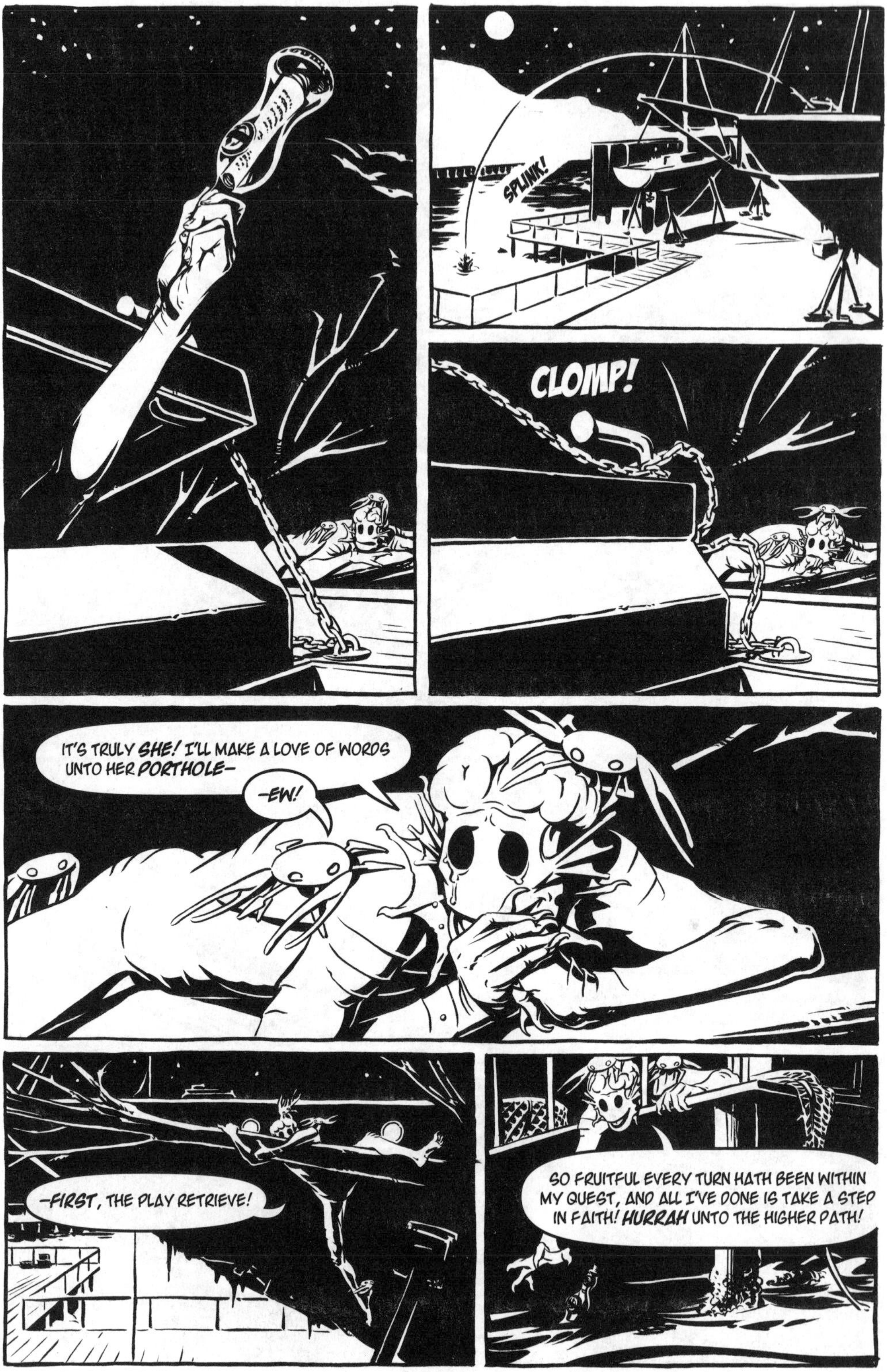
SPLINK!
CLOMP!
IT'S TRULY SHE! I'LL MAKE A LOVE OF WORDS UNTO HER PORTHOLE-
-EW!
-FIRST, THE PLAY RETRIEVE!
SO FRUITFUL EVERY TURN HATH BEEN WITHIN MY QUEST, AND ALL I'VE DONE IS TAKE A STEP IN FAITH! HURRAH UNTO THE HIGHER PATH!

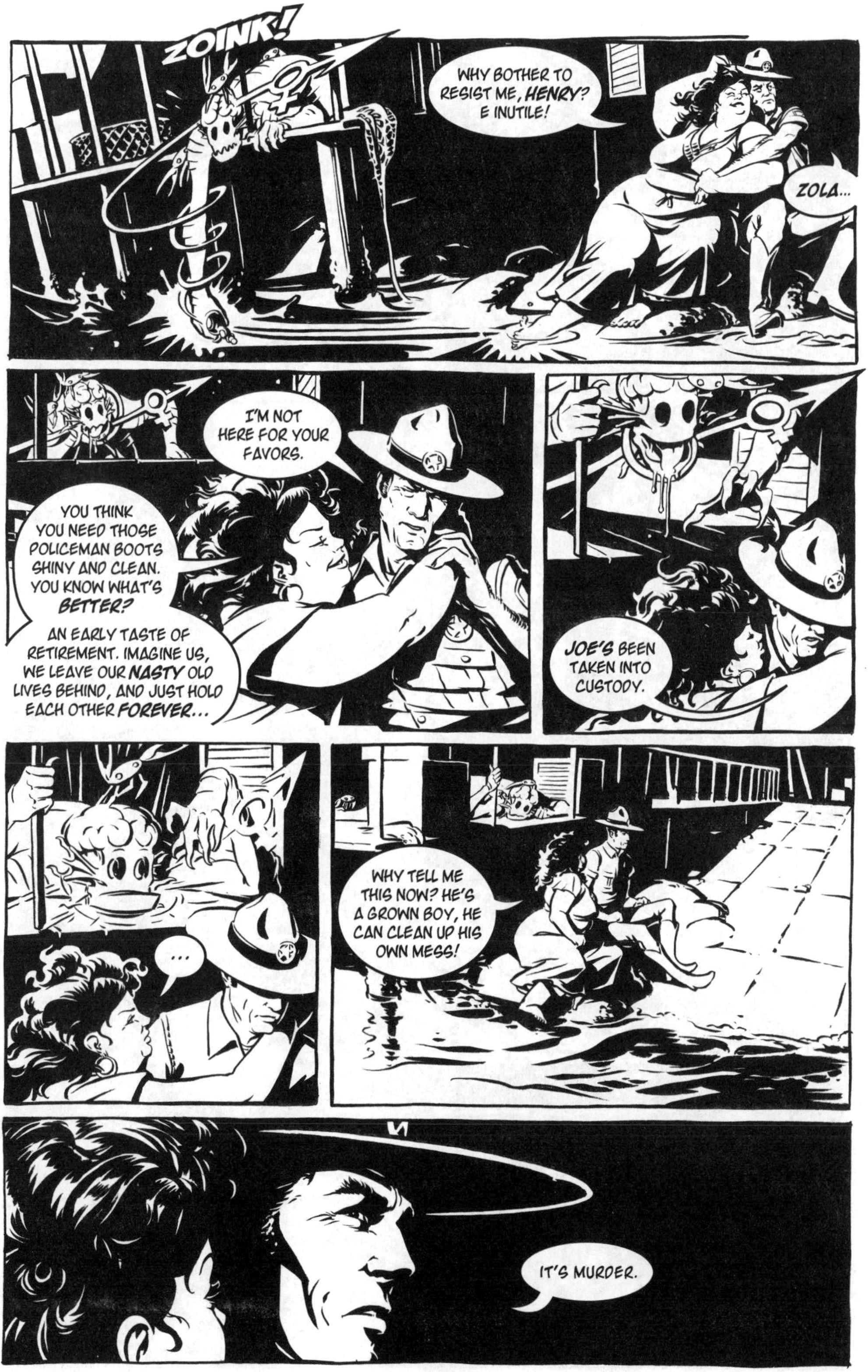
ZOINK!
WHY BOTHER TO RESIST ME, HENRY? E INUTILE!
ZOLA...
I'M NOT HERE FOR YOUR FAVORS.
YOU THINK YOU NEED THOSE POLICEMAN BOOTS SHINY AND CLEAN. YOU KNOW WHAT'S BETTER?
AN EARLY TASTE OF RETIREMENT. IMAGINE US, WE LEAVE OUR NASTY OLD LIVES BEHIND, AND JUST HOLD EACH OTHER FOREVER...
JOE'S BEEN TAKEN INTO CUSTODY.
...
WHY TELL ME THIS NOW? HE'S A GROWN BOY, HE CAN CLEAN UP HIS OWN MESS!
IT'S MURDER.

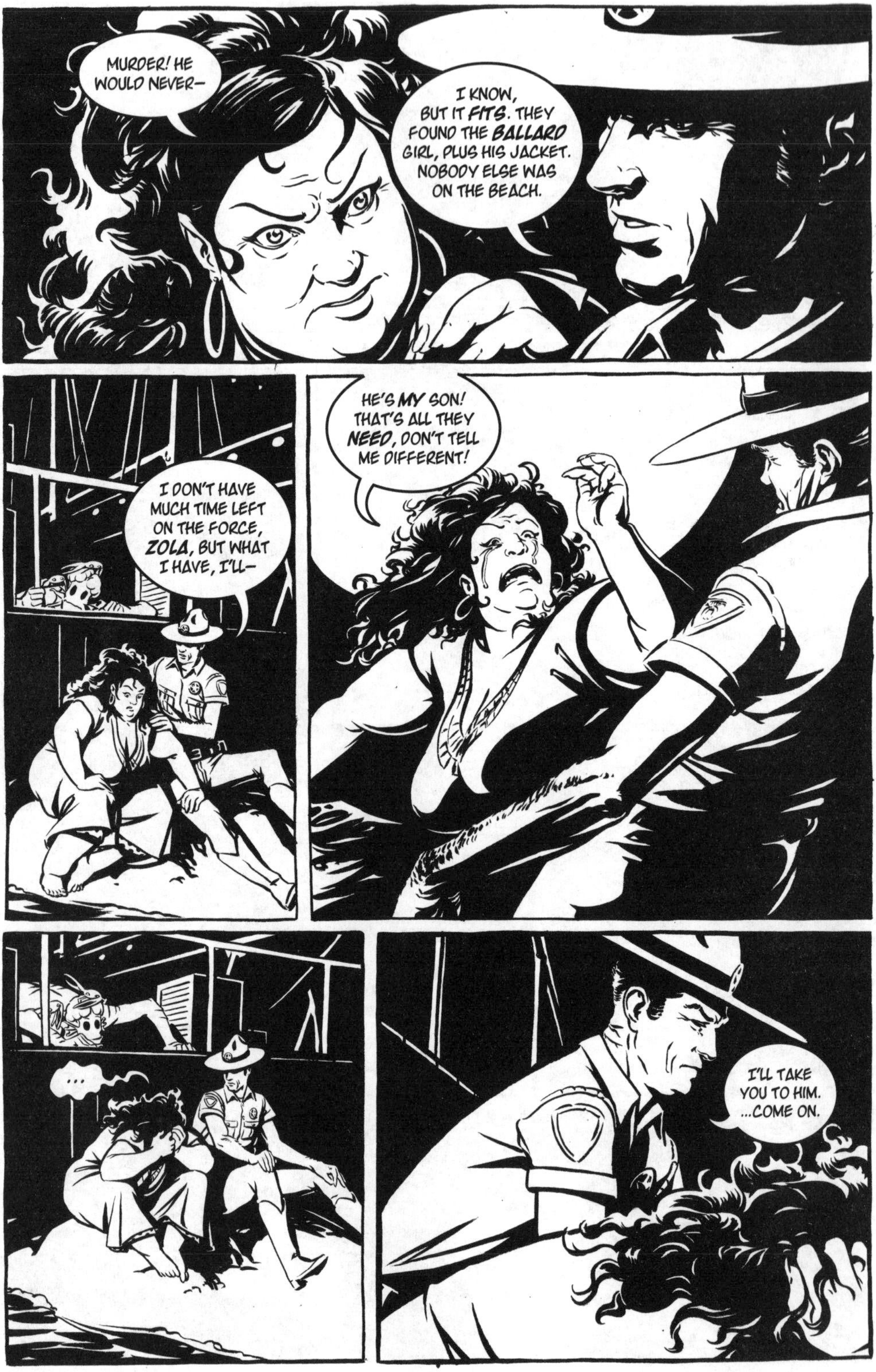
MURDER! HE WOULD NEVER–
I KNOW, BUT IT FITS. THEY FOUND THE BALLARD GIRL, PLUS HIS JACKET. NOBODY ELSE WAS ON THE BEACH.
I DON'T HAVE MUCH TIME LEFT ON THE FORCE, ZOLA, BUT WHAT I HAVE, I'LL–
HE'S MY SON! THAT'S ALL THEY NEED, DON'T TELL ME DIFFERENT!
...
I'LL TAKE YOU TO HIM. ...COME ON.

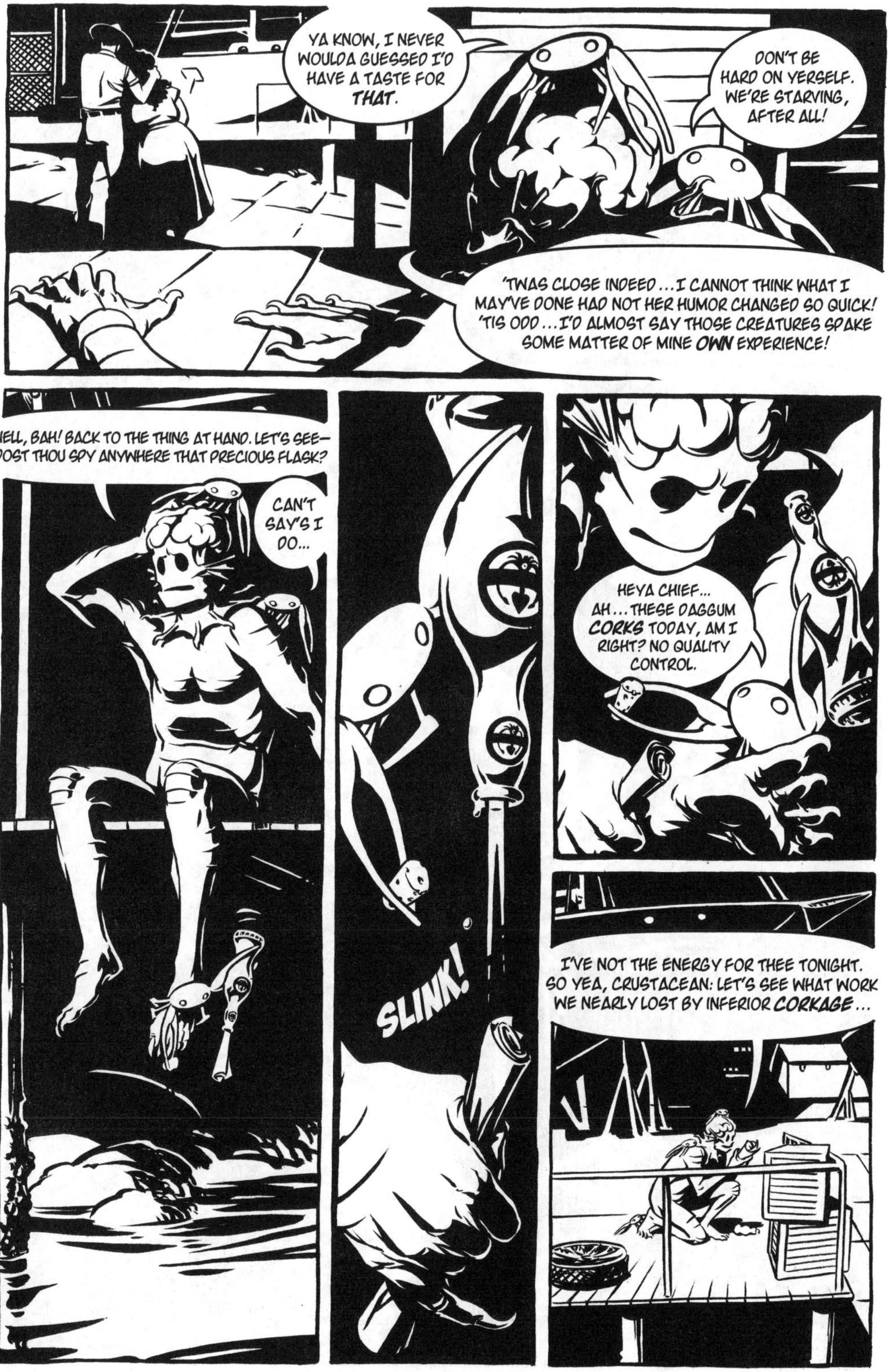
YA KNOW, I NEVER WOULDA GUESSED I'D HAVE A TASTE FOR THAT.
DON'T BE HARD ON YERSELF. WE'RE STARVING, AFTER ALL!
'TWAS CLOSE INDEED... I CANNOT THINK WHAT I MAY'VE DONE HAD NOT HER HUMOR CHANGED SO QUICK! 'TIS ODD... I'D ALMOST SAY THOSE CREATURES SPAKE SOME MATTER OF MINE OWN EXPERIENCE!
WELL, BAH! BACK TO THE THING AT HAND. LET'S SEE-DOST THOU SPY ANYWHERE THAT PRECIOUS FLASK?
CAN'T SAY'S I DO...
SLINK!
HEYA CHIEF... AH... THESE DAGGUM CORKS TODAY, AM I RIGHT? NO QUALITY CONTROL.
I'VE NOT THE ENERGY FOR THEE TONIGHT. SO YEA, CRUSTACEAN: LET'S SEE WHAT WORK WE NEARLY LOST BY INFERIOR CORKAGE...

72

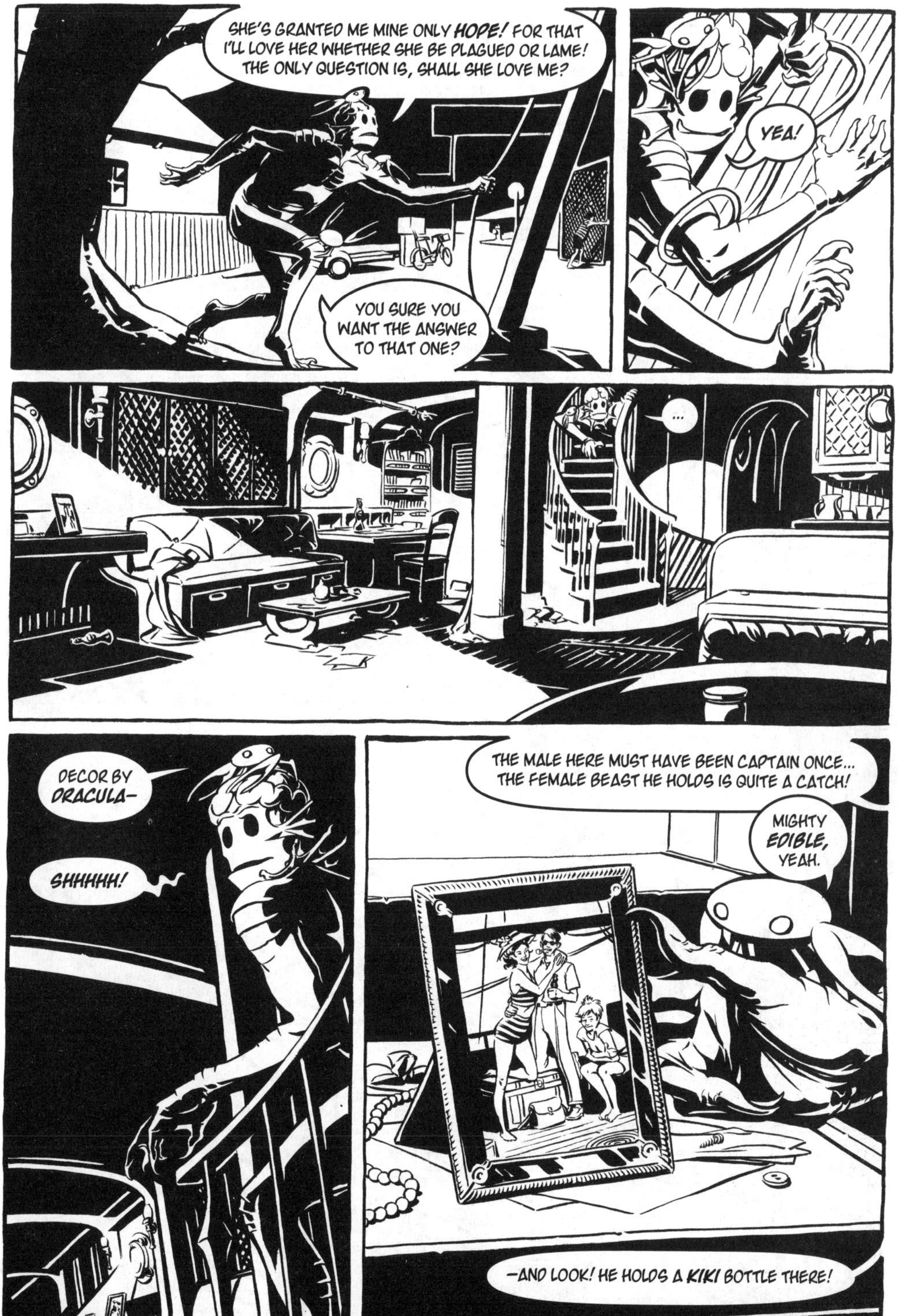
SHE'S GRANTED ME MINE ONLY HOPE! FOR THAT I'LL LOVE HER WHETHER SHE BE PLAGUED OR LAME! THE ONLY QUESTION IS, SHALL SHE LOVE ME?
YOU SURE YOU WANT THE ANSWER TO THAT ONE?
YEA!
...
DECOR BY DRACULA–
SHHHHH!
THE MALE HERE MUST HAVE BEEN CAPTAIN ONCE... THE FEMALE BEAST HE HOLDS IS QUITE A CATCH!
MIGHTY EDIBLE, YEAH.
–AND LOOK! HE HOLDS A KIKI BOTTLE THERE!

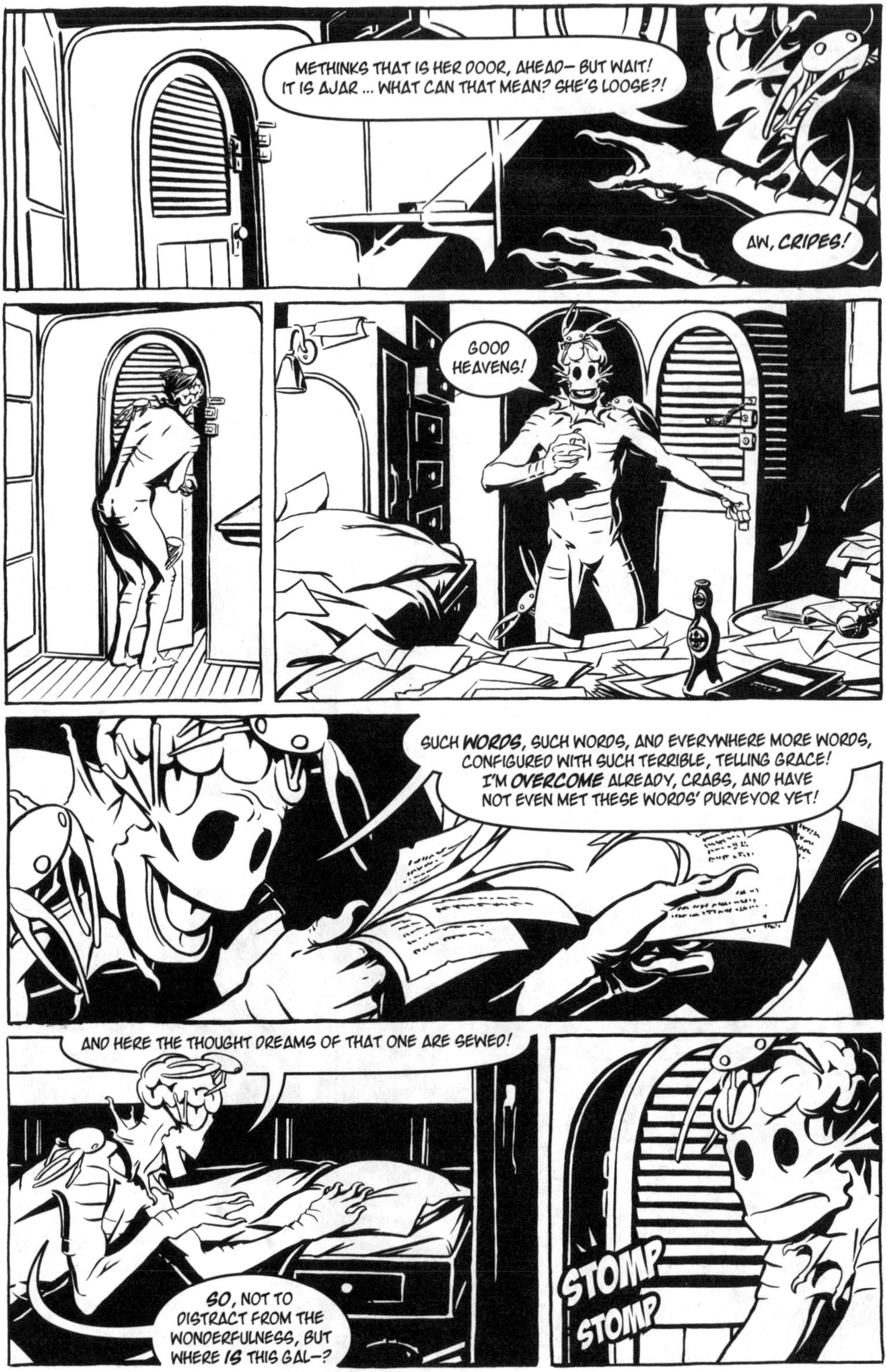
METHINKS THAT IS HER DOOR, AHEAD— BUT WAIT! IT IS AJAR ... WHAT CAN THAT MEAN? SHE'S LOOSE?!
AW, CRIPES!
GOOD HEAVENS!
SUCH WORDS, SUCH WORDS, AND EVERYWHERE MORE WORDS, CONFIGURED WITH SUCH TERRIBLE, TELLING GRACE! I'M OVERCOME ALREADY, CRABS, AND HAVE NOT EVEN MET THESE WORDS' PURVEYOR YET!
AND HERE THE THOUGHT DREAMS OF THAT ONE ARE SEWED!
SO, NOT TO DISTRACT FROM THE WONDERFULNESS, BUT WHERE IS THIS GAL—?
STOMP
STOMP

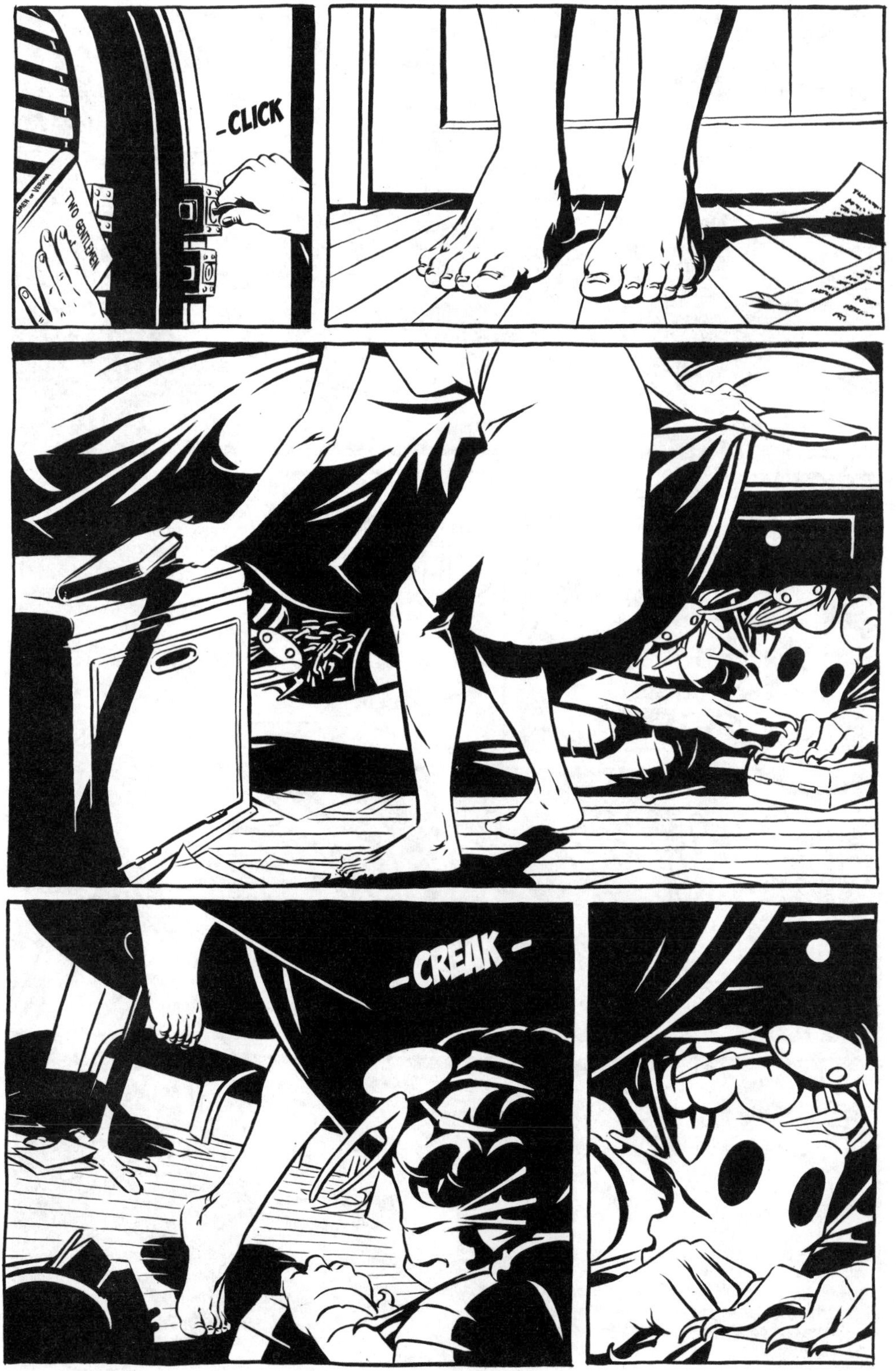
-CLICK
TWO GENTLEMEN
-CREAK-

DEAR LORD, THANK YOU FOR THIS NIGHT, AND THANK YOU FOR *BOBBY, ZOLA, JOE,* AND EVERYONE ELSE I KNOW AND LOVE...

THANK YOU FOR LIFE, LOVE, BEAUTY, ART, THE IMAGINATION, AND ALL THE OTHER GOOD THINGS IN LIFE. HELP TODAY TO BE A GOOD DAY FOR EVERYONE. IN *JESUS'* NAME. AMEN.

?

—AND FORGIVE ME OF MY SINS. *AMEN.*

BEDTIME FOR *BONKERS—*

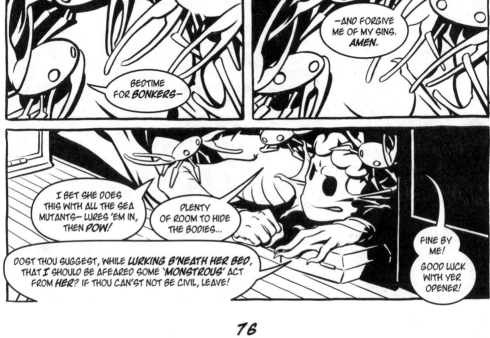

I BET SHE DOES THIS WITH ALL THE SEA MUTANTS— LURES 'EM IN, THEN *POW!*

PLENTY OF ROOM TO HIDE THE BODIES...

DOST THOU SUGGEST, WHILE *LURKING B'NEATH HER BED,* THAT *I* SHOULD BE AFEARED SOME *'MONSTROUS'* ACT FROM *HER?* IF THOU CAN'ST NOT BE CIVIL, LEAVE!

FINE BY ME!

GOOD LUCK WITH YER OPENER!

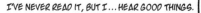

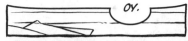

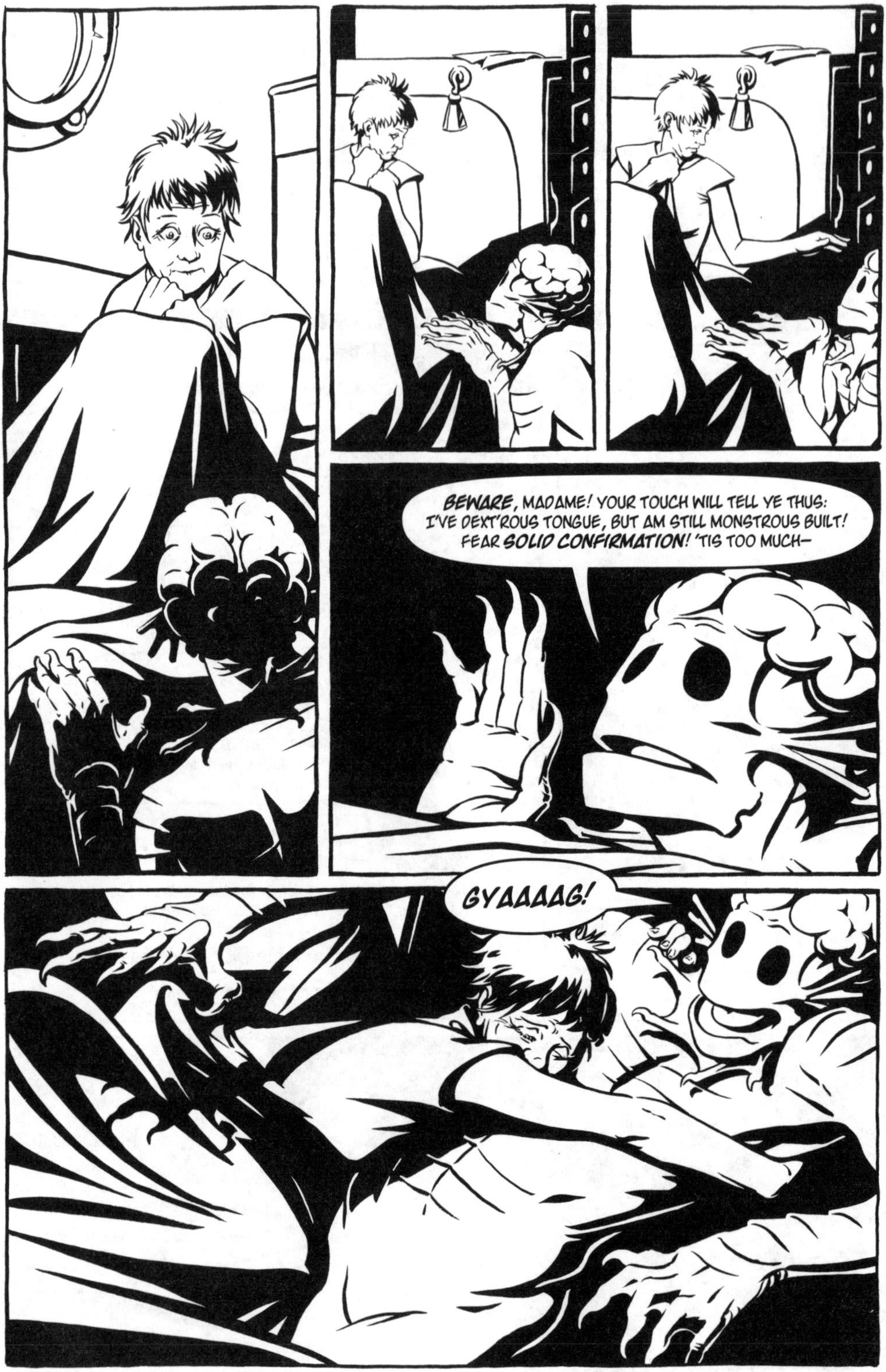
BEWARE, MADAME! YOUR TOUCH WILL TELL YE THUS: I'VE DEXT'ROUS TONGUE, BUT AM STILL MONSTROUS BUILT! FEAR SOLID CONFIRMATION! 'TIS TOO MUCH—
GYAAAAG!

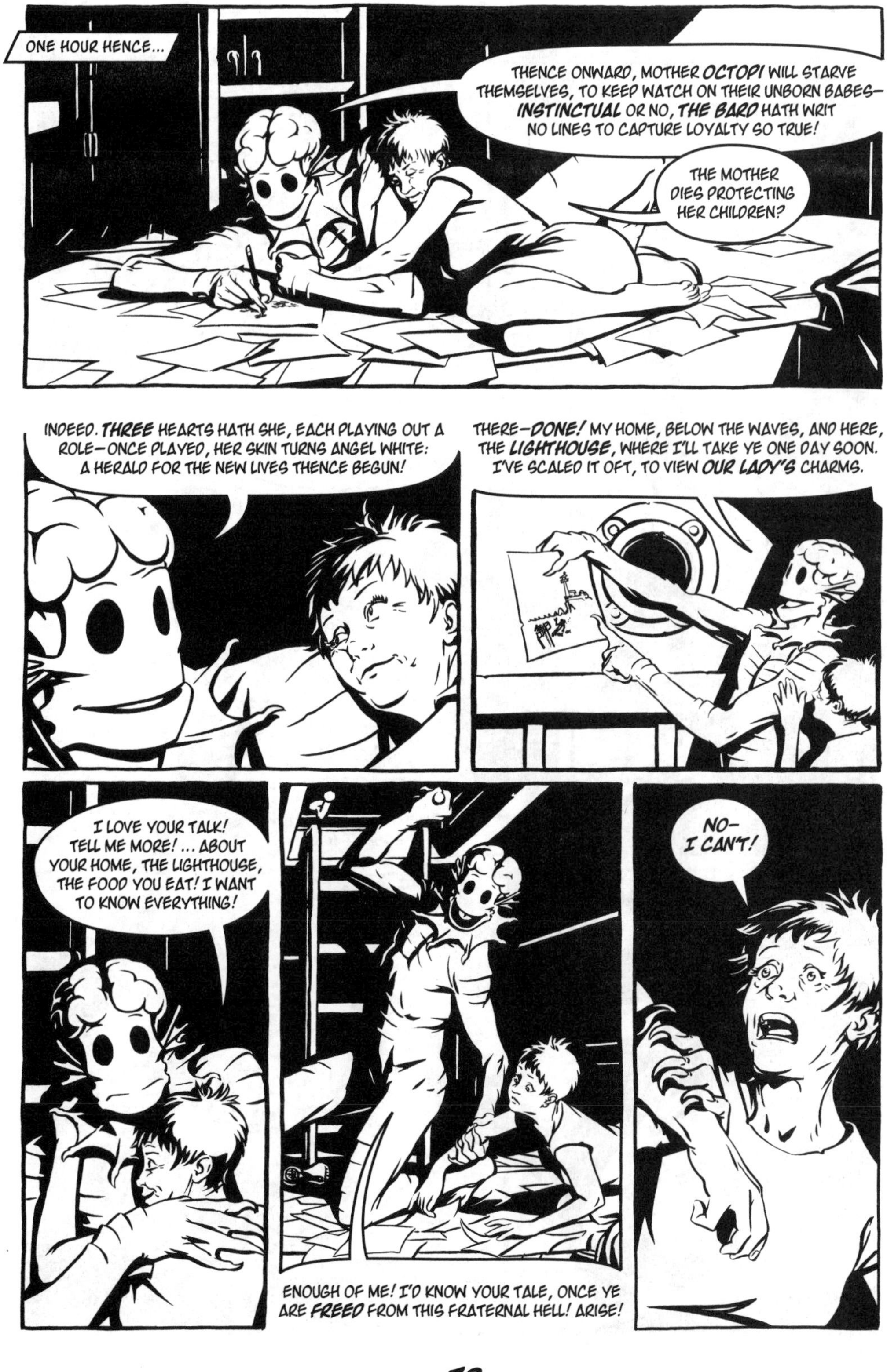
ONE HOUR HENCE...
THENCE ONWARD, MOTHER OCTOPI WILL STARVE THEMSELVES, TO KEEP WATCH ON THEIR UNBORN BABES—INSTINCTUAL OR NO, THE BARD HATH WRIT NO LINES TO CAPTURE LOYALTY SO TRUE!
THE MOTHER DIES PROTECTING HER CHILDREN?
INDEED. THREE HEARTS HATH SHE, EACH PLAYING OUT A ROLE—ONCE PLAYED, HER SKIN TURNS ANGEL WHITE: A HERALD FOR THE NEW LIVES THENCE BEGUN!
THERE—DONE! MY HOME, BELOW THE WAVES, AND HERE, THE LIGHTHOUSE, WHERE I'LL TAKE YE ONE DAY SOON. I'VE SCALED IT OFT, TO VIEW OUR LADY'S CHARMS.
I LOVE YOUR TALK! TELL ME MORE! ... ABOUT YOUR HOME, THE LIGHTHOUSE, THE FOOD YOU EAT! I WANT TO KNOW EVERYTHING!
ENOUGH OF ME! I'D KNOW YOUR TALE, ONCE YE ARE FREED FROM THIS FRATERNAL HELL! ARISE!
NO—I CAN'T!

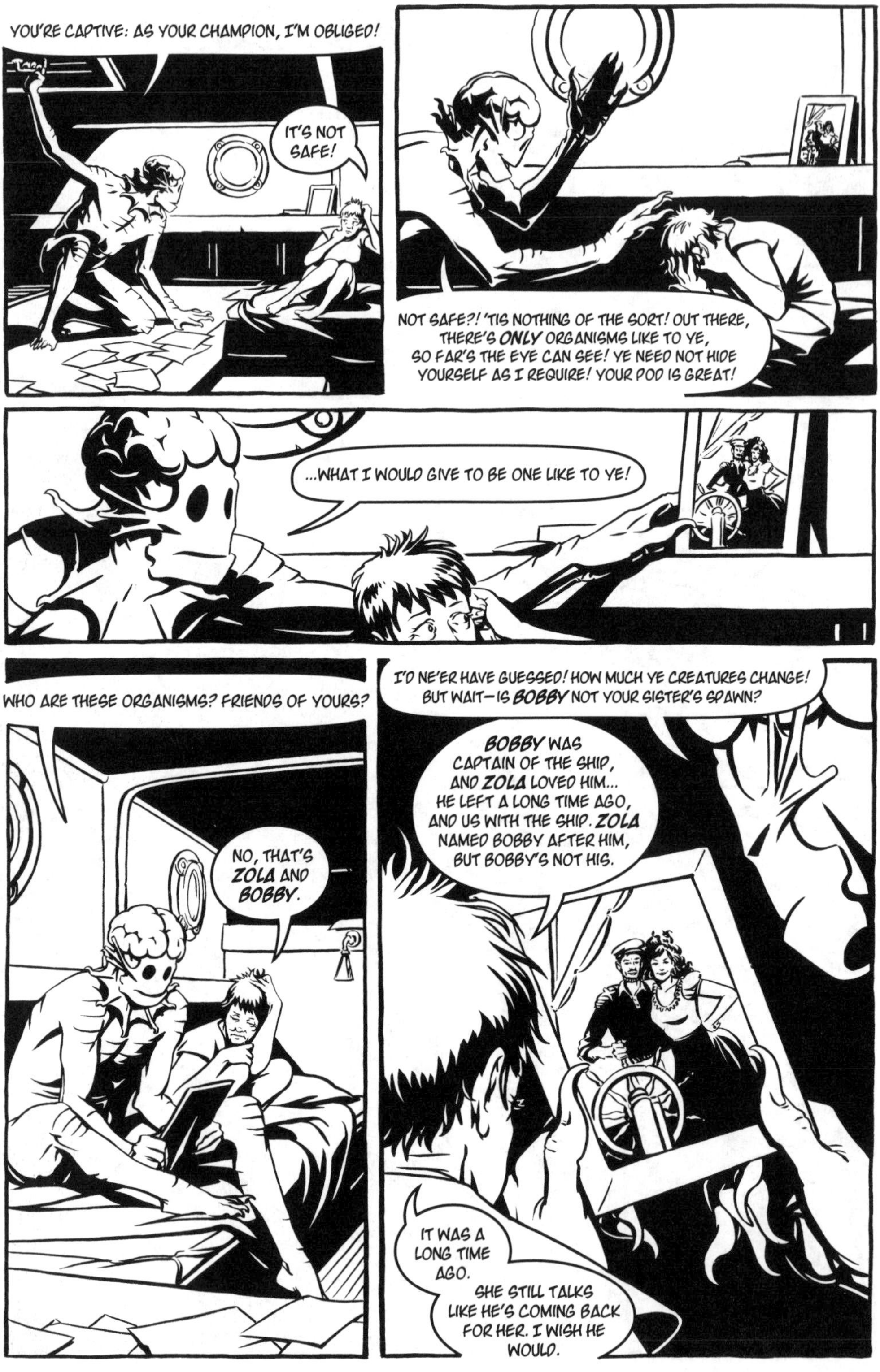
YOU'RE CAPTIVE: AS YOUR CHAMPION, I'M OBLIGED!
IT'S NOT SAFE!
NOT SAFE?! 'TIS NOTHING OF THE SORT! OUT THERE, THERE'S ONLY ORGANISMS LIKE TO YE, SO FAR'S THE EYE CAN SEE! YE NEED NOT HIDE YOURSELF AS I REQUIRE! YOUR POD IS GREAT!
...WHAT I WOULD GIVE TO BE ONE LIKE TO YE!
WHO ARE THESE ORGANISMS? FRIENDS OF YOURS?
NO, THAT'S ZOLA AND BOBBY.
I'D NE'ER HAVE GUESSED! HOW MUCH YE CREATURES CHANGE! BUT WAIT—IS BOBBY NOT YOUR SISTER'S SPAWN?
BOBBY WAS CAPTAIN OF THE SHIP, AND ZOLA LOVED HIM... HE LEFT A LONG TIME AGO, AND US WITH THE SHIP. ZOLA NAMED BOBBY AFTER HIM, BUT BOBBY'S NOT HIS.
IT WAS A LONG TIME AGO.
SHE STILL TALKS LIKE HE'S COMING BACK FOR HER. I WISH HE WOULD.

YE SAILED WITH HIM ACROSS THE SEA! FROM WHENCE?

HE TAUGHT US *ENGLISH*, TOO...

FROM *ITALY*, AFTER THE SECOND WAR. HE WAS *BRITISH*, AND HE TALKED WELL: SORT OF LIKE YOU...

HE WOULD READ FROM THESE *PLAYS*—THEY WERE HIS TREASURES! *ZOLA* DIDN'T LIKE TO LISTEN. I DON'T KNOW WHY. I LIKED TO...

I ALMOST THOUGHT HE *DID* COME BACK... WHEN YOU SPOKE!

TWO GENTLEMEN of VERONA

I SEE. AND ART YE ... DISAPPOINTED, THEN?

OH, NO, NO! YOU HAVE A MONSTER'S *BODY*, BUT ... I CAN SEE YOU. I SEE HIM IN YOU.

YET HERE'S DISTINCTION, WENCH: I'LL NOT LEAVE YE! I'M HERE FOR **NAUGHT BUT BENEFIT** TO YE! SO, THEN, RELEASE WHATEVER STOCK YE'VE LEFT IN THESE BETRAYORS. WE HAVE **LIFE** TO LIVE!

I CAN'T LEAVE THE BOAT—IT'S NOT SAFE!!

O, **FIE!** YOUR SISTER'S PUT YE HERE AND MADE YE LIKE IT! WELL, I'VE COME PURSUING ENDS TO **MINE OWN** ILLS: SO HERE, I'LL MAKE AN END TO **YOURS** AS WELL—ARISE!

YOU'RE FREE AT LAST!

AAAAAAAAAAAAAAA

I'M SORRY! **GIULIETTA**, CALM YOURSELF!

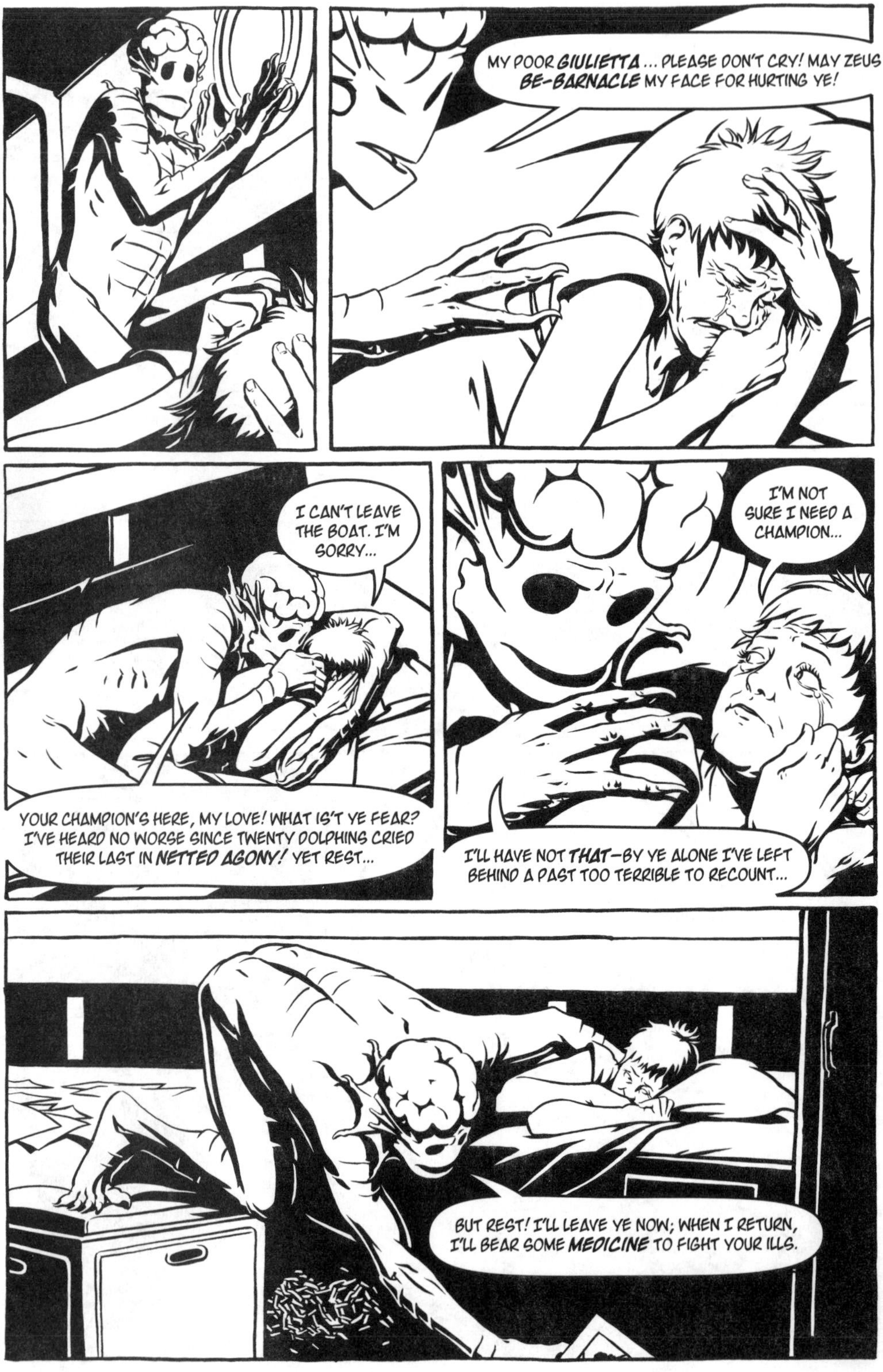
MY POOR GIULIETTA ... PLEASE DON'T CRY! MAY ZEUS BE-BARNACLE MY FACE FOR HURTING YE!
I CAN'T LEAVE THE BOAT. I'M SORRY...
YOUR CHAMPION'S HERE, MY LOVE! WHAT IS'T YE FEAR? I'VE HEARD NO WORSE SINCE TWENTY DOLPHINS CRIED THEIR LAST IN NETTED AGONY! YET REST...
I'M NOT SURE I NEED A CHAMPION...
I'LL HAVE NOT THAT—BY YE ALONE I'VE LEFT BEHIND A PAST TOO TERRIBLE TO RECOUNT...
BUT REST! I'LL LEAVE YE NOW; WHEN I RETURN, I'LL BEAR SOME MEDICINE TO FIGHT YOUR ILLS.

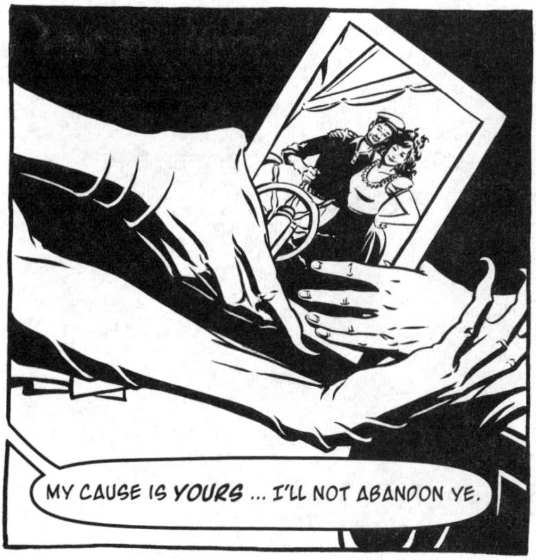
MY CAUSE IS *YOURS* ... I'LL NOT ABANDON YE.

CHAPTER FOUR
crying

89

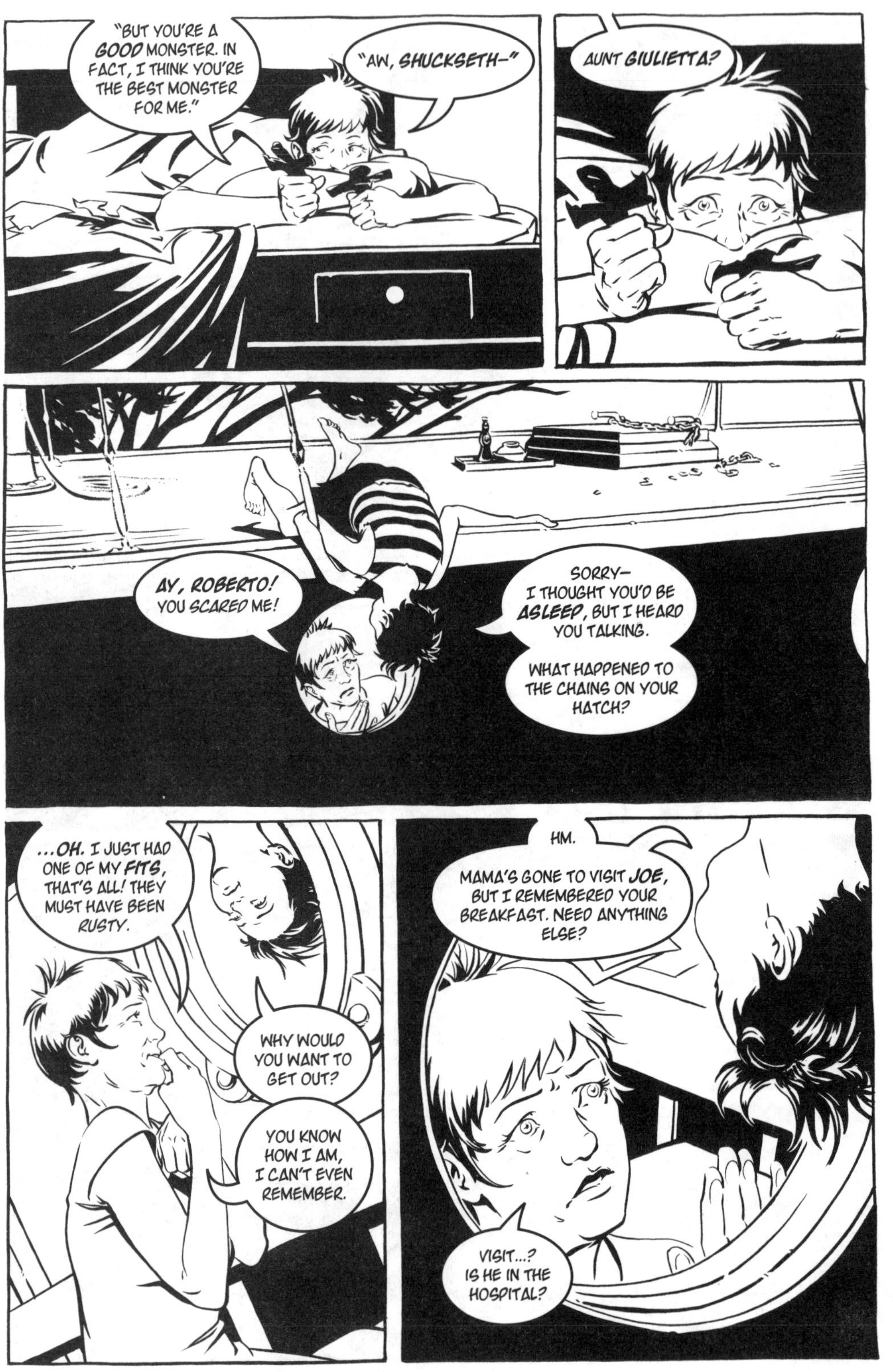
"BUT YOU'RE A GOOD MONSTER. IN FACT, I THINK YOU'RE THE BEST MONSTER FOR ME."
"AW, SHUCKSETH–"
AUNT GIULIETTA?
AY, ROBERTO! YOU SCARED ME!
SORRY– I THOUGHT YOU'D BE ASLEEP, BUT I HEARD YOU TALKING.
WHAT HAPPENED TO THE CHAINS ON YOUR HATCH?
...OH. I JUST HAD ONE OF MY FITS, THAT'S ALL! THEY MUST HAVE BEEN RUSTY.
WHY WOULD YOU WANT TO GET OUT?
YOU KNOW HOW I AM, I CAN'T EVEN REMEMBER.
HM.
MAMA'S GONE TO VISIT JOE, BUT I REMEMBERED YOUR BREAKFAST. NEED ANYTHING ELSE?
VISIT...? IS HE IN THE HOSPITAL?

The Daily
SOUTHWEST[ERN]

August 6th, 1963

LIGHTHOUSE KILLER CAPTURED!

Police link high school running back with rash of summertime disappearances. Trial Tuesday.

By JOHN CULLICOTT
(Ass't Managing Editor)

In an unparalleled act of deductive reasoning, local police have linked Joe Marina, a senior at Santa Lucia High, with the murder of his school-mate, Jane Ballard. The first part of the Ballard girl's body was found washed up last week...

DEAR LORD...

'LIGHTHOUSE KILLER'...?

THEY SAY HE PUSHED HER OFF THE LIGHTHOUSE LAST *FRIDAY*... MAYBE OTHERS TOO.

CAPTAIN *CRAW* SAYS THEY'RE WRONG.

HE SAYS *MR. HARRISON*, THE LIGHT-HOUSE KEEPER, ALWAYS LOCKS IT FROM BELOW SO NO ONE CAN GET TO THE *TOP* WHEN HE'S NOT *THERE*.

HARRISON— WHERE HAVE I HEARD HIS NAME BEFORE?

HE'S... A *FRIEND* OF MOMMA'S.

OF COURSE!!! HE WAS *HERE* THAT NIGHT, I SAW HIM! IF I CAN EXPLAIN—OH, *BOBBY!* WE COULD HELP *JOE* CLEAR HIS NAME!

YES! DON'T WORRY BOBBY, WE'RE GOING TO HELP JOE, AND—

AUNT GIULIETTA?

—HM?

HOW CAN YOU HELP IF YOU CAN'T LEAVE YOUR CABIN?

...

91

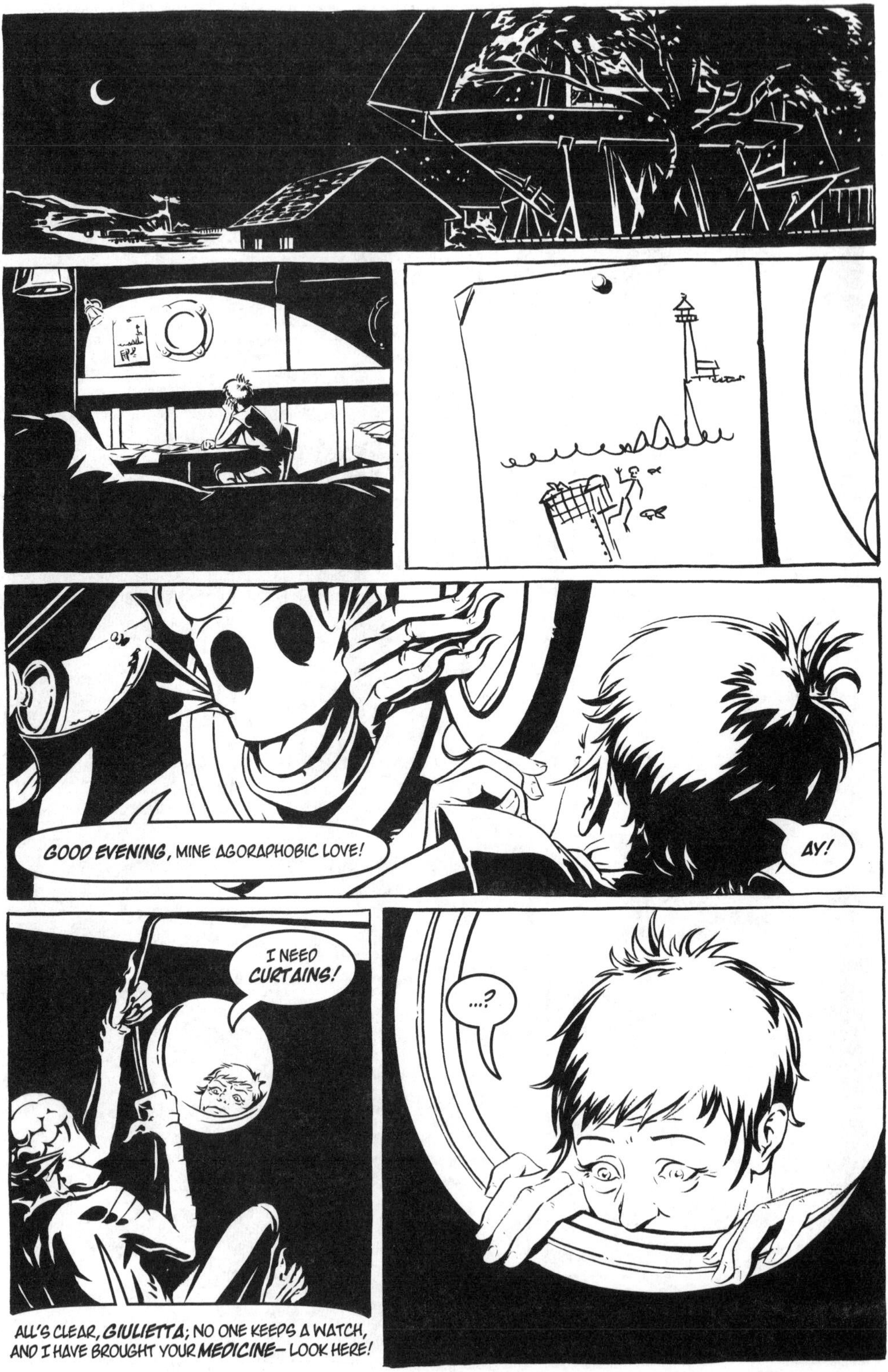
GOOD EVENING, MINE AGORAPHOBIC LOVE!
AY!
I NEED CURTAINS!
...?
ALL'S CLEAR, GIULIETTA; NO ONE KEEPS A WATCH, AND I HAVE BROUGHT YOUR MEDICINE— LOOK HERE!

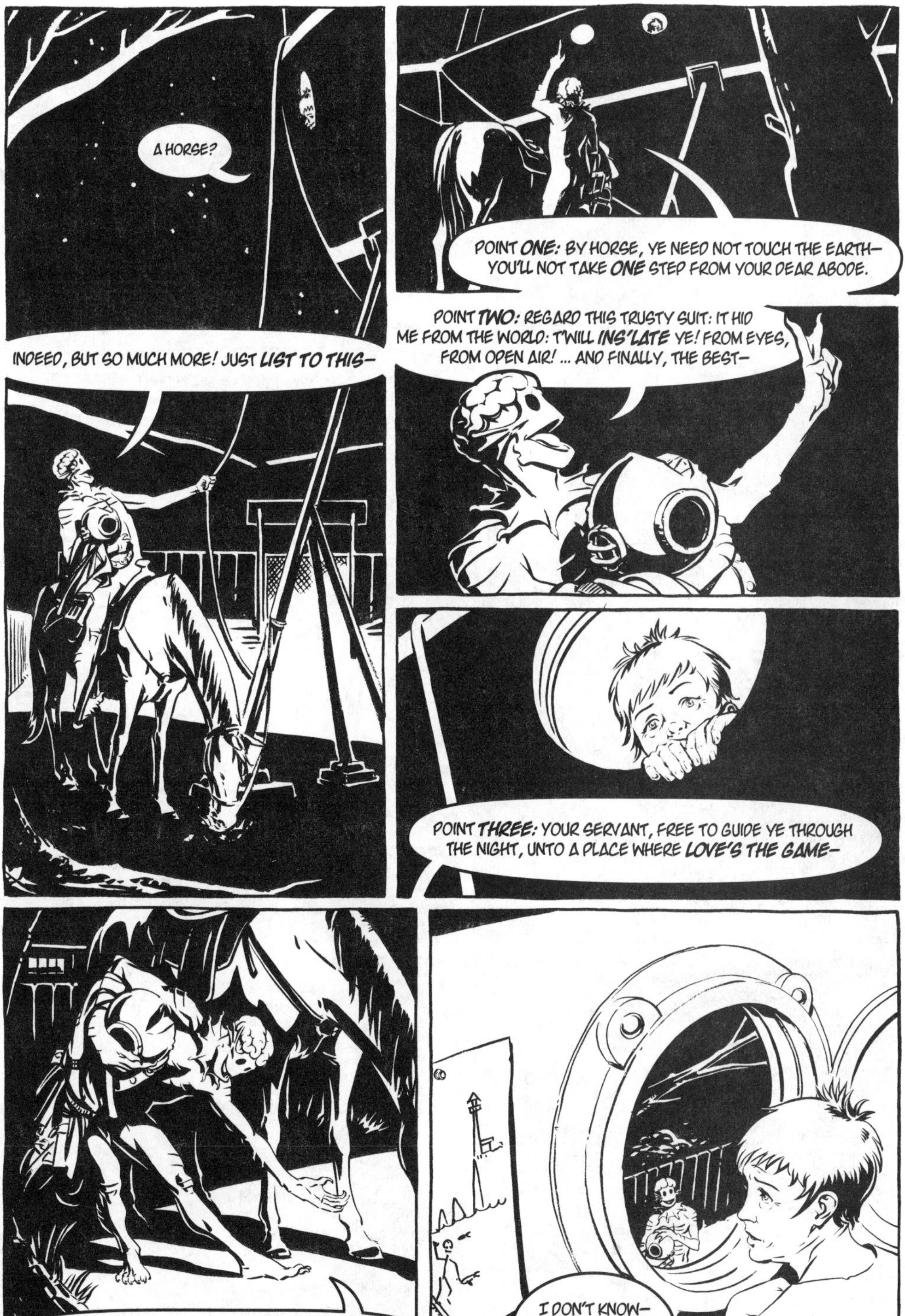
A HORSE?
POINT ONE: BY HORSE, YE NEED NOT TOUCH THE EARTH– YOU'LL NOT TAKE ONE STEP FROM YOUR DEAR ABODE.
INDEED, BUT SO MUCH MORE! JUST LIST TO THIS–
POINT TWO: REGARD THIS TRUSTY SUIT: IT HID ME FROM THE WORLD: T'WILL INS'LATE YE! FROM EYES, FROM OPEN AIR! ... AND FINALLY, THE BEST–
POINT THREE: YOUR SERVANT, FREE TO GUIDE YE THROUGH THE NIGHT, UNTO A PLACE WHERE LOVE'S THE GAME–
AND ALL EYES TURN TO THEIR OWN LOVES, PRYING NOT INTO OUR DELICATE AFFAIR ... YE SEE?
I DON'T KNOW– I DON'T KNOW WHAT TO SAY.

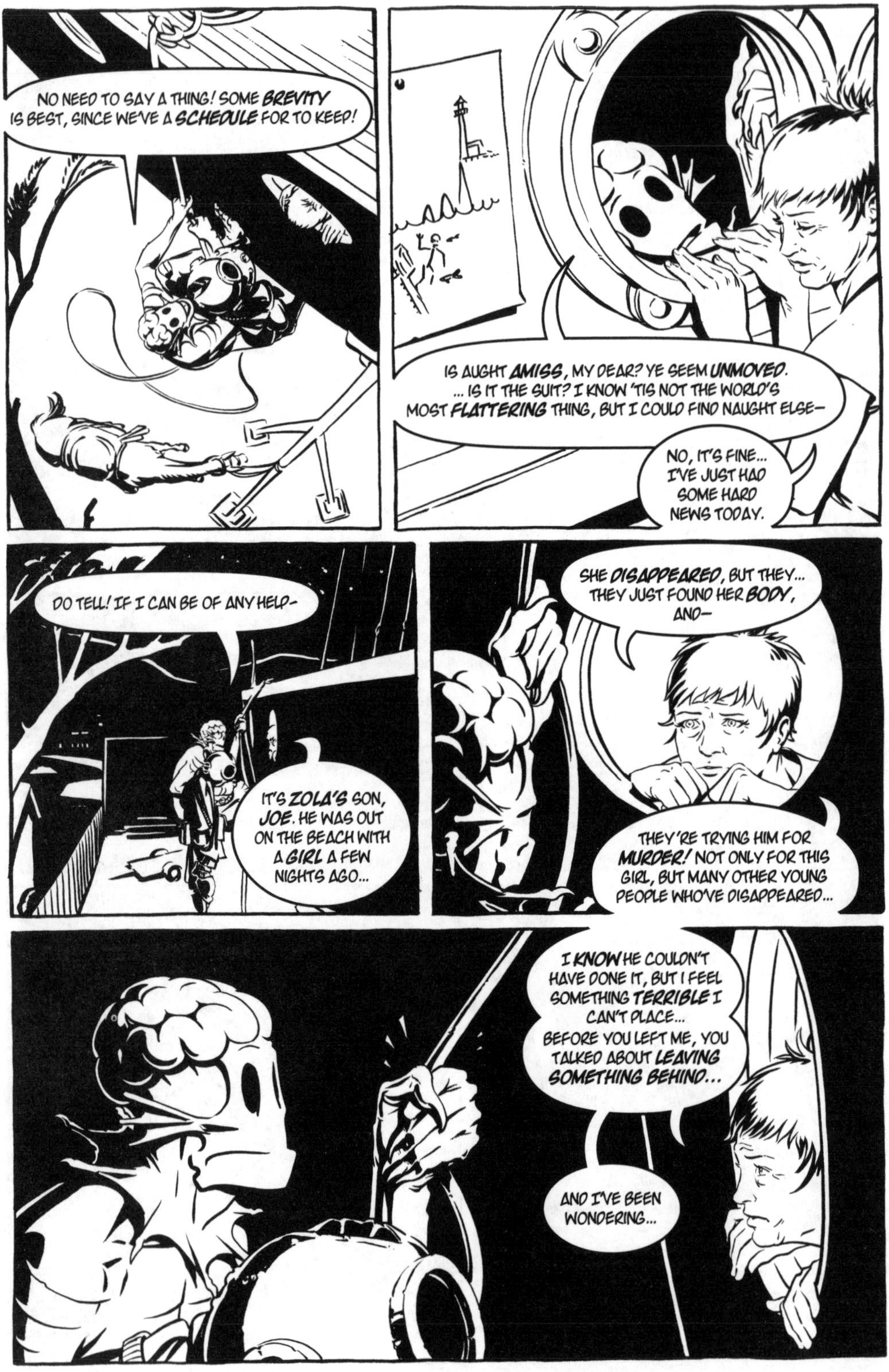
NO NEED TO SAY A THING! SOME BREVITY IS BEST, SINCE WE'VE A SCHEDULE FOR TO KEEP!
IS AUGHT AMISS, MY DEAR? YE SEEM UNMOVED. ... IS IT THE SUIT? I KNOW 'TIS NOT THE WORLD'S MOST FLATTERING THING, BUT I COULD FIND NAUGHT ELSE—
NO, IT'S FINE... I'VE JUST HAD SOME HARD NEWS TODAY.
DO TELL! IF I CAN BE OF ANY HELP-
IT'S ZOLA'S SON, JOE. HE WAS OUT ON THE BEACH WITH A GIRL A FEW NIGHTS AGO...
SHE DISAPPEARED, BUT THEY... THEY JUST FOUND HER BODY, AND—
THEY'RE TRYING HIM FOR MURDER! NOT ONLY FOR THIS GIRL, BUT MANY OTHER YOUNG PEOPLE WHO'VE DISAPPEARED...
I KNOW HE COULDN'T HAVE DONE IT, BUT I FEEL SOMETHING TERRIBLE I CAN'T PLACE...
BEFORE YOU LEFT ME, YOU TALKED ABOUT LEAVING SOMETHING BEHIND...
AND I'VE BEEN WONDERING...

95

INNOCENT AS AN *ANGELFISH*, EH?

BEGONE, FOUL *DEMON!* THOU'RT NOT MY *JUDGE!*

GRUE?!

FORGIVE ME, LOVE! I WAS ... *RECITING* SOME OLD LINES; A LITTLE *MONOLOGUE* OR SOME SUCH SILLINESS! SHALL WE DESCEND AND RIDE?

...ALL RIGHT.

WHICH *PLAY* WAS IT FROM?

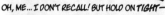

OH, ME ... I DON'T RECALL! BUT HOLD ON *TIGHT—*

I'VE NAMED HIM *ROCINANTE.* HE'S A GEM... ART COMFORTABLE, MY LOVE? YE LOOK DIVINE!

I CAN'T SCRATCH MY NOSE, BUT I'M OKAY.

I *THANK* YE FOR YOUR BRAVERY! YE'LL SEE, *GIULIETTA*— YE ARE *SAFE* AS SAFE CAN BE!

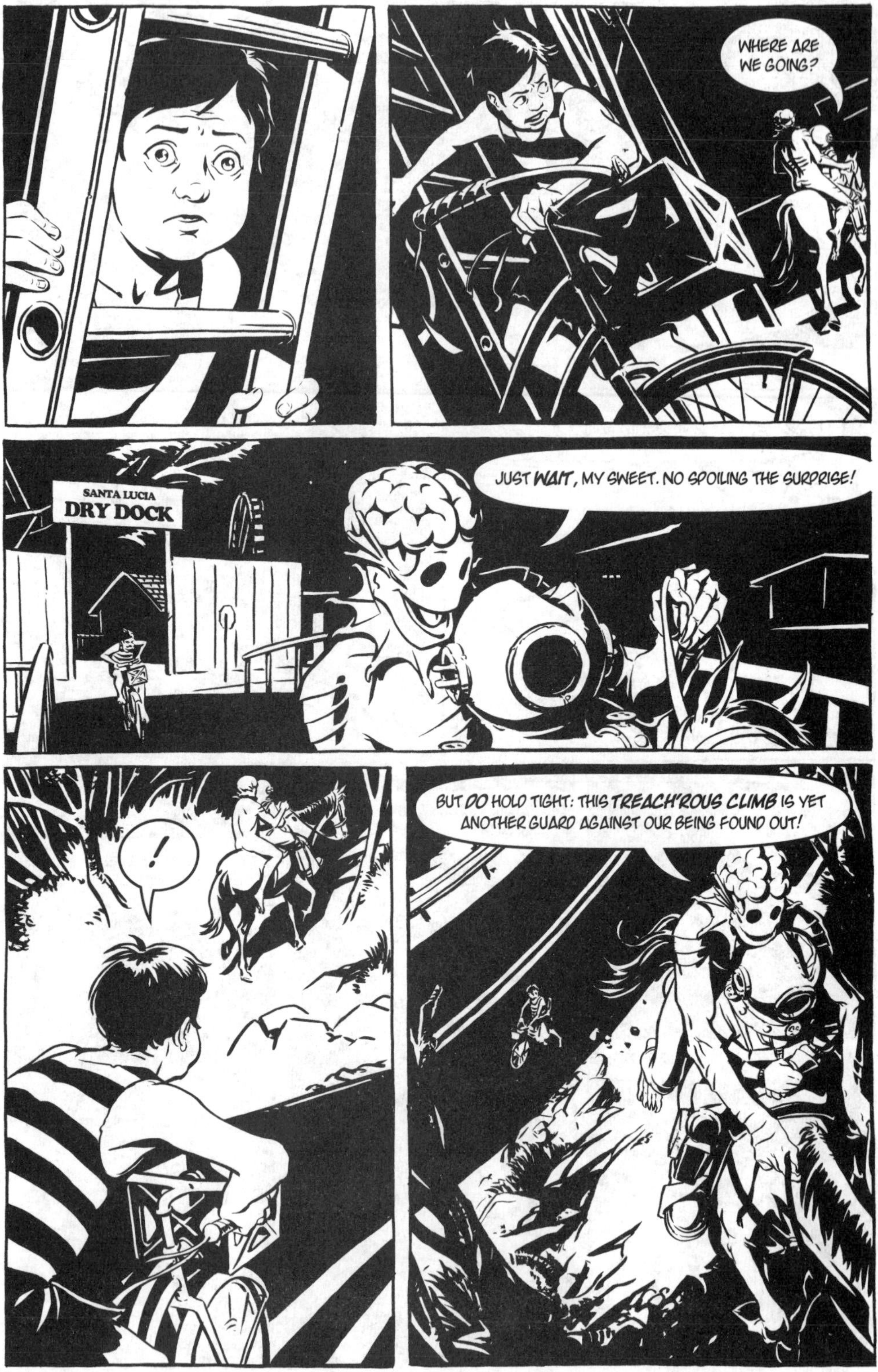
WHERE ARE WE GOING?
SANTA LUCIA DRY DOCK
JUST WAIT, MY SWEET. NO SPOILING THE SURPRISE!
!
BUT DO HOLD TIGHT: THIS TREACH'ROUS CLIMB IS YET ANOTHER GUARD AGAINST OUR BEING FOUND OUT!

SO TELL ME, *LARRY*, IS THIS SOME *NEW* KIND OF IDIOCY? SOMETHING BEYOND MY *TIME*?

SORRY, CAPTAIN.

SORRY DON'T GET A *STOLEN HORSE* BACK, SON. NOT THE *SECOND* TIME, EITHER.

CAPTAIN CRAW!

YOU CAN SEE *JOE* TOMORROW, *BOBBY*. NO MORE VISITS TODAY.

A MONSTER HAS *GIULIETTA!* IT'S *TAKING HER AWAY!*

CONFOUND IT, BOBBY, WHAT'S GOTTEN INTO YOU? GO HOME!

Y' SHOULDN'T BE OUT THIS LATE, KID!

HE'S GOT HER IN A DIVING SUIT ON A *WHITE HORSE!* I *SAW* HIM!

...WHITE HORSE, HUH?

...

WANT ME TO COME WITH YOU, CAPTAIN?

LARRY, I DON'T, IN FACT, WANT YOU TO GO *ANYWHERE* WITH ME, EVER.

BEHOLD, **LOVE'S SHRINE**, WHERE CELLULOID ANOINTS NEW LOVERS' LIPS, AND SOOTHES THEIR BUTTERFLIES!

AS YE CAN SEE, I'VE **SANCTUARY** MADE UPON OUR HILL. THESE ROPES SHALL GUARD AGAINST ALL OUTSIDE GRIEVANCES ... WILL YE DISMOUNT?

...IT'S BEAUTIFUL.

CLICK

—I FEEL **CHARMING**, OH SO **CHARMING**—

—IT'S ALARMING HOW **CHARMING** I FEEEEEEL—

I KNOW NOT IF YE LIKE SUCH THINGS — BUT I HAVE BROUGHT A **TRINKET** FROM THE BRINE. 'TWAS IN A WRECK, SOME ERAS OLD, AND FULL UNTOUCHED...

100

WHO ELSE WAS MEANT TO HAVE THIS THING? 'TIS YOURS...

IT WAS AFTER THE WAR, AND ZOLA AND I WERE WITHOUT OUR PARENTS. SHE WAS SEVENTEEN. I SHOULD HAVE BEEN TAKING CARE OF HER, BUT IT WAS ZOLA THAT KEPT US SAFE...

PEOPLE CELEBRATED IN THE STREETS, IN **NAPLES**, WHERE WE LIVED. I REMEMBER I WAS ALWAYS HUNGRY. EVEN HUNGER DIDN'T TAKE AWAY FROM **ZOLA'S** BEAUTY! EVERY YOUNG MAN LOOKED AT HER.

BUT IT WAS THEN, WHEN **ROBERT** LOOKED AT HER, SHE WAS STRUCK BY THE SAME THING!

ROBERT WAS BRITISH, AND VERY RICH FROM HIS FAMILY'S BUSINESS—THAT WAS **KIKI COLA**. **ZOLA** KNEW OUR HARD TIMES WOULD BE OVER.

AFTER THEY COURTED ONLY A WEEK, HE RETURNED TO **ENGLAND**, SAYING HE WOULD BE BACK. IT TOOK SOME MONTHS, BUT HE SENT US MONEY, SO WE MANAGED.

WHEN HE CAME BACK, HE TOOK US TO **SPAIN**, WHERE HIS FAMILY HAD THE **MARIETTA**.

I WAS VERY NERVOUS, LEAVING HOME AND MOVING ALL AROUND. I COULDN'T BELIEVE WHEN HE WANTED TO SAIL TO **AMERICA**, TO CALIFORNIA! BUT WE DID.

ROBERT HAD THE **MARIETTA** PACKED FULL OF CRATES, FILLED WITH **KIKI COLA** BOTTLES TO INTRODUCE IN **AMERICA**. THE SEA WAS SO WIDE OPEN AND EMPTY... IT WAS MORE COMFORTABLE TO ME.

ZOLA HATED THE TRIP.

BUT I LIKED TO LISTEN. THAT WAS MY MISTAKE. I GAVE HIM MY **ATTENTION** ... AND I LEARNED ENGLISH FASTER THAN **ZOLA**.

HE WOULD TRY TO KEEP HER OCCUPIED WITH READING FROM HIS **PLAYS**. SHE DIDN'T LIKE TO LISTEN. SHE SAID WHEN SHE GOT TO CALIFORNIA, SHE WOULD ACT IN **HOLLYWOOD** FILMS, WITH **REAL** WORDS...

WHEN WE REACHED THE **PANAMA CANAL**, THEY WERE FIGHTING A LOT, AND I TRIED TO STAY OUT OF THE WAY. SOMETIMES **ROBERT** WOULD COME FIND ME, WHEN **ZOLA** WAS BELOW. I LET HIM READ TO ME, EVEN THOUGH I KNEW IT WAS PART OF THEIR TROUBLE...

AT **CALIFORNIA**, THE BOAT RAN AGROUND JUST BEFORE THE HARBOR, AND THE COAST GUARD HAD TO BRING IT INTO THE DRY DOCK.

ONCE WE WERE THERE, **ROBERT** FOUND ANOTHER BOAT IN THE HARBOR, AND DECIDED TO BUY IT WHILE THE **MARIETTA** WAS BEING REPAIRED. JUST FOR DAY SAILING, HE SAID.

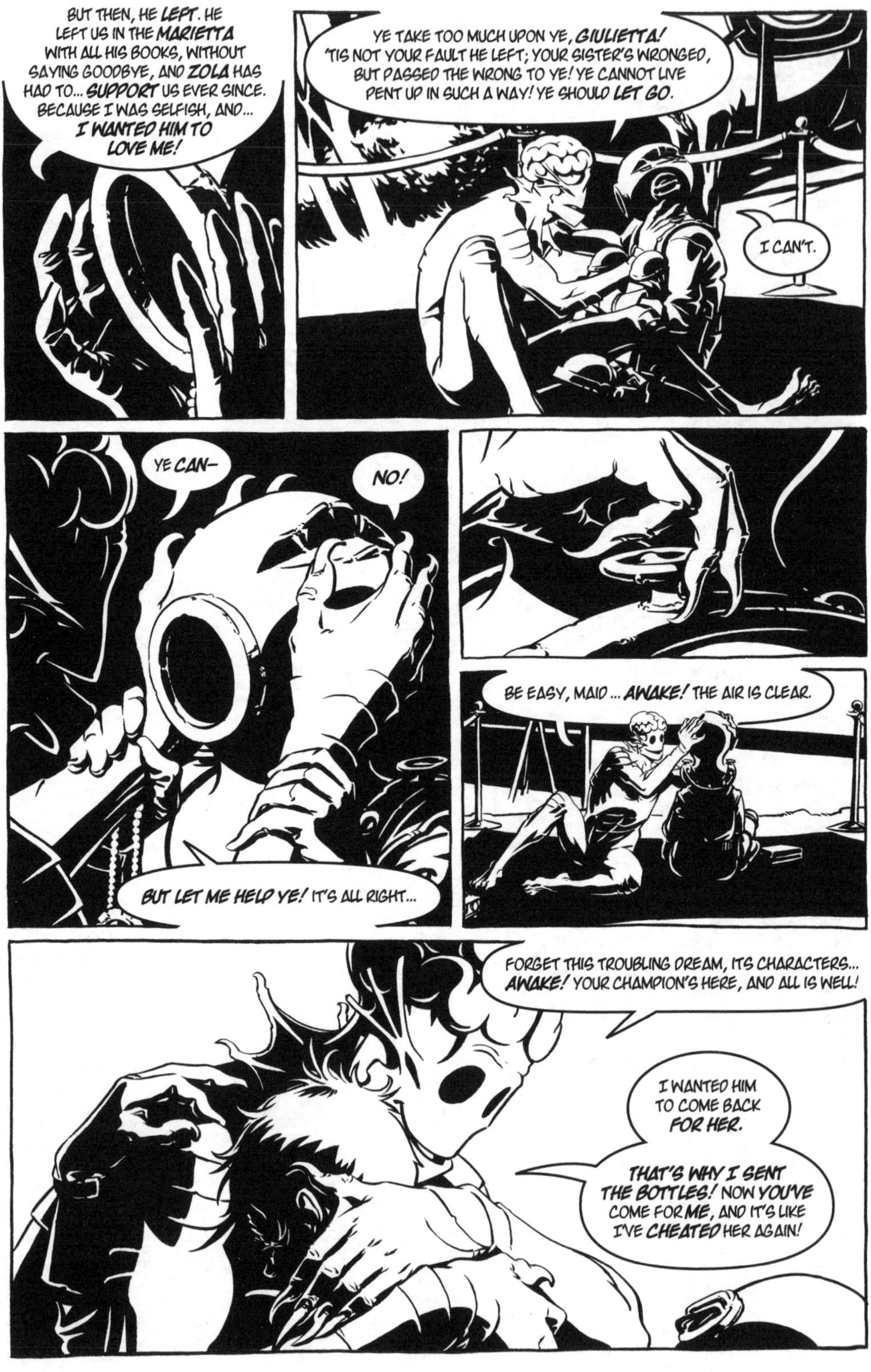
BUT THEN, HE LEFT. HE LEFT US IN THE MARIETTA WITH ALL HIS BOOKS, WITHOUT SAYING GOODBYE, AND ZOLA HAS HAD TO... SUPPORT US EVER SINCE. BECAUSE I WAS SELFISH, AND... I WANTED HIM TO LOVE ME!
YE TAKE TOO MUCH UPON YE, GIULIETTA! 'TIS NOT YOUR FAULT HE LEFT; YOUR SISTER'S WRONGED, BUT PASSED THE WRONG TO YE! YE CANNOT LIVE PENT UP IN SUCH A WAY! YE SHOULD LET GO.
I CAN'T.
YE CAN-
NO!
BUT LET ME HELP YE! IT'S ALL RIGHT...
BE EASY, MAID... AWAKE! THE AIR IS CLEAR.
FORGET THIS TROUBLING DREAM, ITS CHARACTERS... AWAKE! YOUR CHAMPION'S HERE, AND ALL IS WELL!
I WANTED HIM TO COME BACK FOR HER.
THAT'S WHY I SENT THE BOTTLES! NOW YOU'VE COME FOR ME, AND IT'S LIKE I'VE CHEATED HER AGAIN!

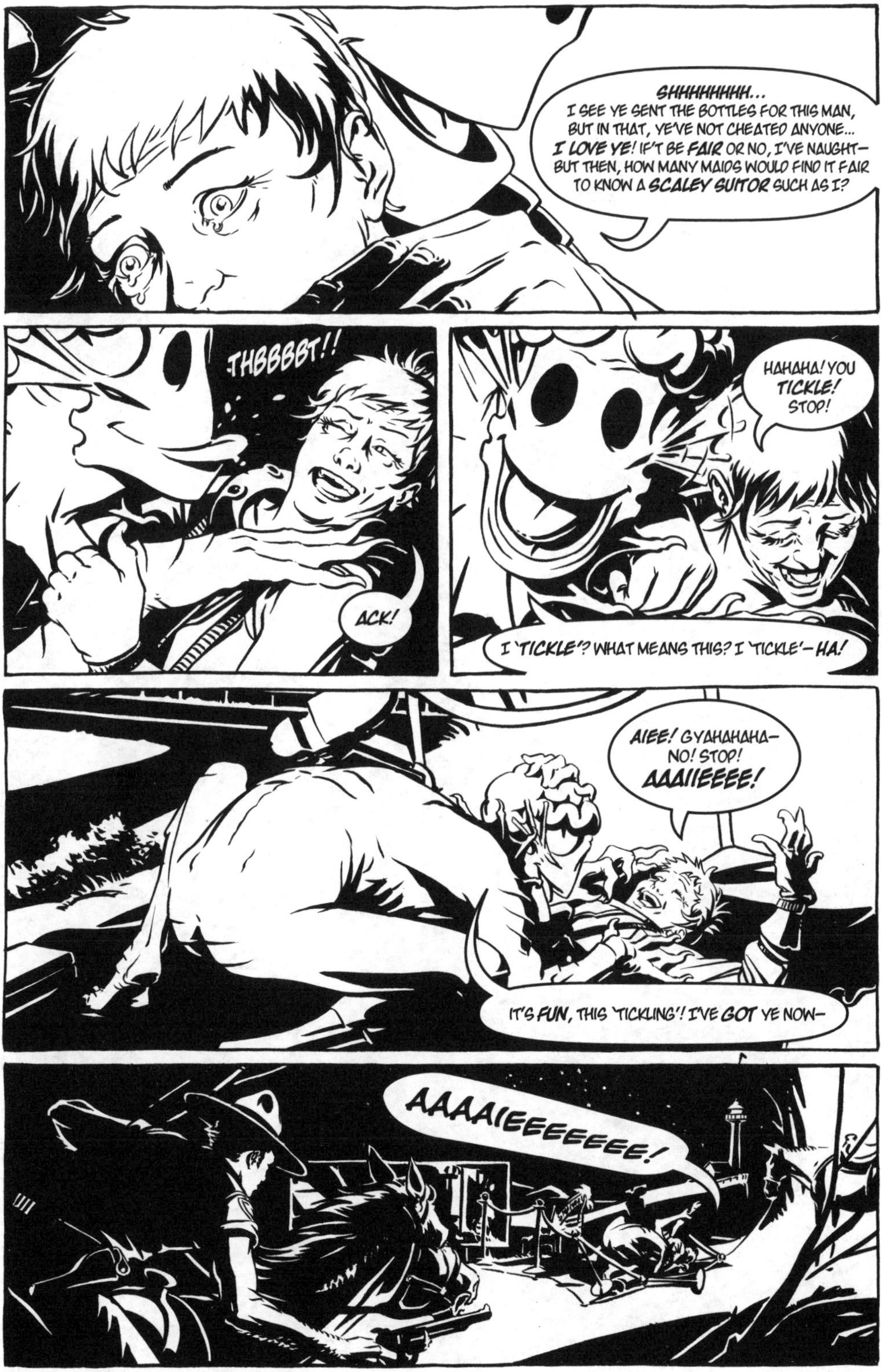
SHHHHHHHH...
I SEE YE SENT THE BOTTLES FOR THIS MAN,
BUT IN THAT, YE'VE NOT CHEATED ANYONE...
I LOVE YE! IF'T BE FAIR OR NO, I'VE NAUGHT-
BUT THEN, HOW MANY MAIDS WOULD FIND IT FAIR
TO KNOW A SCALEY SUITOR SUCH AS I?
THBBBBT!!
ACK!
HAHAHA! YOU TICKLE! STOP!
I 'TICKLE'? WHAT MEANS THIS? I 'TICKLE'—HA!
AIEE! GYAHAHAHA-
NO! STOP!
AAAIIEEEE!
IT'S FUN, THIS 'TICKLING'! I'VE GOT YE NOW-
AAAAIEEEEEEEE!

106

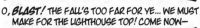

O, *BLAST!* THE FALL'S TOO FAR FOR YE... WE MUST MAKE FOR THE LIGHTHOUSE TOP! COME NOW—

THE *LIGHTHOUSE*— BUT WHAT IF IT'S LOCKED?!

FEAR NOT: I SCALED IT WITH A FEMALE TWICE YOUR WEIGHT! I'LL SCALE IT 'GAIN, AND TWICE AS FAST!

SCREEEEEECH!

WHERE ARE YOU, DAMMIT?! COME ON—

—AAAUUGH!

AAAAAAAAAAAAAUGH!!!!

HOLD ON, OLD GIRL!!

HELO!! HELP ME!!!

SHUT UP! DON'T HAVE A— GIULIETTA! NO!!! WHAT'S *WRONG* WITH YE?! HE'LL *HEAR* YE! QUIET DOWN!

SKRTTCH!!

BANG!

DRAT!

I HOPE YOU'RE PLEASED!!! HE'S COMING FOR US NOW, AND I DON'T KNOW WHAT'S TO BE DONE! *DO YE?!*

YOU'LL KILL HIM— LIKE YOU KILLED THEM ALL!

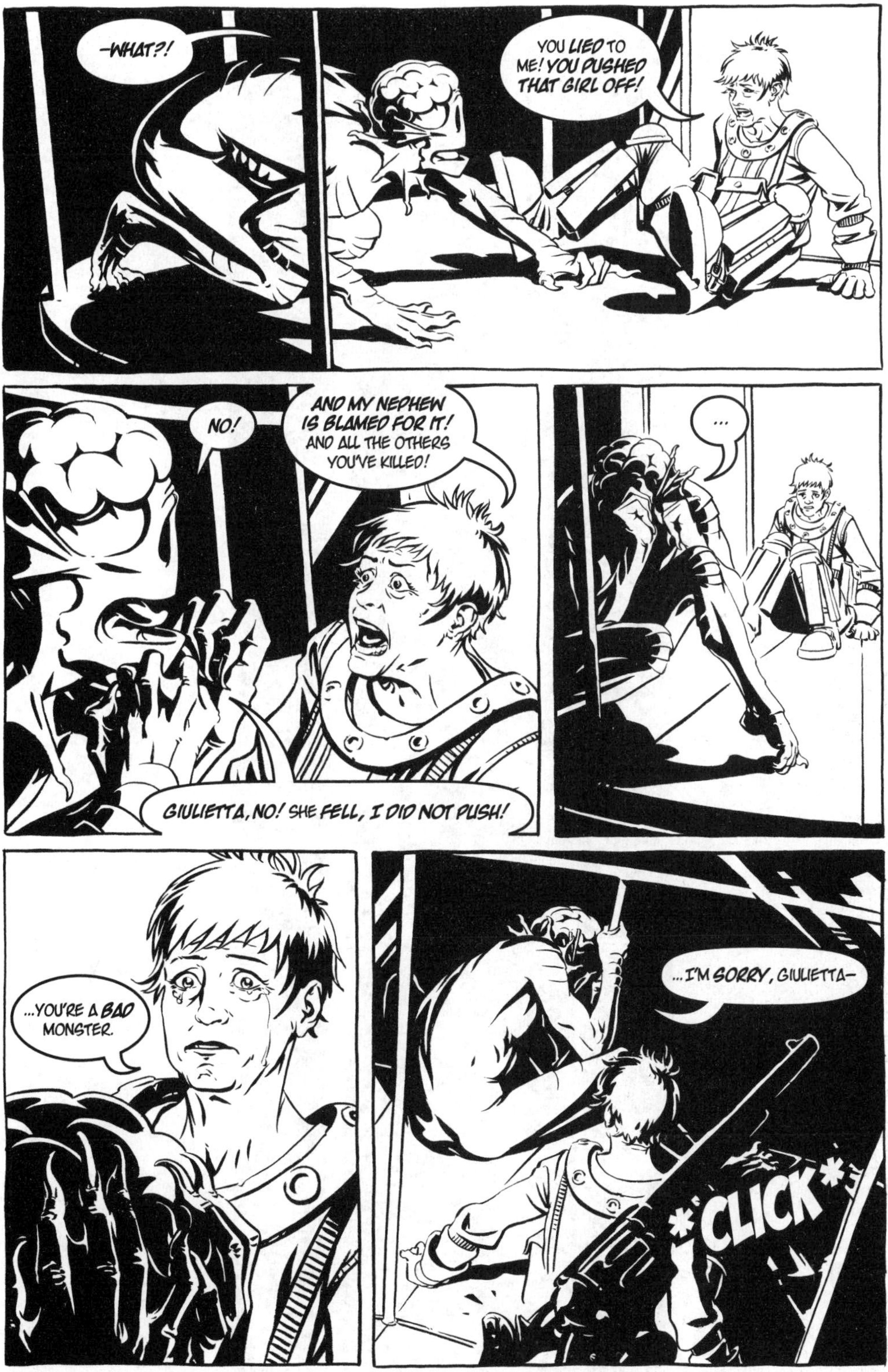
-WHAT?!
YOU LIED TO ME! YOU PUSHED THAT GIRL OFF!
NO!
AND MY NEPHEW IS BLAMED FOR IT! AND ALL THE OTHERS YOU'VE KILLED!
GIULIETTA, NO! SHE FELL, I DID NOT PUSH!
...
...YOU'RE A BAD MONSTER.
...I'M SORRY, GIULIETTA-
CLICK

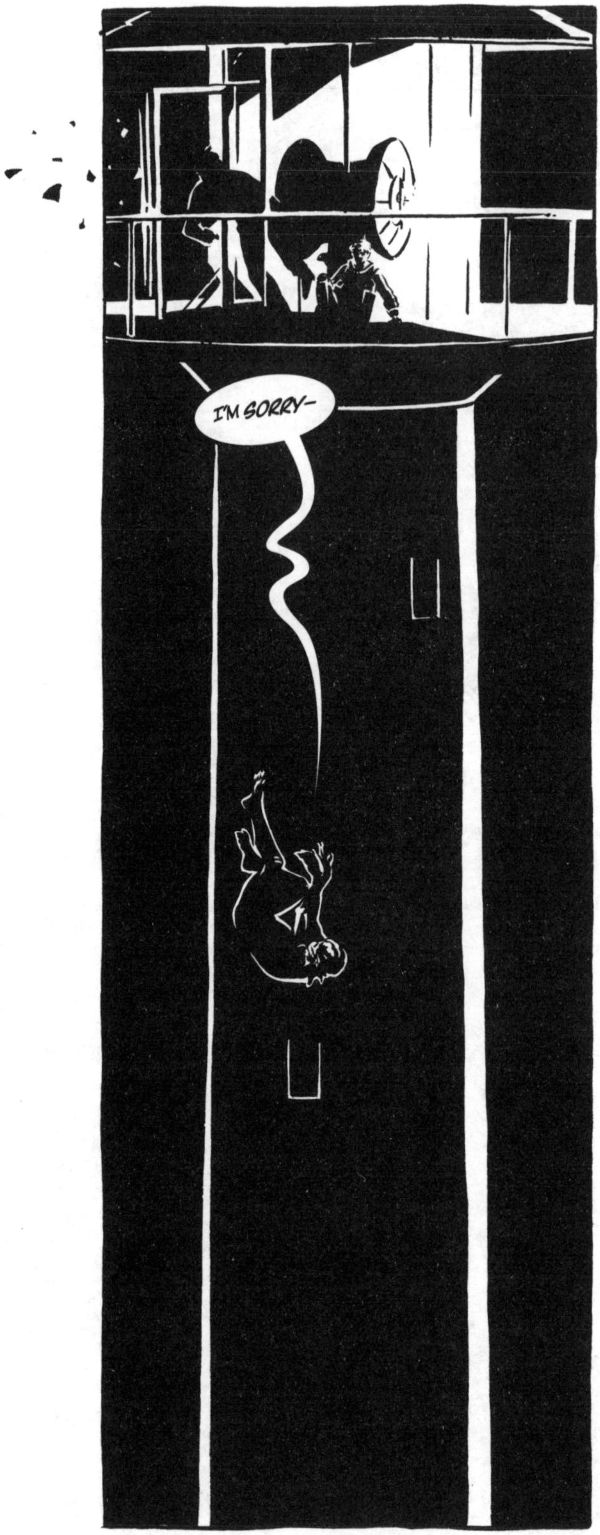
I'M SORRY-

CHAPTER FIVE
it's over

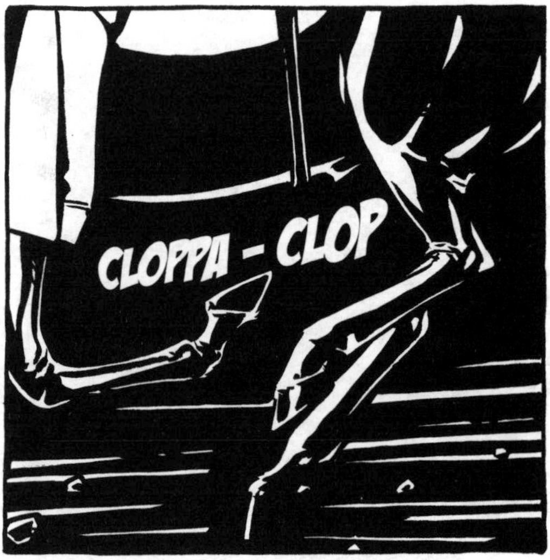
CLOPPA - CLOP

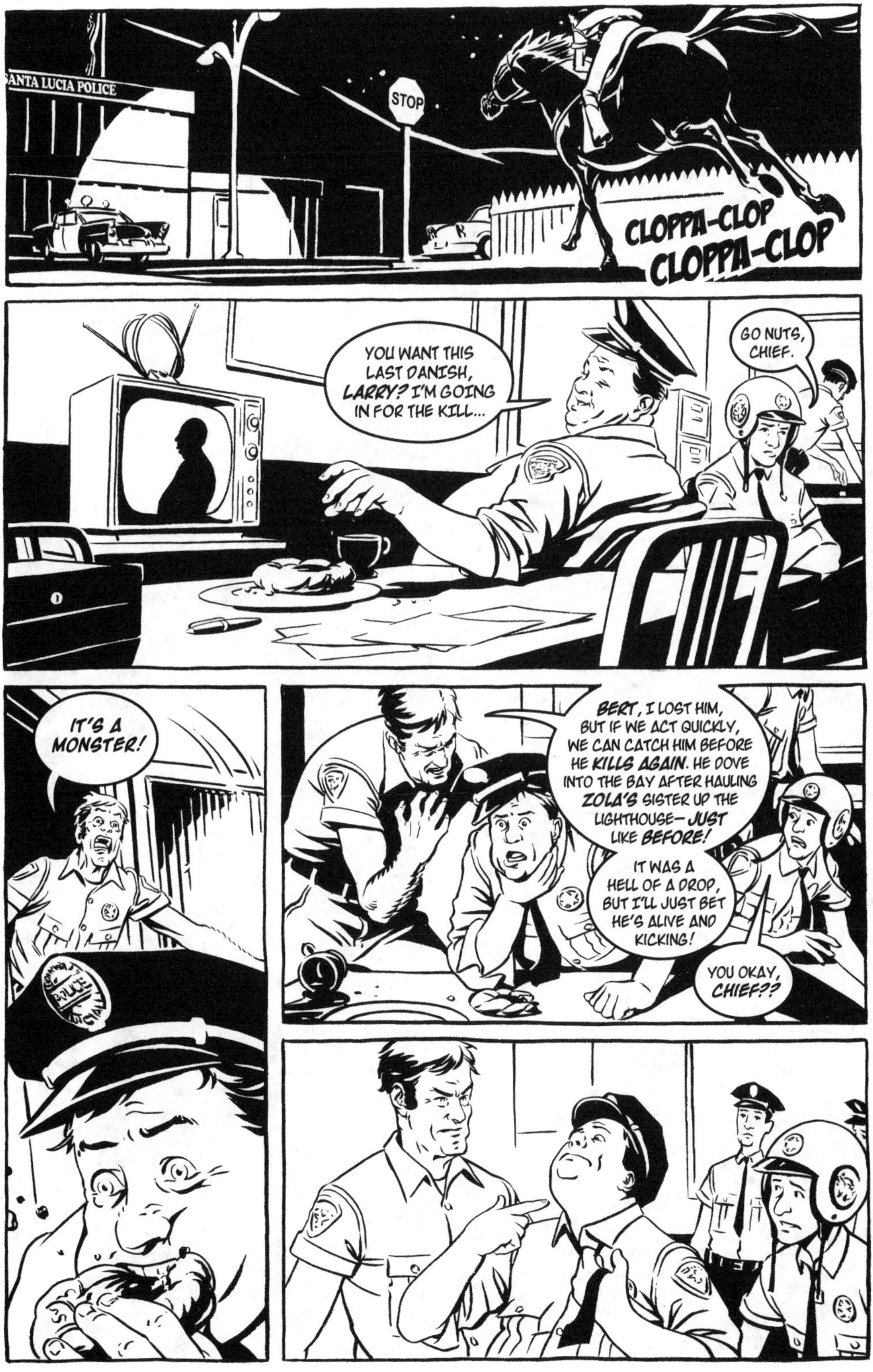
SANTA LUCIA POLICE
STOP
CLOPPA-CLOP
CLOPPA-CLOP
YOU WANT THIS LAST DANISH, LARRY? I'M GOING IN FOR THE KILL...
GO NUTS, CHIEF.
IT'S A MONSTER!
BERT, I LOST HIM, BUT IF WE ACT QUICKLY, WE CAN CATCH HIM BEFORE HE KILLS AGAIN. HE DOVE INTO THE BAY AFTER HAULING ZOLA'S SISTER UP THE LIGHTHOUSE— JUST LIKE BEFORE!
IT WAS A HELL OF A DROP, BUT I'LL JUST BET HE'S ALIVE AND KICKING!
YOU OKAY, CHIEF??

114

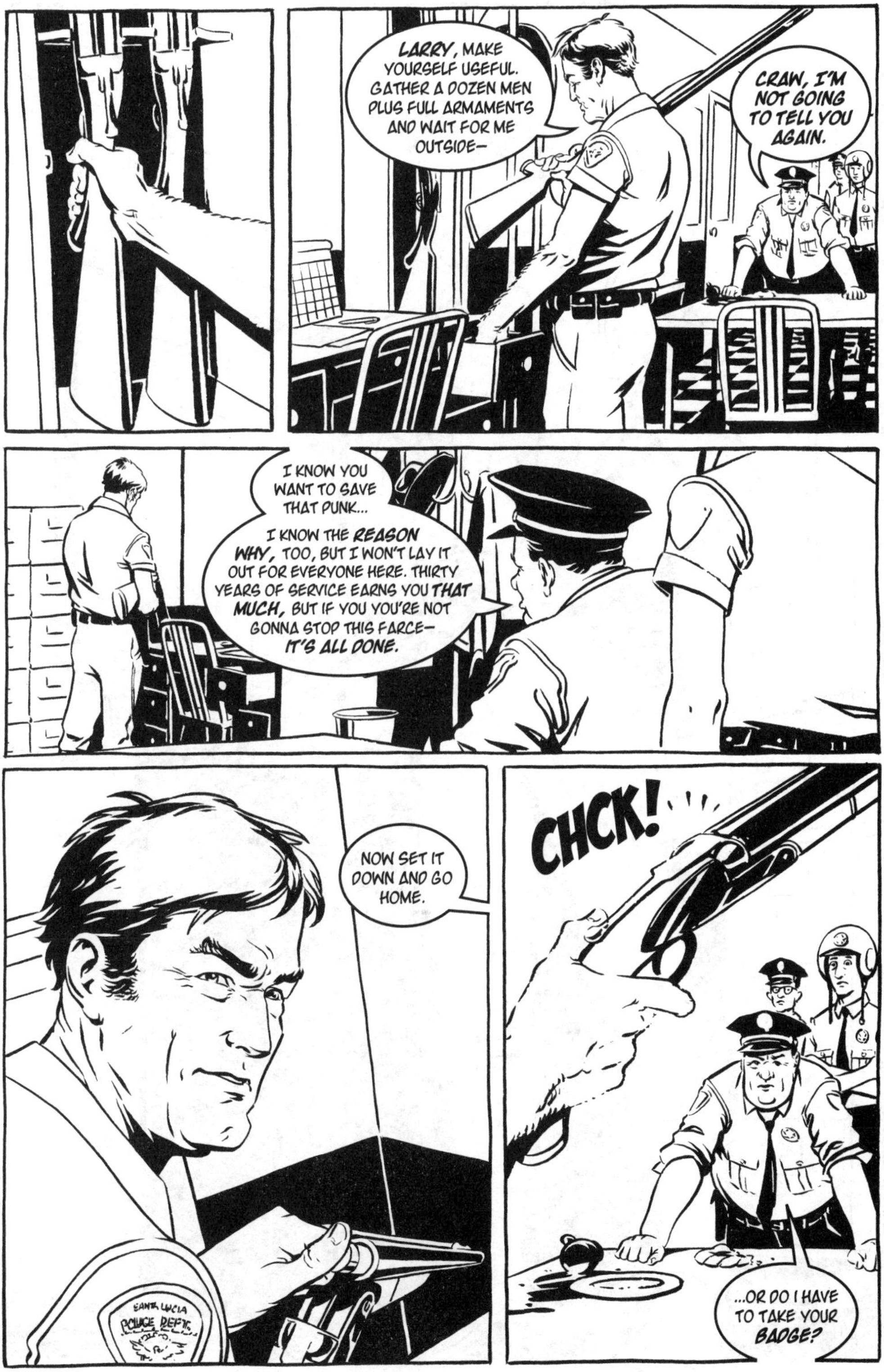
LARRY, MAKE YOURSELF USEFUL. GATHER A DOZEN MEN PLUS FULL ARMAMENTS AND WAIT FOR ME OUTSIDE–
CRAW, I'M NOT GOING TO TELL YOU AGAIN.
I KNOW YOU WANT TO SAVE THAT PUNK...
I KNOW THE REASON WHY, TOO, BUT I WON'T LAY IT OUT FOR EVERYONE HERE. THIRTY YEARS OF SERVICE EARNS YOU THAT MUCH, BUT IF YOU YOU'RE NOT GONNA STOP THIS FARCE– IT'S ALL DONE.
NOW SET IT DOWN AND GO HOME.
SANTA LUCIA POLICE DEPT.
CHCK!
...OR DO I HAVE TO TAKE YOUR BADGE?

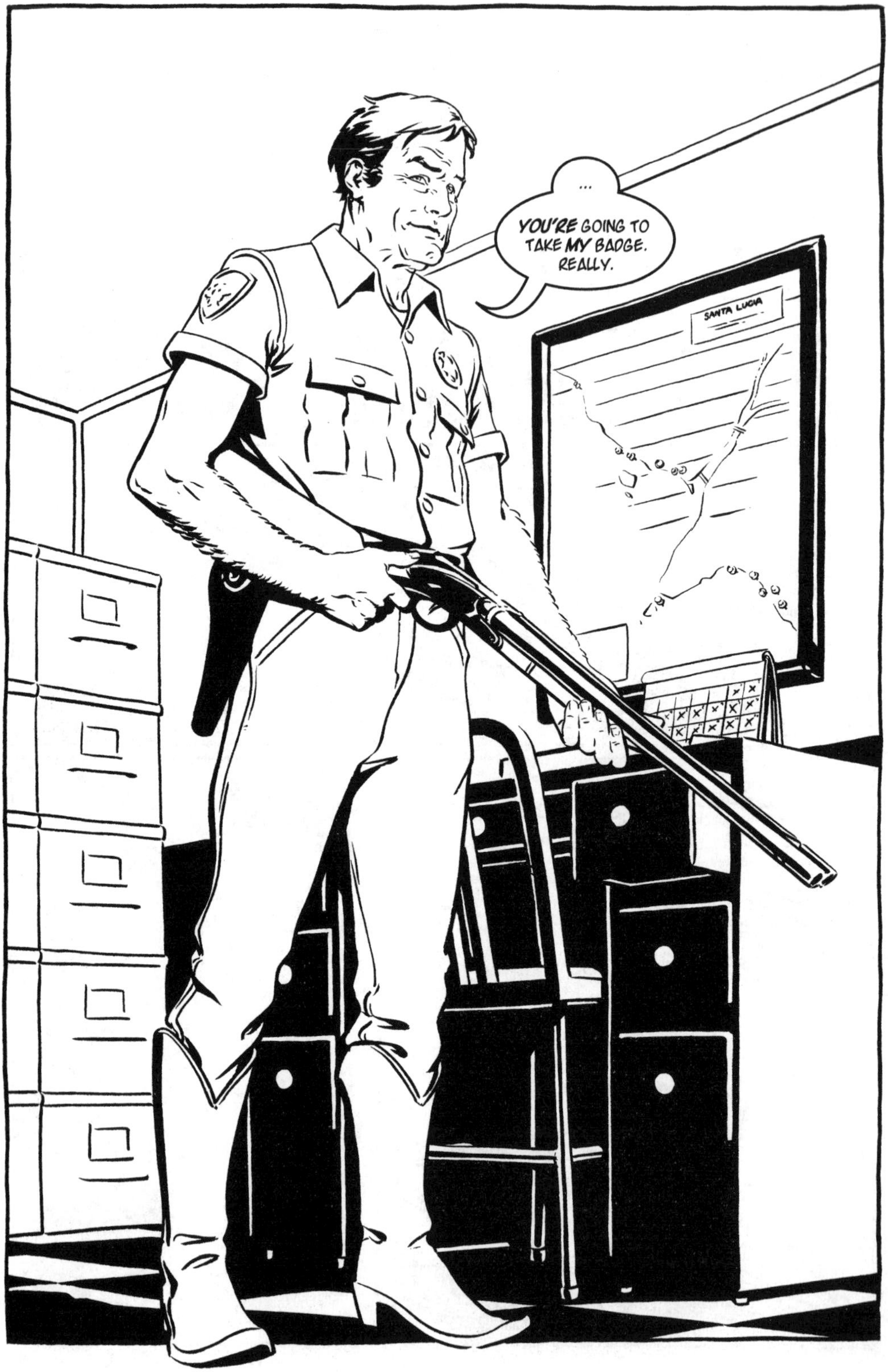
...
YOU'RE GOING TO TAKE MY BADGE. REALLY.
SANTA LUCIA

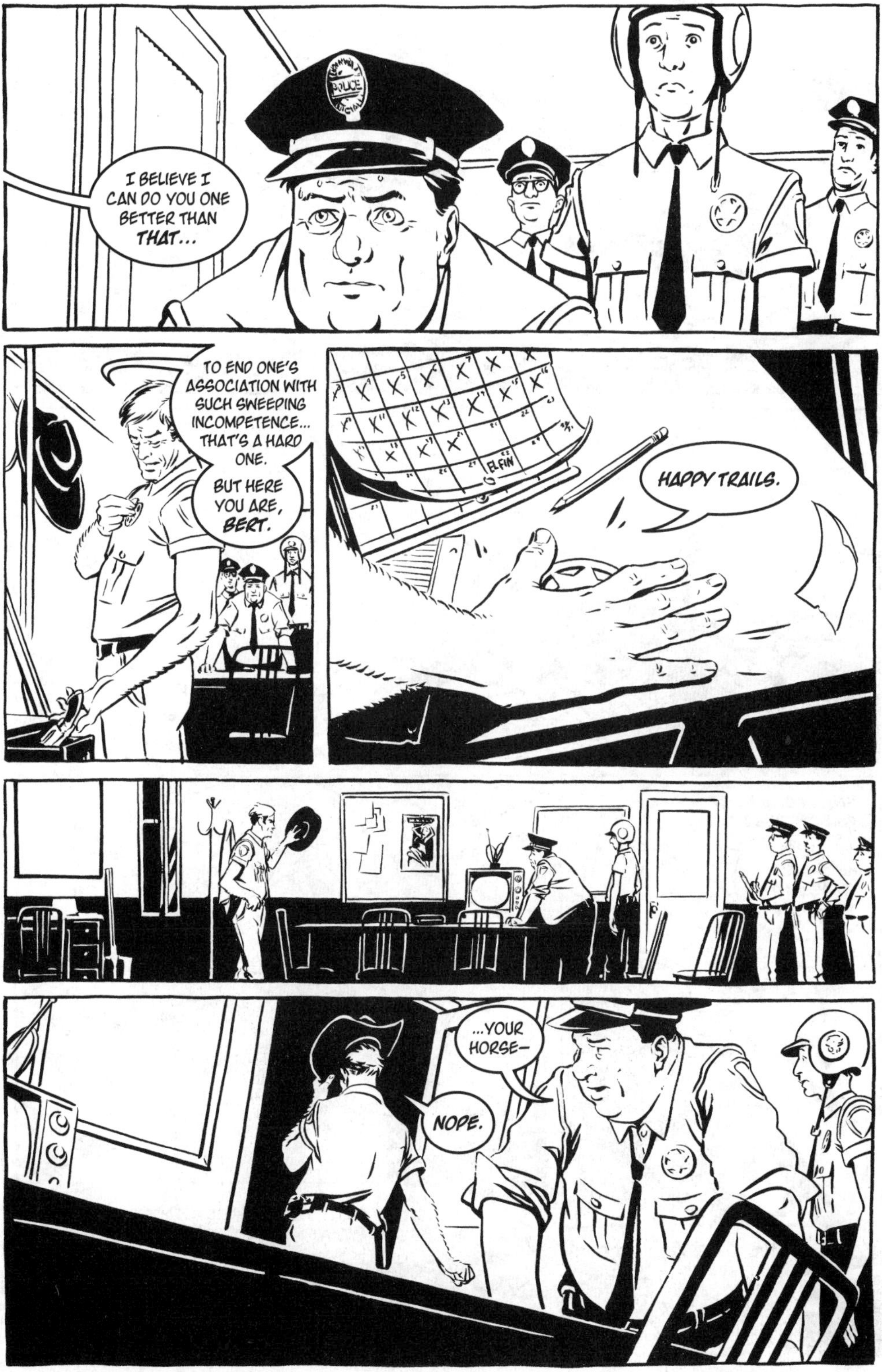
I BELIEVE I CAN DO YOU ONE BETTER THAN THAT...
TO END ONE'S ASSOCIATION WITH SUCH SWEEPING INCOMPETENCE... THAT'S A HARD ONE.
BUT HERE YOU ARE, BERT.
ELFIN
HAPPY TRAILS.
...YOUR HORSE-
NOPE.

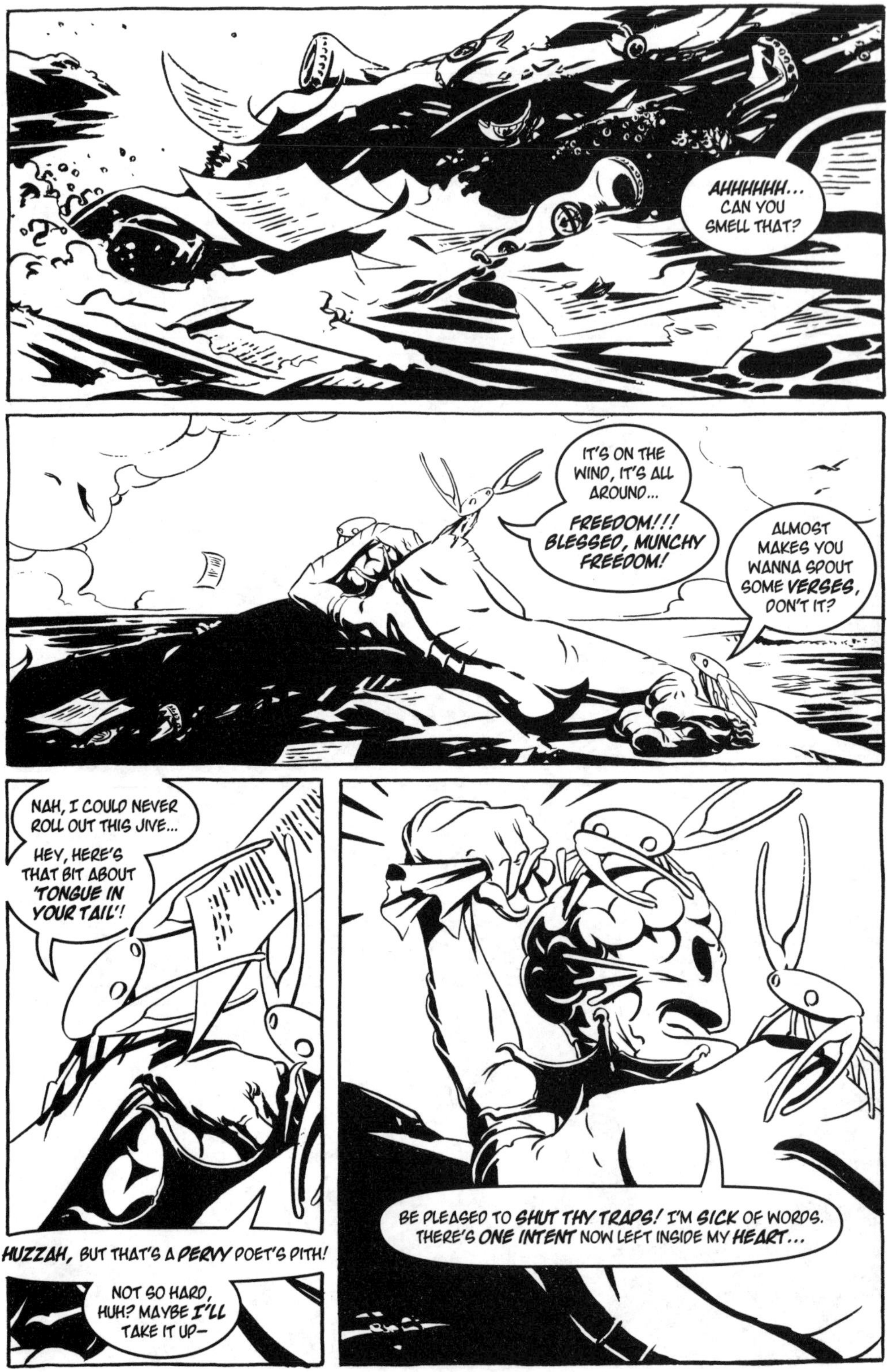
AHHHHHH... CAN YOU SMELL THAT?
IT'S ON THE WIND, IT'S ALL AROUND...
FREEDOM!!! BLESSED, MUNCHY FREEDOM!
ALMOST MAKES YOU WANNA SPOUT SOME VERSES, DON'T IT?
NAH, I COULD NEVER ROLL OUT THIS JIVE...
HEY, HERE'S THAT BIT ABOUT 'TONGUE IN YOUR TAIL'!
HUZZAH, BUT THAT'S A PERVY POET'S PITH!
NOT SO HARD, HUH? MAYBE I'LL TAKE IT UP—
BE PLEASED TO SHUT THY TRAPS! I'M SICK OF WORDS.
THERE'S ONE INTENT NOW LEFT INSIDE MY HEART...

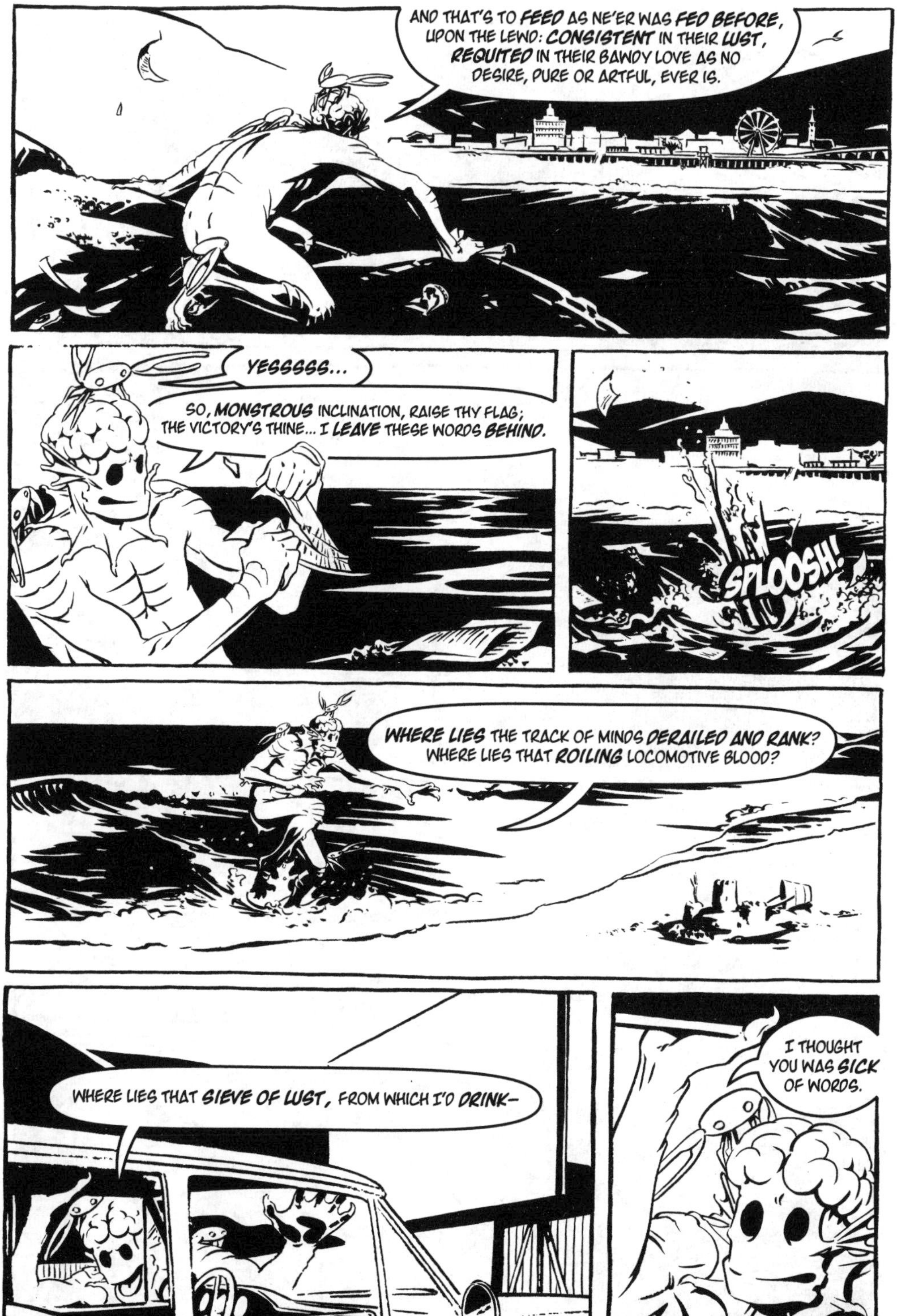
AND THAT'S TO FEED AS NE'ER WAS FED BEFORE, UPON THE LEWD: CONSISTENT IN THEIR LUST, REQUITED IN THEIR BAWDY LOVE AS NO DESIRE, PURE OR ARTFUL, EVER IS.
YESSSSS...
SO, MONSTROUS INCLINATION, RAISE THY FLAG; THE VICTORY'S THINE... I LEAVE THESE WORDS BEHIND.
SPLOOSH!
WHERE LIES THE TRACK OF MINDS DERAILED AND RANK? WHERE LIES THAT ROILING LOCOMOTIVE BLOOD?
WHERE LIES THAT SIEVE OF LUST, FROM WHICH I'D DRINK—
I THOUGHT YOU WAS SICK OF WORDS.

AUNT *GIULIETTA?* YOU DIDN'T EAT YOUR LUNCH—

OH.

IT'S ALL RIGHT, YOU DON'T HAVE TO COME OUT. I'LL JUST SET IT ON THE TABLE FOR YOU.

OKAY.

AND DON'T WORRY ABOUT THAT MONSTER. I BET WE'VE SEEN THE LAST OF— ...HIM.

AUNT *GIULIETTA*... WHO DREW THIS PICTURE?

THE *MONSTER* WAS MY... I MEAN, THOUGHT HE WAS—

HE WAS YOUR *FRIEND?!* I DON'T... WAS I WRONG TO GO TO THE POLICE?

NO, NO, ROBERTO! HE'S A *BAD* THING. YOU DID'T DO ANY- THING WRONG!

I'M SORRY!

-CLUNK-

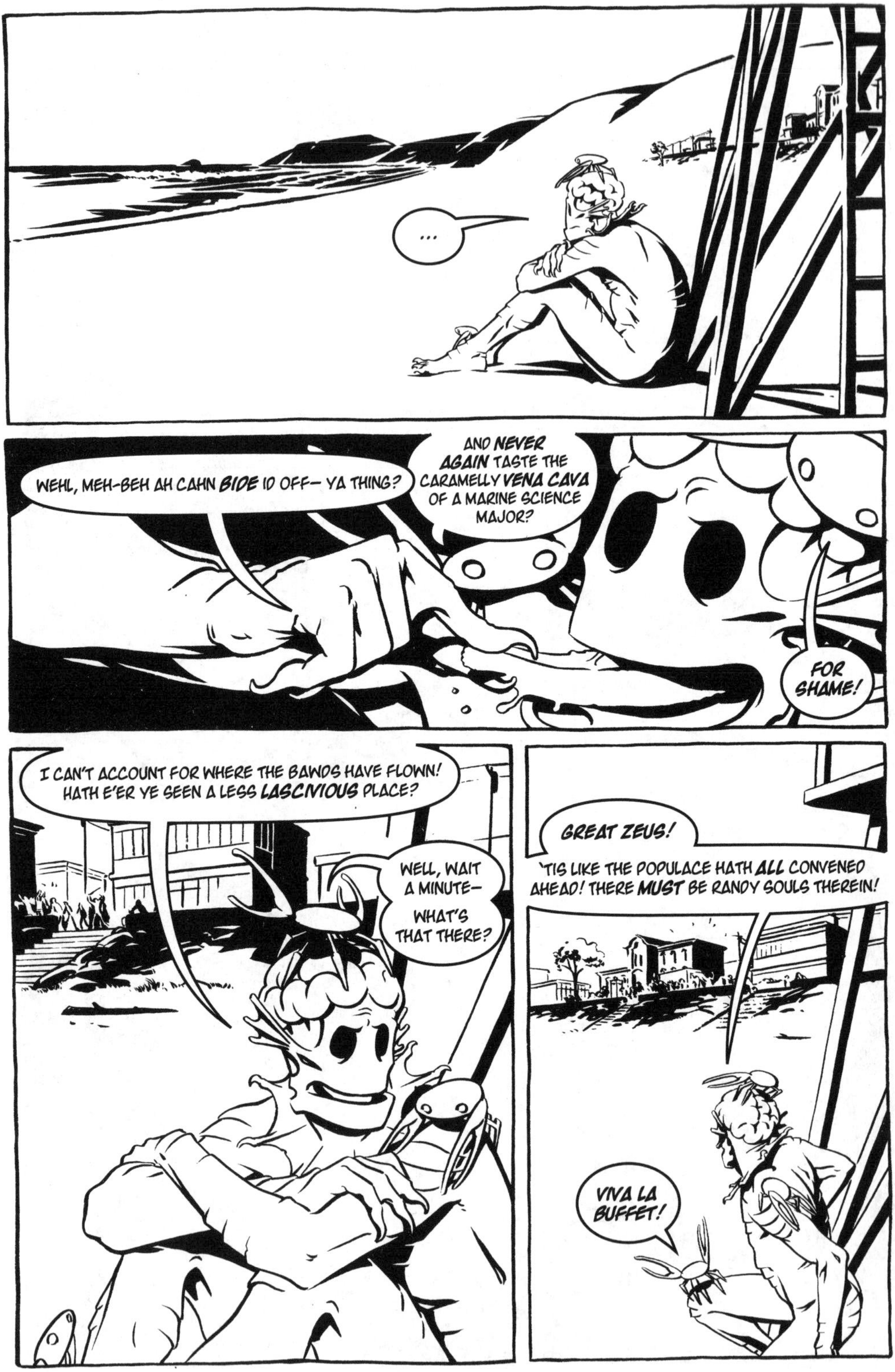
...
WEHL, MEH-BEH AH CAHN BIDE ID OFF— YA THING?
AND NEVER AGAIN TASTE THE CARAMELLY VENA CAVA OF A MARINE SCIENCE MAJOR?
FOR SHAME!
I CAN'T ACCOUNT FOR WHERE THE BAWDS HAVE FLOWN! HATH E'ER YE SEEN A LESS LASCIVIOUS PLACE?
WELL, WAIT A MINUTE—
WHAT'S THAT THERE?
GREAT ZEUS!
'TIS LIKE THE POPULACE HATH ALL CONVENED AHEAD! THERE MUST BE RANDY SOULS THEREIN!
VIVA LA BUFFET!

123

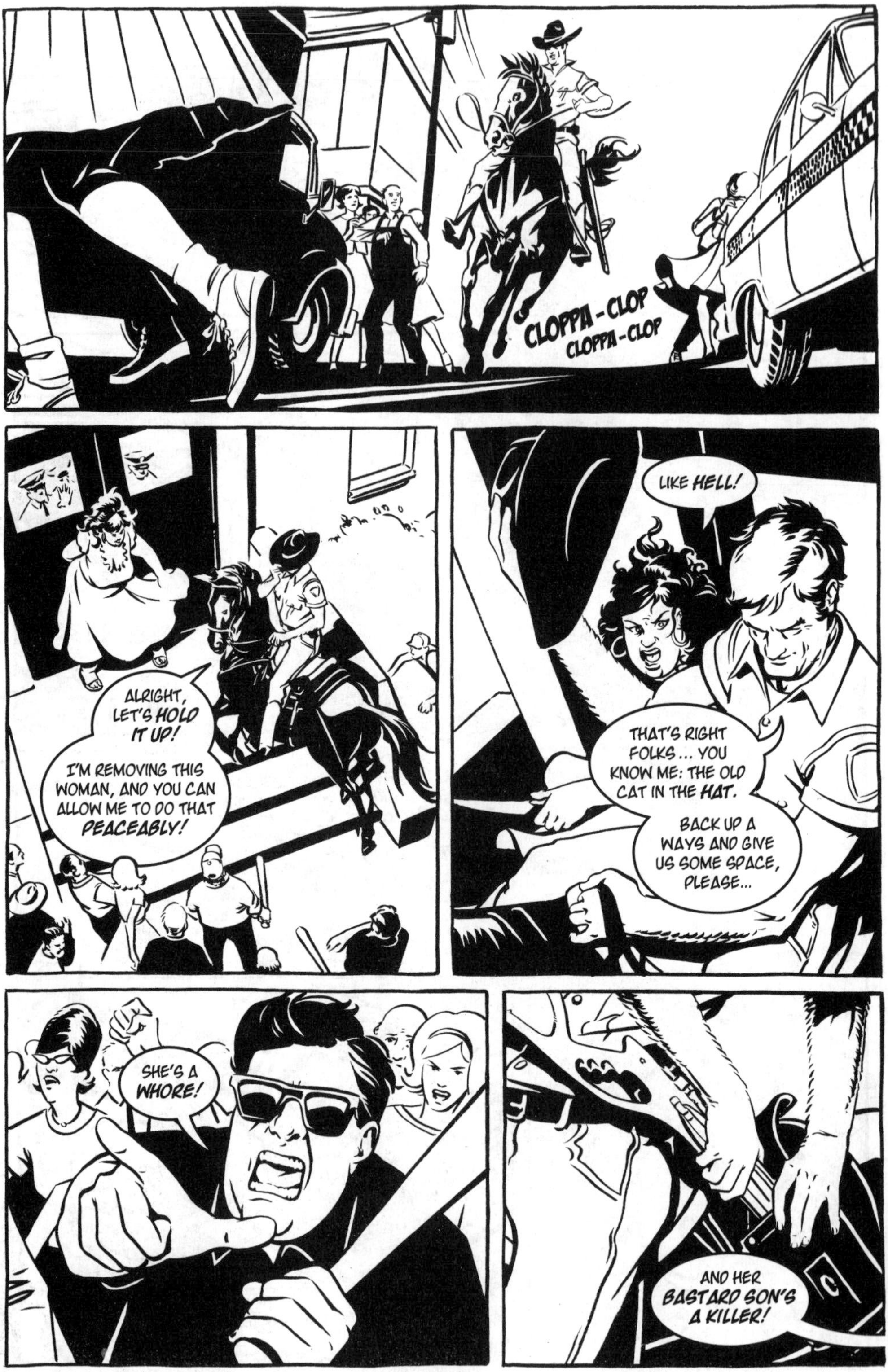
CLOPPA-CLOP
CLOPPA-CLOP
ALRIGHT, LET'S HOLD IT UP!
I'M REMOVING THIS WOMAN, AND YOU CAN ALLOW ME TO DO THAT PEACEABLY!
LIKE HELL!
THAT'S RIGHT FOLKS... YOU KNOW ME: THE OLD CAT IN THE HAT.
BACK UP A WAYS AND GIVE US SOME SPACE, PLEASE...
SHE'S A WHORE!
AND HER BASTARD SON'S A KILLER!

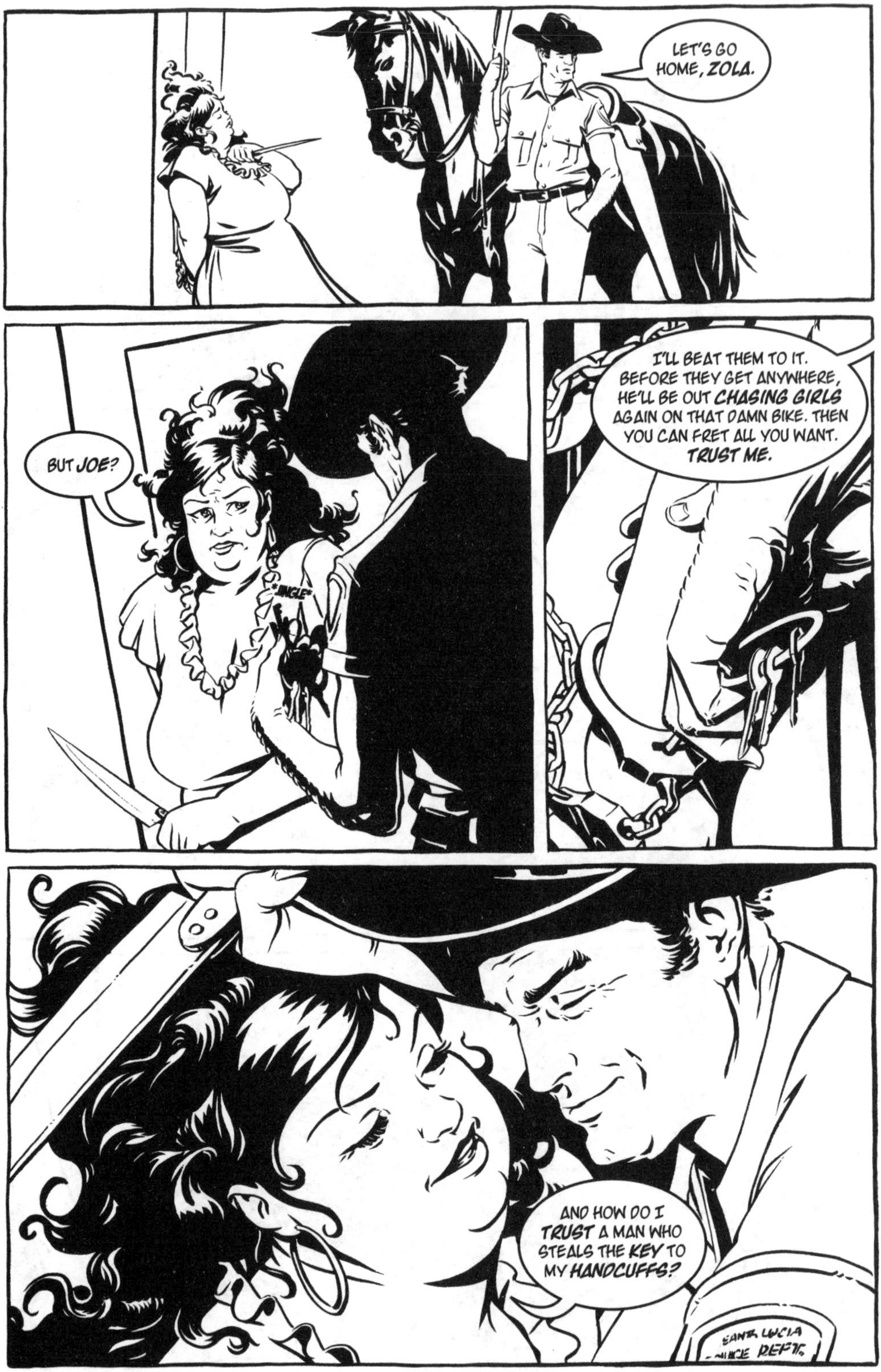
LET'S GO HOME, ZOLA.
BUT JOE?
JINGLE
I'LL BEAT THEM TO IT. BEFORE THEY GET ANYWHERE, HE'LL BE OUT CHASING GIRLS AGAIN ON THAT DAMN BIKE. THEN YOU CAN FRET ALL YOU WANT. TRUST ME.
AND HOW DO I TRUST A MAN WHO STEALS THE KEY TO MY HANDCUFFS?

WELL *THAT* WAS A WHOLE LOT OF NOTHIN'.

THOU HAST NO *CENTRAL NERVOUS SYSTEM*, CRAB. THIS MAN HATH SHOWN HIS METTLE, AND IT'S PAST THE *BEST I'VE PLIED!* I'D WELL TO DEAL SO PLAIN...

I'LL TAKE HIS CUE! I'LL *LAY ME OUT*, ALL PARTS, TO *GIULIETTA!* MAYHAP BY THIS I SHALL BE FREED OF MINE PROPENSITIES! *COME CRABS!*

NO CHANCE— ONE, THAT CRITTER YOU'RE SO *IMPRESSED* WITH IS *AFTER YOUR HIDE*, AND HE'S HEADED BACK TO THE SHIP—

TWO, YOU'D HAVE TA BEAT 'EM THERE, AN THEY'S GOT A *QUADRUPED!*

GEOFFREY, THIS ABSOLUTELY IS THE *OPPOSITE OF CAPITAL!* IF I DON'T GET SOME CHEESE, *I'M GOING TO DIE!*

FLAP FLAP

127

CLACK

WHAT A WORLD...

BEACHSIDE KILLER: CHAINS OR CHAIR?

A MOB'S AN *UGLY* THING, ISN'T IT, MISS? I AVERTED MY EYES TOO!

WHERE'LL IT BE, THEN?

EH?

ALRIGHT... WHAT'S THE GAME, MISS? YOU A *FOREIGN TYPE?* ABLO INGLES?

NO OFFENSE, JUST LAST TIME I HAULED A *FOREIGN TYPE* THEY THOUGHT MY CAB WAS SOME KINDA PUBLIC SERVICE!

YOU *DO* KNOW YOU GOTTA PAY A FARE, RIGHT? *UNCLE SAM* KIND, UNDERSTAND? NO *LIRA*, NO PESOS, NO *FORTUNE TELLING—*

128

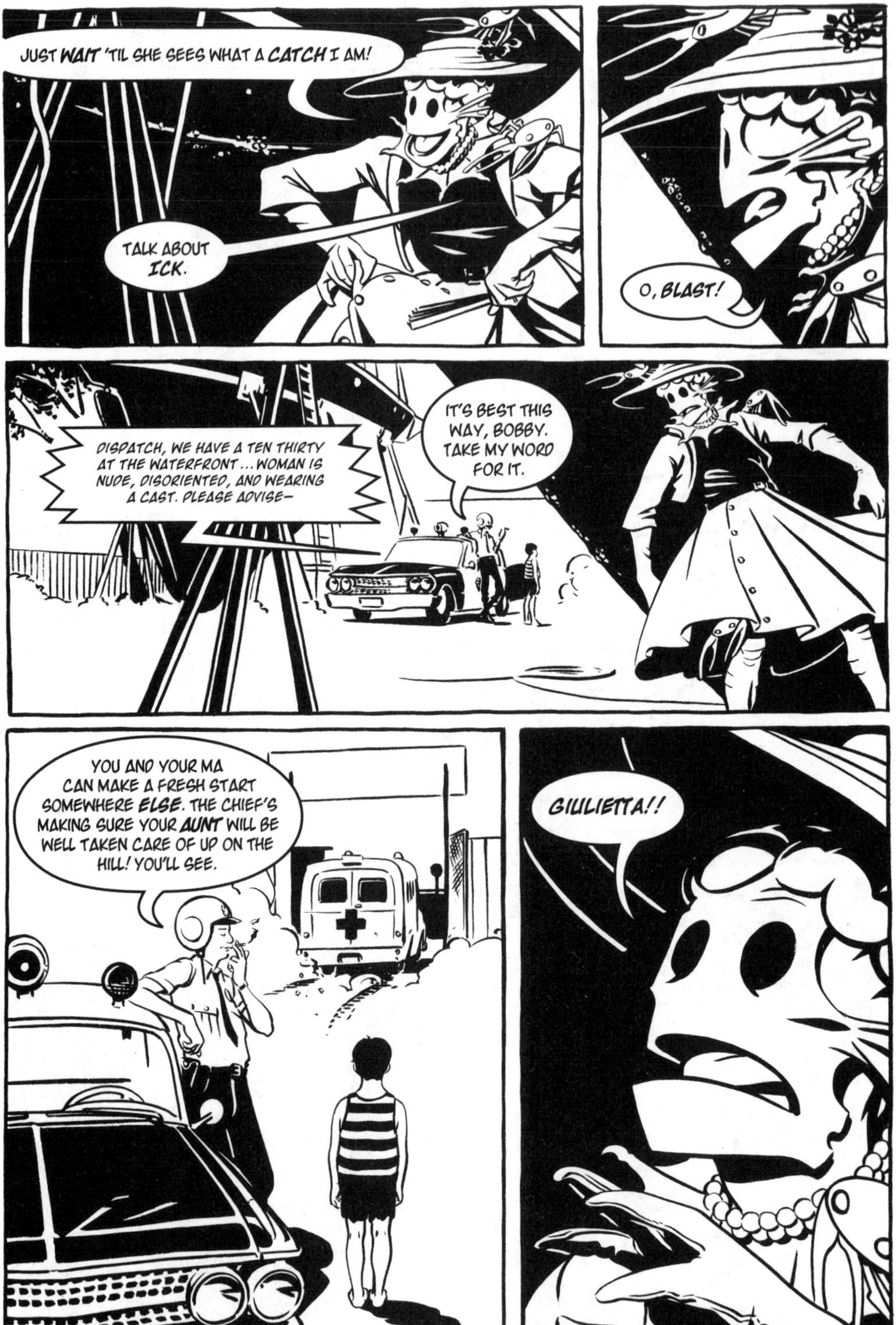
JUST WAIT 'TIL SHE SEES WHAT A CATCH I AM!
TALK ABOUT ICK.
O, BLAST!
DISPATCH, WE HAVE A TEN THIRTY AT THE WATERFRONT... WOMAN IS NUDE, DISORIENTED, AND WEARING A CAST. PLEASE ADVISE–
IT'S BEST THIS WAY, BOBBY. TAKE MY WORD FOR IT.
YOU AND YOUR MA CAN MAKE A FRESH START SOMEWHERE ELSE. THE CHIEF'S MAKING SURE YOUR AUNT WILL BE WELL TAKEN CARE OF UP ON THE HILL! YOU'LL SEE.
GIULIETTA!!

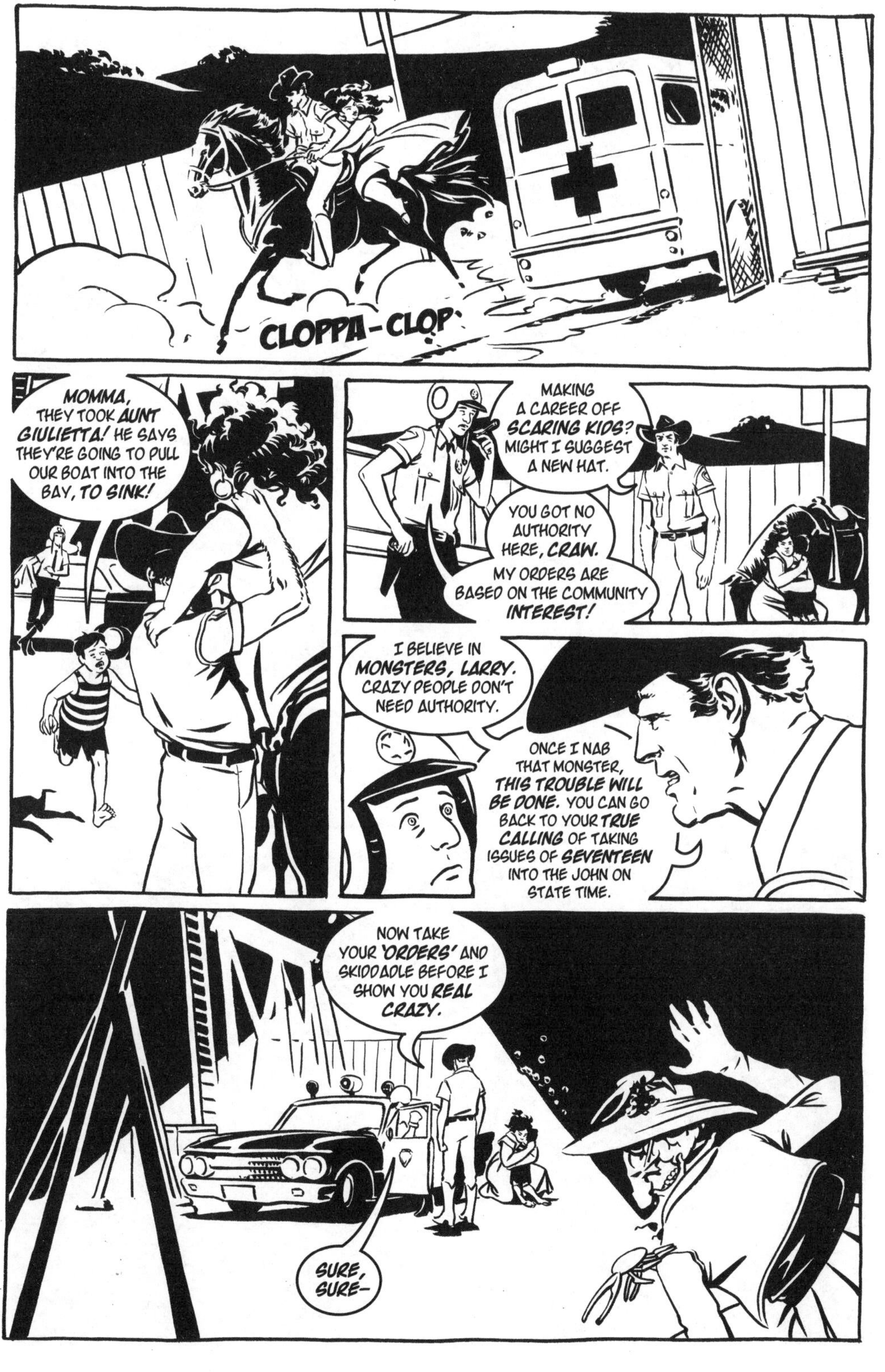

CLOPPA-CLOP
MOMMA, THEY TOOK AUNT GIULIETTA! HE SAYS THEY'RE GOING TO PULL OUR BOAT INTO THE BAY, TO SINK!
MAKING A CAREER OFF SCARING KIDS? MIGHT I SUGGEST A NEW HAT.
YOU GOT NO AUTHORITY HERE, CRAW.
MY ORDERS ARE BASED ON THE COMMUNITY INTEREST!
I BELIEVE IN MONSTERS, LARRY. CRAZY PEOPLE DON'T NEED AUTHORITY.
ONCE I NAB THAT MONSTER, THIS TROUBLE WILL BE DONE. YOU CAN GO BACK TO YOUR TRUE CALLING OF TAKING ISSUES OF SEVENTEEN INTO THE JOHN ON STATE TIME.
NOW TAKE YOUR 'ORDERS' AND SKIDDADLE BEFORE I SHOW YOU REAL CRAZY.
SURE, SURE-

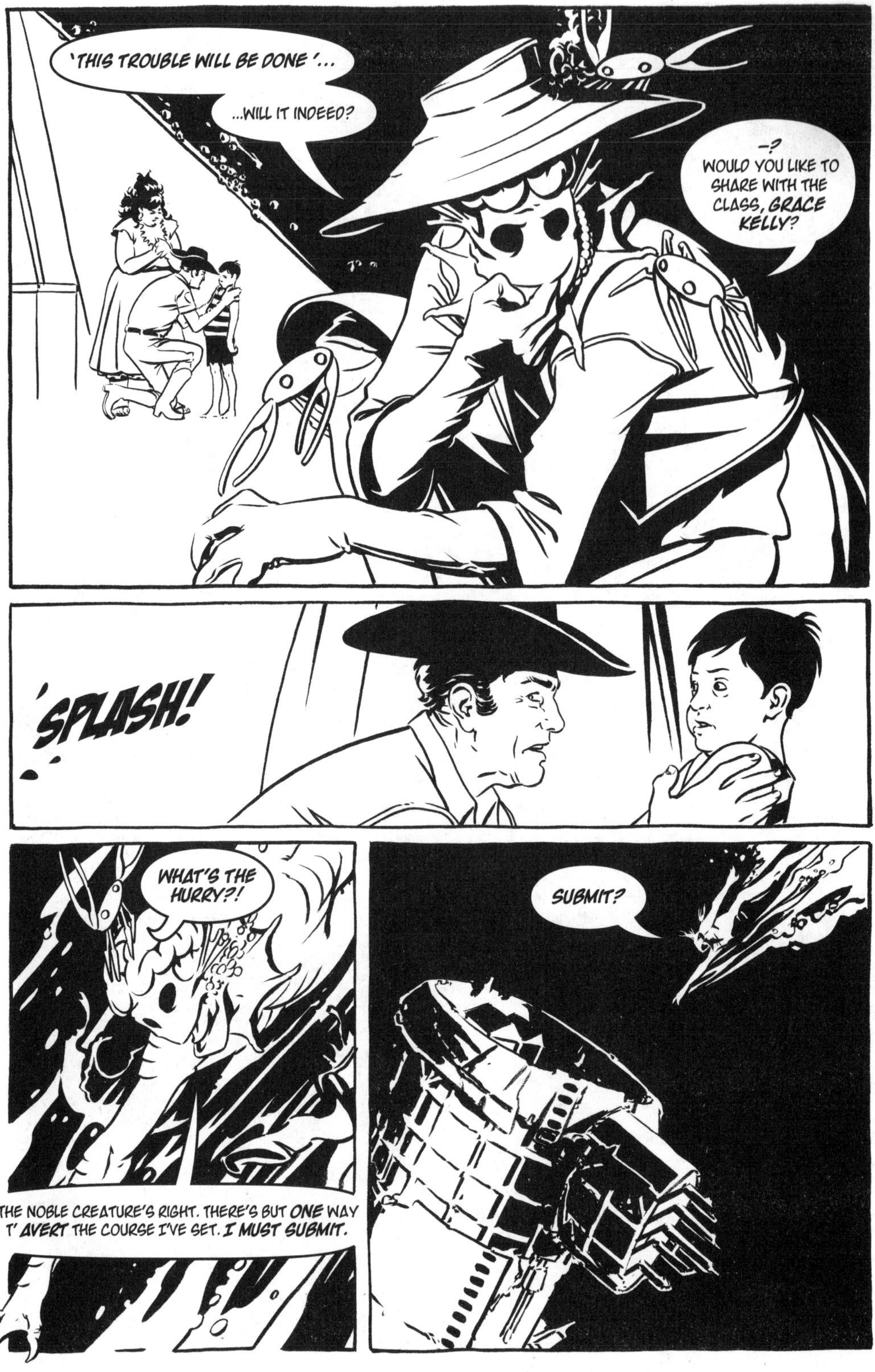
'THIS TROUBLE WILL BE DONE '...
...WILL IT INDEED?
-?
WOULD YOU LIKE TO SHARE WITH THE CLASS, GRACE KELLY?
'SPLASH!
WHAT'S THE HURRY?!
SUBMIT?
THE NOBLE CREATURE'S RIGHT. THERE'S BUT ONE WAY T' AVERT THE COURSE I'VE SET. I MUST SUBMIT.

BUT I'VE ONE CHANCE TO ACT FOR THE IDEAL...

I THOUGHT I'D SAVE MYSELF FROM MONSTERS' WAYS. I'VE **SWUM ENOUGH** TO SEE THAT SHALL NOT **BE**...

HOORAH TO THAT!

TO **PLUMB THE TRENCH**, RETRIEVE MY CHEST OF SPOILS, AND TURN ME IN TO THE AUTHORITIES!

HEH.

HAW. HAW. HAHA!

EH-HAH, HEH...

...HAHA! AHAHAHA HAHA-HA HAHA!

—ER... *COUGH*.

YOU'RE SERIOUS?

...SO IF YOU MAKE IT **BACK** FROM BELOW, YOU'LL TURN YOURSELF IN, AN' BE A **MARTYR** TO A BUNCH OF **FAST FOOD**?

WHY DON'T YA JUST SKIP AIRING THE DIRTY LAUNDRY AND TURN YOURSELF IN NOW, IF ALL YA WANTS A **DEATH SENTENCE**?

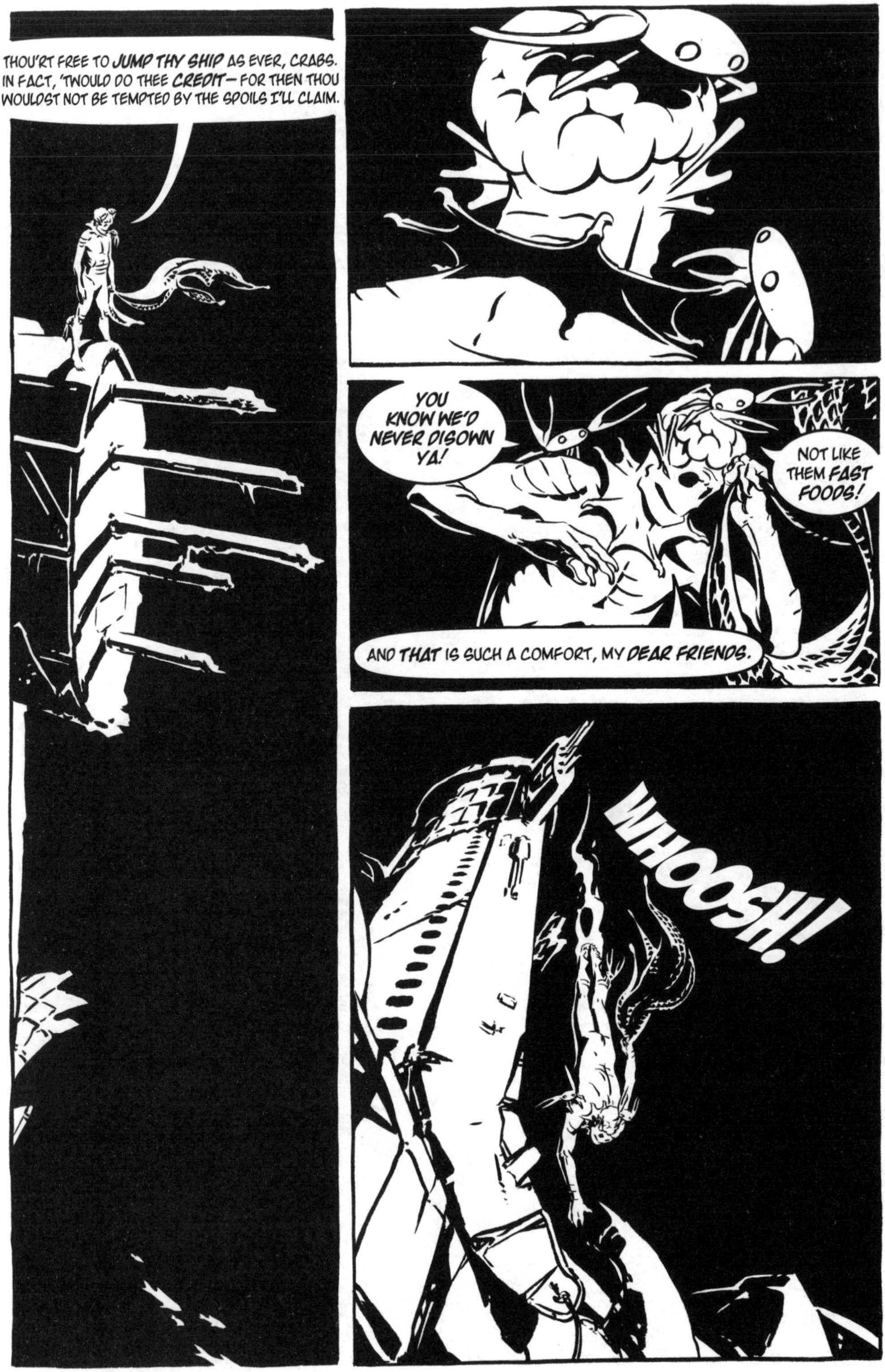
THOU'RT FREE TO JUMP THY SHIP AS EVER, CRABS. IN FACT, 'TWOULD DO THEE CREDIT— FOR THEN THOU WOULDST NOT BE TEMPTED BY THE SPOILS I'LL CLAIM.
YOU KNOW WE'D NEVER DISOWN YA!
NOT LIKE THEM FAST FOODS!
AND THAT IS SUCH A COMFORT, MY DEAR FRIENDS.
WHOOSH!

CHAPTER SIX
love hurts

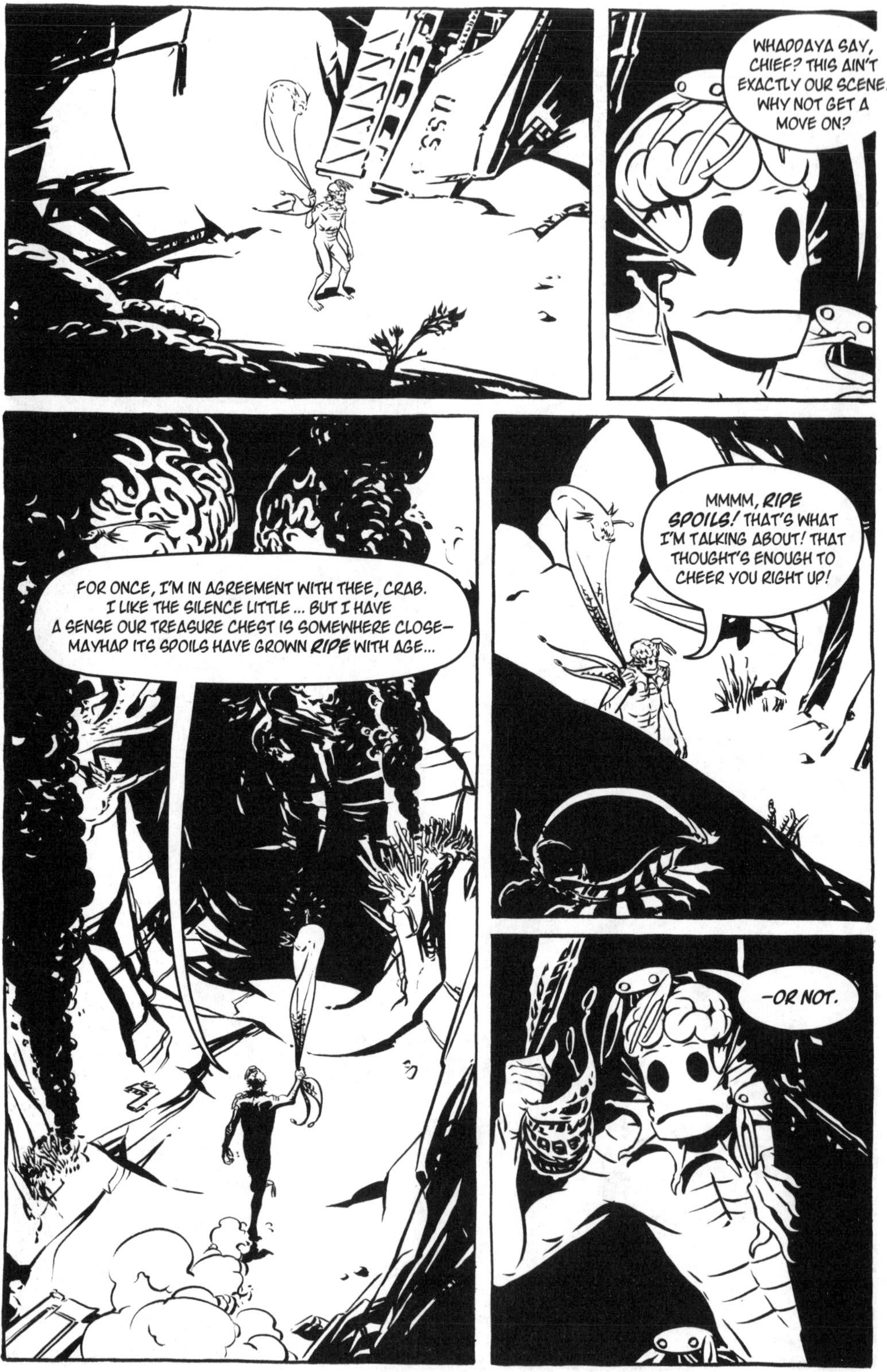
U.S.S.
WHADDAYA SAY, CHIEF? THIS AIN'T EXACTLY OUR SCENE. WHY NOT GET A MOVE ON?
FOR ONCE, I'M IN AGREEMENT WITH THEE, CRAB. I LIKE THE SILENCE LITTLE ... BUT I HAVE A SENSE OUR TREASURE CHEST IS SOMEWHERE CLOSE— MAYHAP ITS SPOILS HAVE GROWN RIPE WITH AGE...
MMMM, RIPE SPOILS! THAT'S WHAT I'M TALKING ABOUT! THAT THOUGHT'S ENOUGH TO CHEER YOU RIGHT UP!
—OR NOT.

141

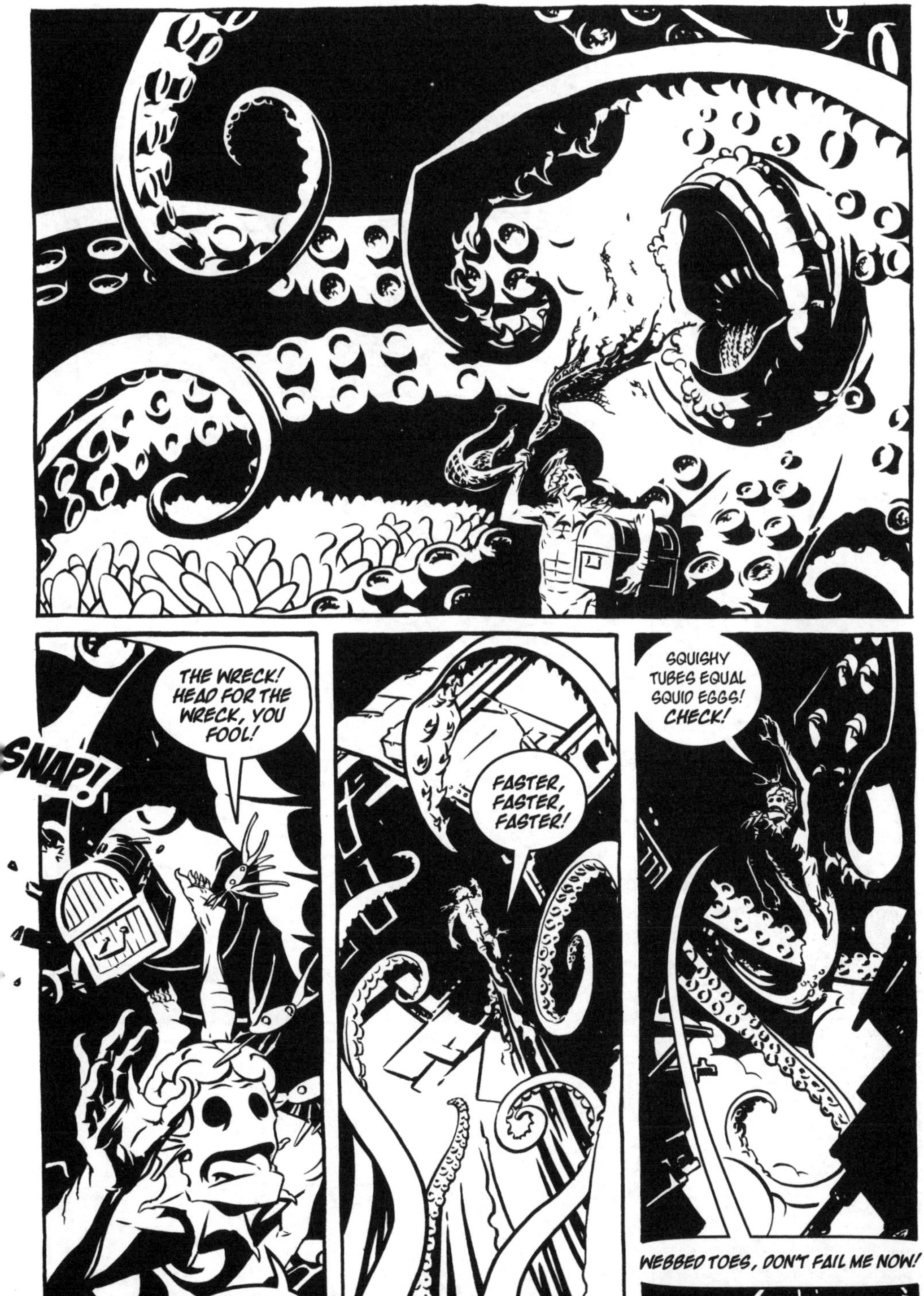
THE WRECK! HEAD FOR THE WRECK, YOU FOOL!
SNAP!
AAAHG!
FASTER, FASTER, FASTER!
SQUISHY TUBES EQUAL SQUID EGGS! CHECK!
WEBBED TOES, DON'T FAIL ME NOW!

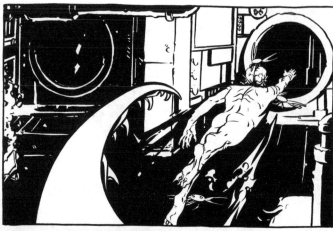

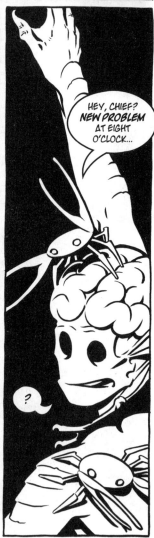

WHO KNOWS HOW LONG OUR TENTACLE RESTRAINT WILL KEEP: IT'S NOW OR NEVER—*HOLD ON TIGHT!*

YEEHAW*!!!*

HEY, CHIEF? *NEW PROBLEM* AT EIGHT O'CLOCK...

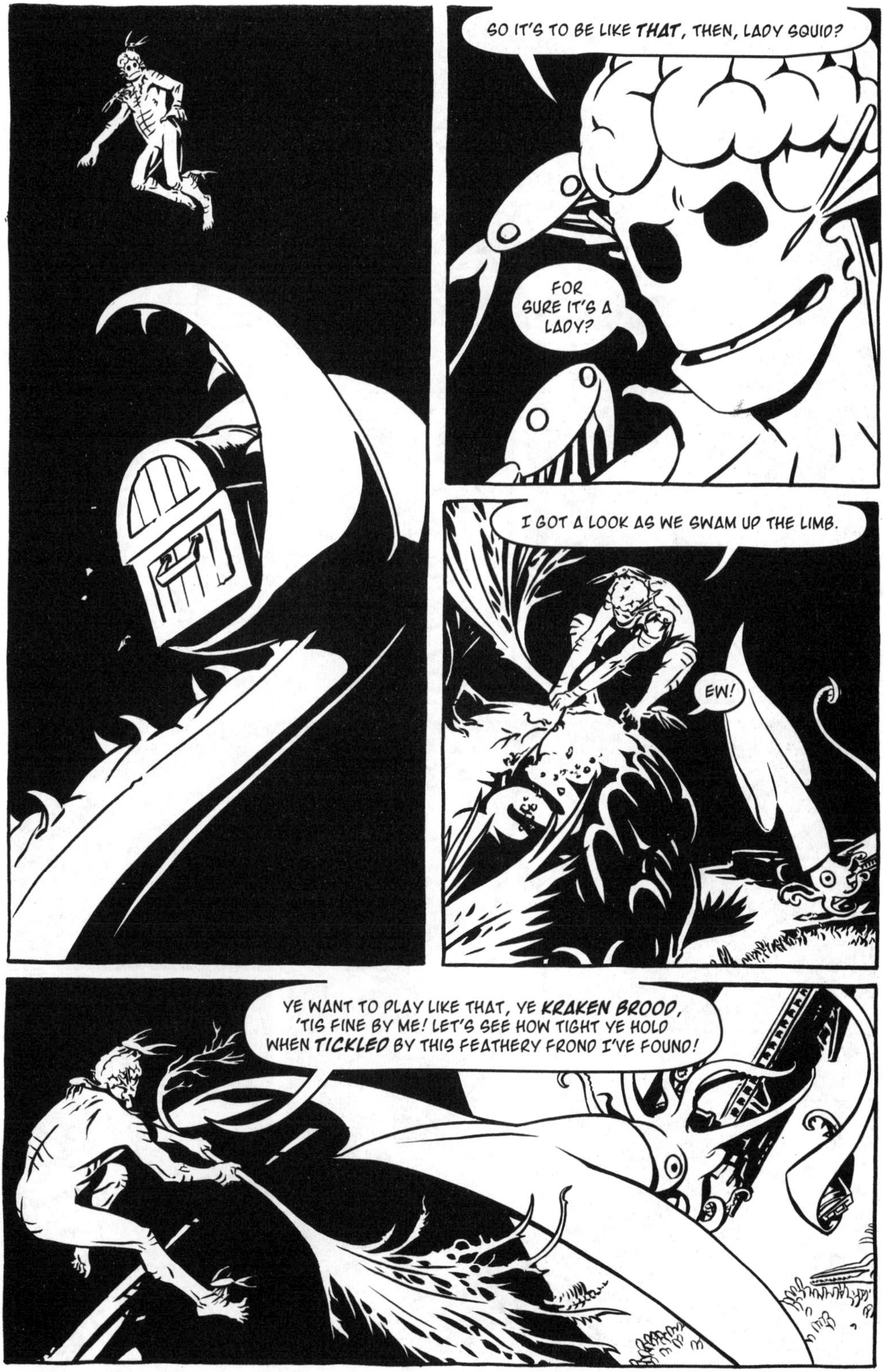
SO IT'S TO BE LIKE THAT, THEN, LADY SQUID?
FOR SURE IT'S A LADY?
I GOT A LOOK AS WE SWAM UP THE LIMB.
EW!
YE WANT TO PLAY LIKE THAT, YE KRAKEN BROOD, 'TIS FINE BY ME! LET'S SEE HOW TIGHT YE HOLD WHEN TICKLED BY THIS FEATHERY FROND I'VE FOUND!

A GOOCHIE-GOOCHIE GOO!

GA-GOO-GOO—

SQRRG!

FWOOOOOOOOOOOOM!

...SQUIDGASM?

150

SPLOOSH!

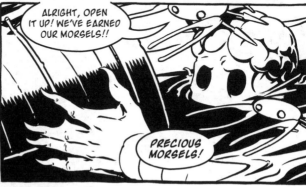

ALRIGHT, OPEN IT UP! WE'VE EARNED OUR MORSELS!!

PRECIOUS MORSELS!

I'M SORRY CRABS: METHINKS WE'D BEST REFRAIN. MY WILL'S SO WEAK, I FEAR I'D EAT THE LOT, AND HAVE NO PROOF OF MINE *INIQUITY!*

YOU'RE A BIMBO-LICKING *SEA MUTANT!!!* HOW MUCH *PROOF* DO YOU THINK THEY *NEED??*

'TIS NOT FOR THEM *ALONE!* WHAT I HAVE DONE, I NEEDS MUST OWN: ELSE MAKE BAD FAITH TO THOSE IDEALS UPHELD IN *SHAK'SPUR'S WORDS—*

THWUMP.

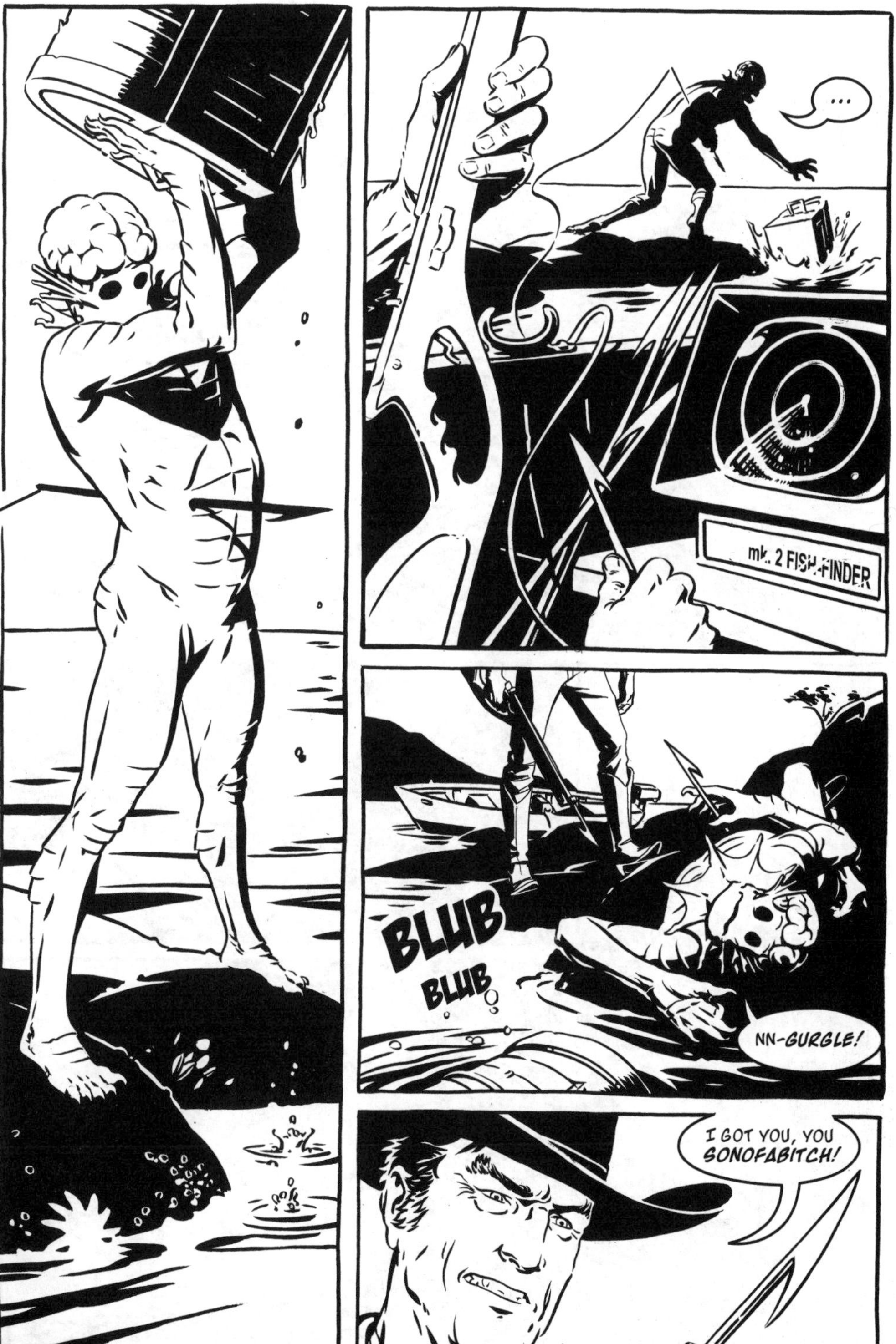
...
mk. 2 FISH-FINDER
BLUB
BLUB
NN-GURGLE!
I GOT YOU, YOU SONOFABITCH!

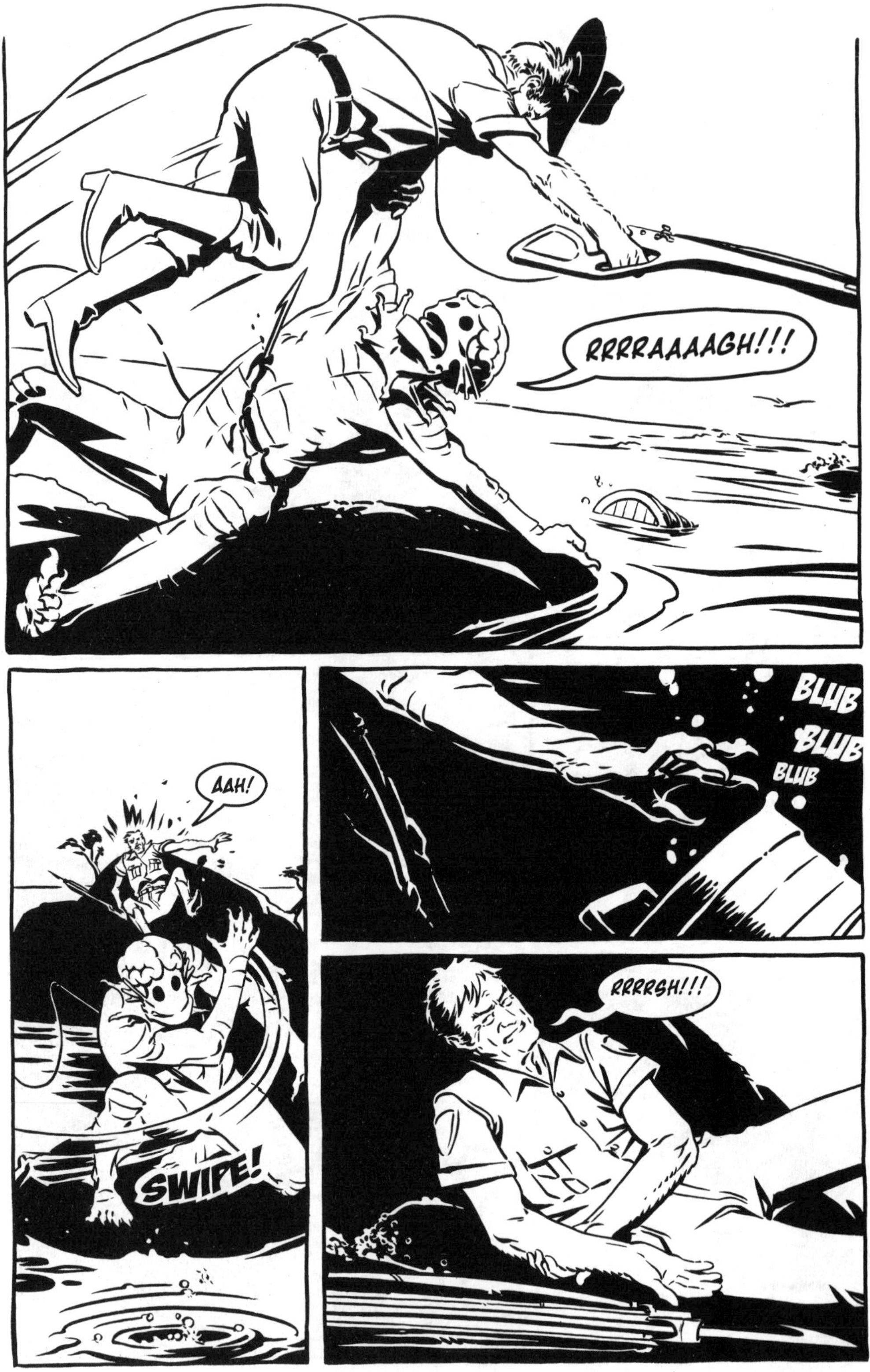
RRRRAAAAAGH!!!
AAH!
SWIPE!
BLUB
BLUB
BLUB
RRRRSH!!!

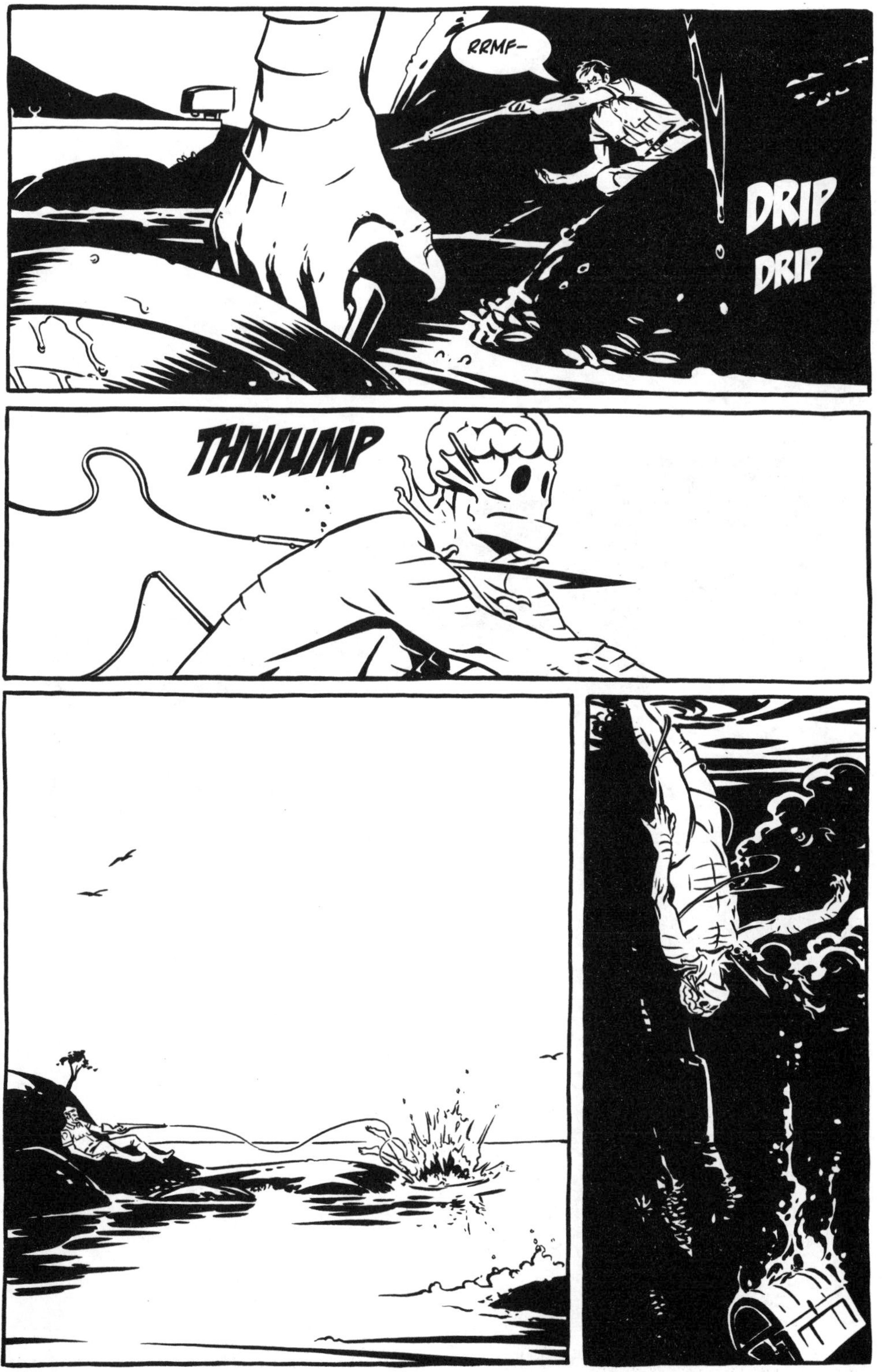
RRMF-
DRIP
DRIP
THWUMP

CHAPTER SEVEN
running scared

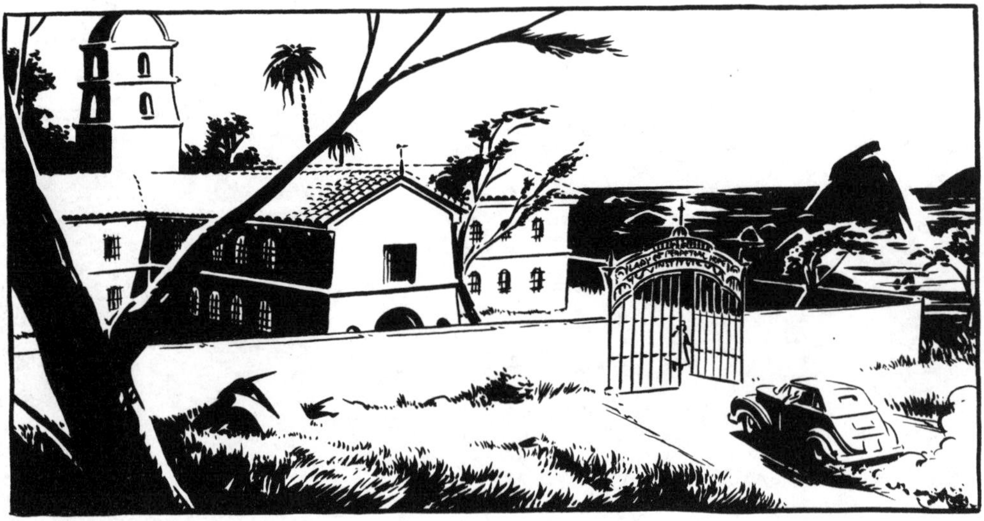
LADY OF PERPETUAL HOPE

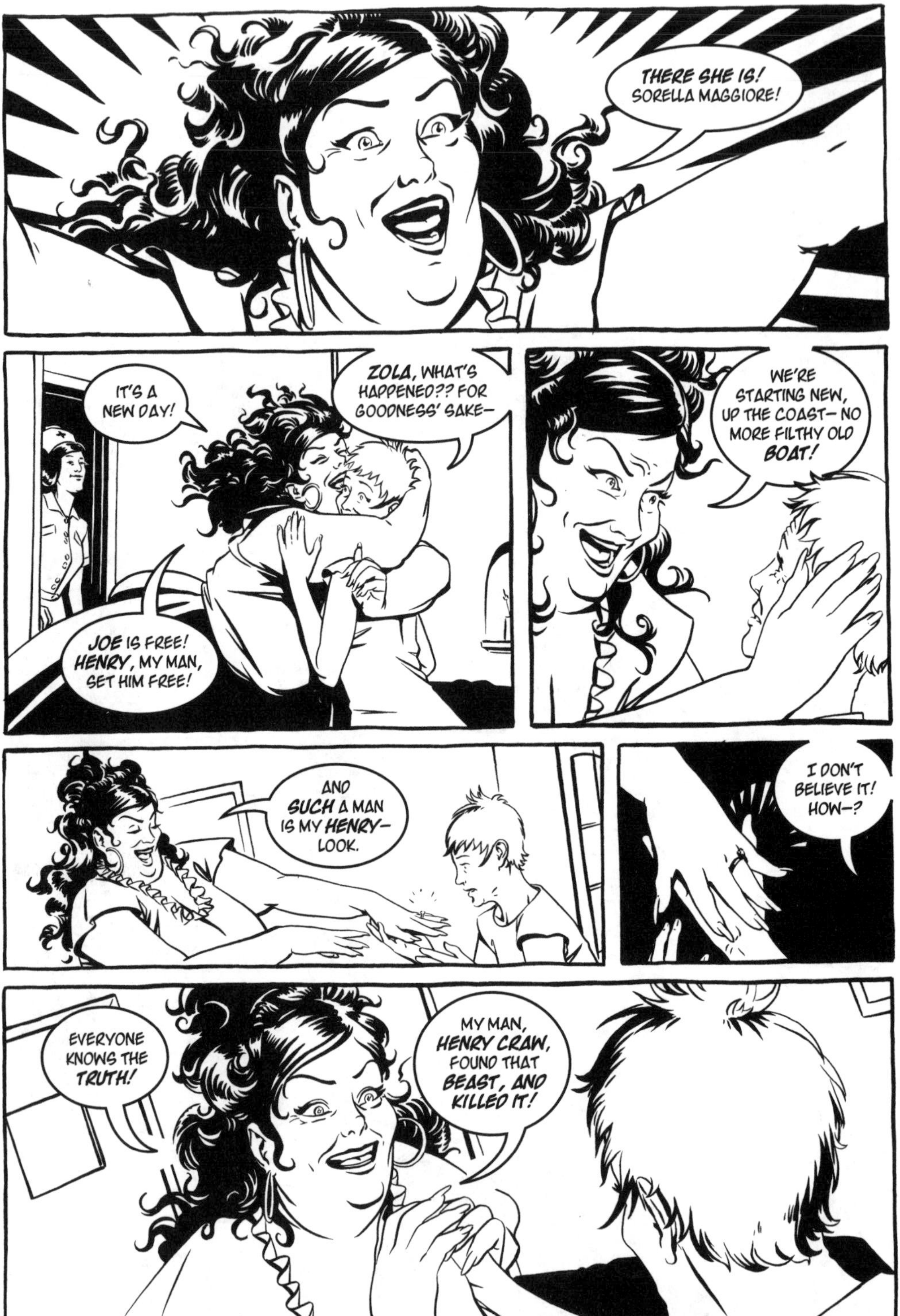
THERE SHE IS! SORELLA MAGGIORE!
IT'S A NEW DAY!
ZOLA, WHAT'S HAPPENED?? FOR GOODNESS' SAKE-
JOE IS FREE! HENRY, MY MAN, SET HIM FREE!
WE'RE STARTING NEW, UP THE COAST- NO MORE FILTHY OLD BOAT!
AND SUCH A MAN IS MY HENRY- LOOK.
I DON'T BELIEVE IT! HOW-?
EVERYONE KNOWS THE TRUTH!
MY MAN, HENRY CRAW, FOUND THAT BEAST, AND KILLED IT!

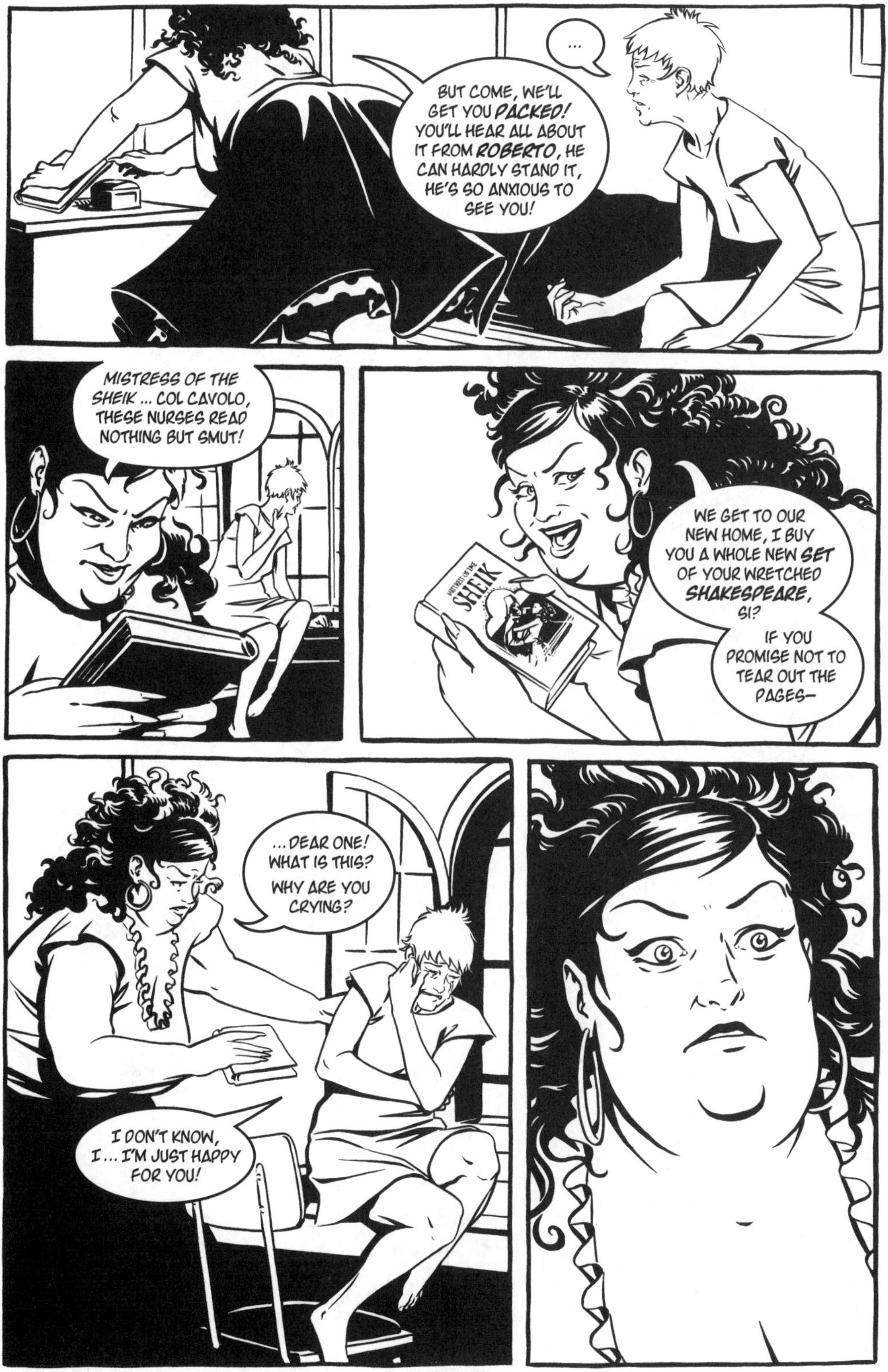
...
BUT COME, WE'LL GET YOU PACKED! YOU'LL HEAR ALL ABOUT IT FROM ROBERTO, HE CAN HARDLY STAND IT, HE'S SO ANXIOUS TO SEE YOU!
MISTRESS OF THE SHEIK ... COL CAVOLO, THESE NURSES READ NOTHING BUT SMUT!
SHEIK
WE GET TO OUR NEW HOME, I BUY YOU A WHOLE NEW SET OF YOUR WRETCHED SHAKESPEARE, SI?
IF YOU PROMISE NOT TO TEAR OUT THE PAGES—
...DEAR ONE! WHAT IS THIS? WHY ARE YOU CRYING?
I DON'T KNOW, I... I'M JUST HAPPY FOR YOU!

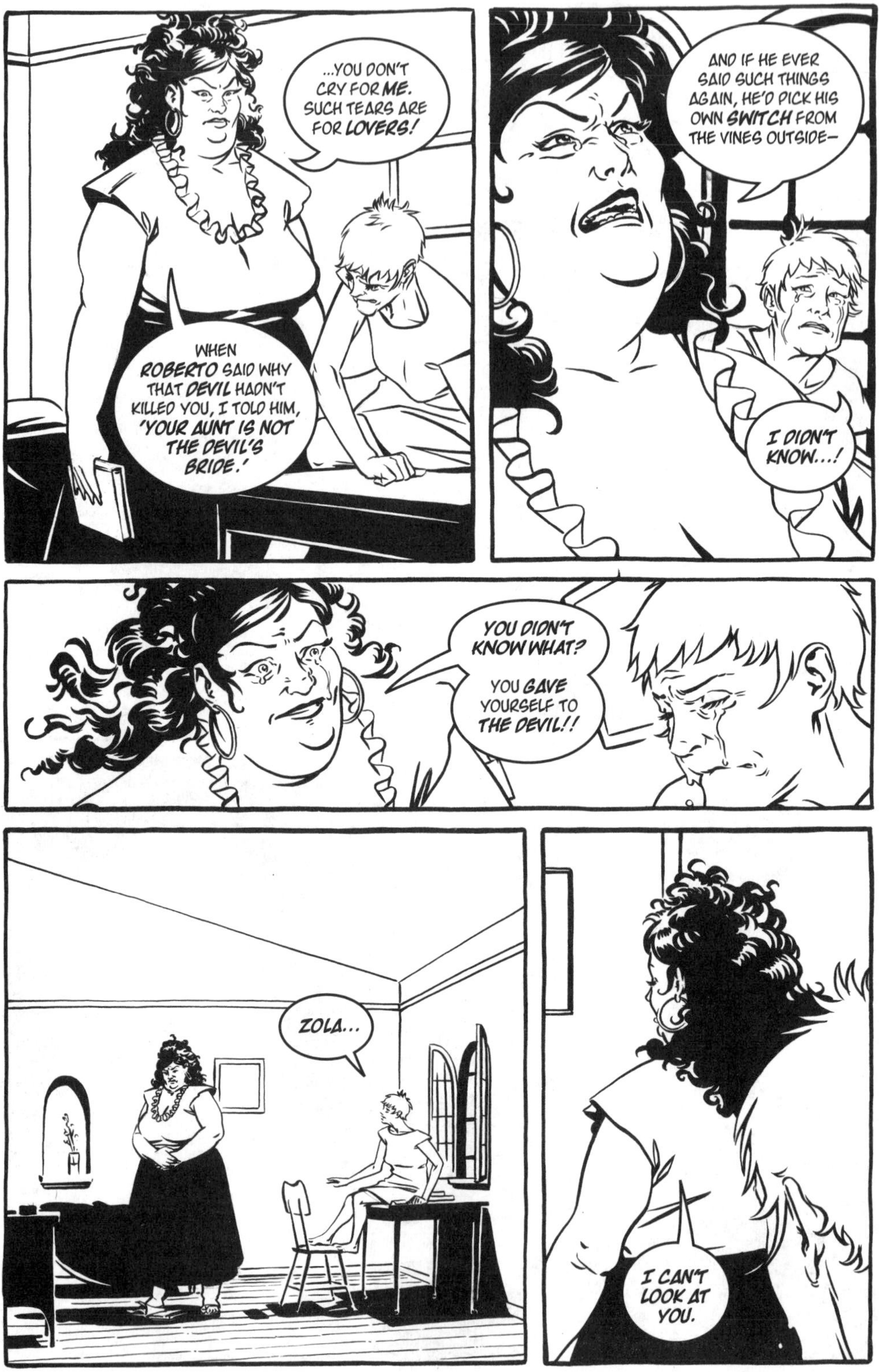
...YOU DON'T CRY FOR ME. SUCH TEARS ARE FOR LOVERS!
WHEN ROBERTO SAID WHY THAT DEVIL HADN'T KILLED YOU, I TOLD HIM, 'YOUR AUNT IS NOT THE DEVIL'S BRIDE.'
AND IF HE EVER SAID SUCH THINGS AGAIN, HE'D PICK HIS OWN SWITCH FROM THE VINES OUTSIDE–
I DIDN'T KNOW...!
YOU DIDN'T KNOW WHAT?
YOU GAVE YOURSELF TO THE DEVIL!!
ZOLA...
I CAN'T LOOK AT YOU.

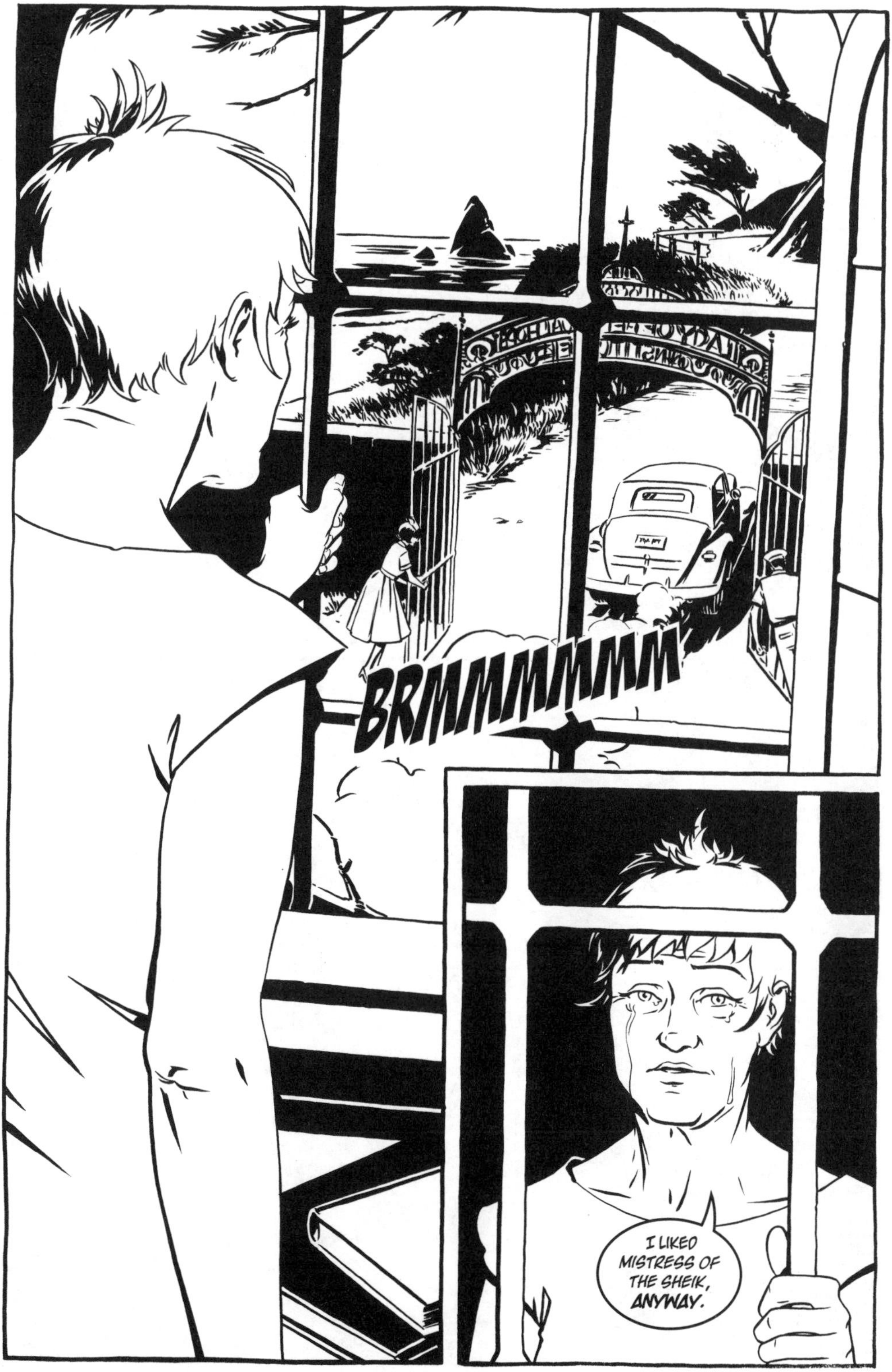
BRMMMMMMM
I LIKED MISTRESS OF THE SHEIK, ANYWAY.

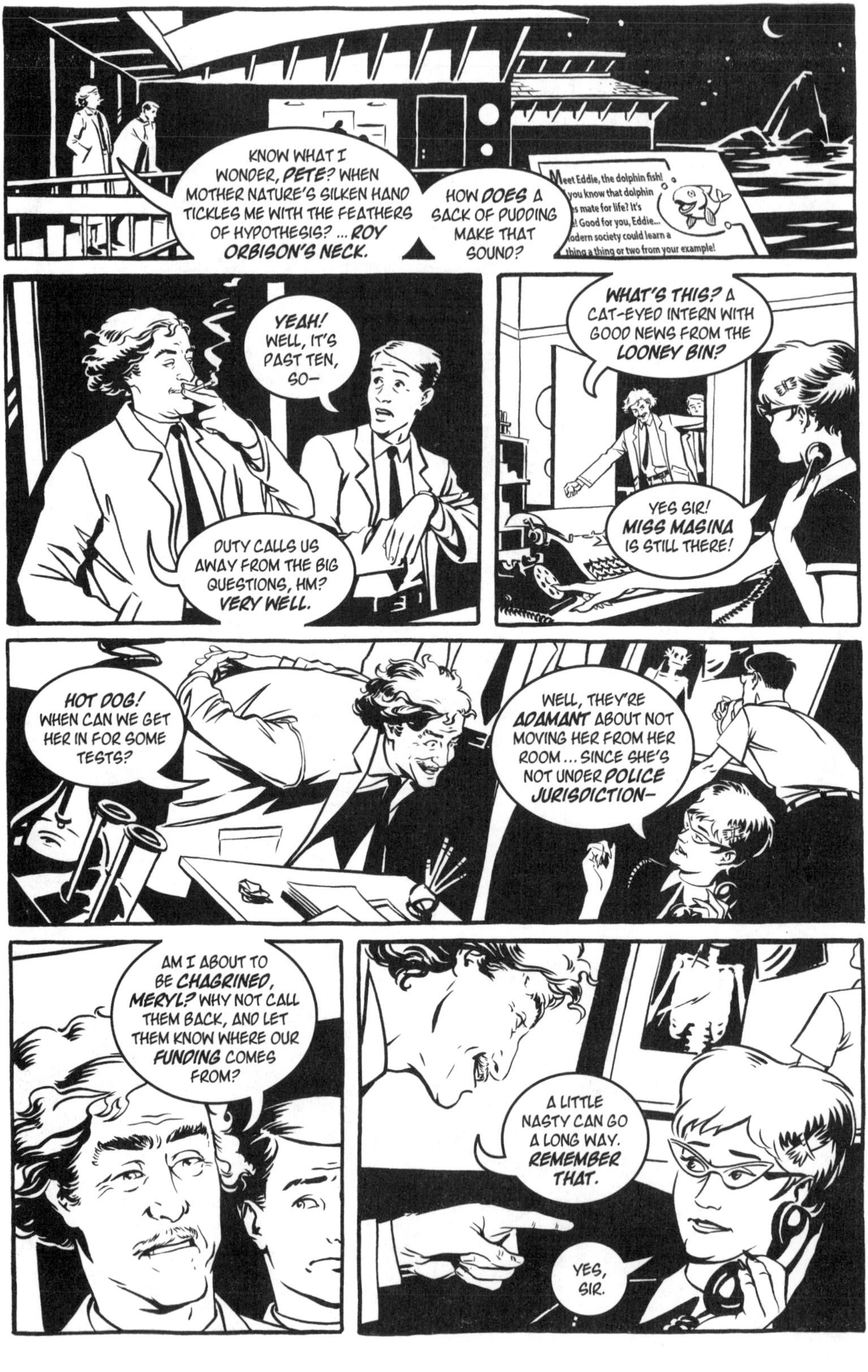

KNOW WHAT I WONDER, PETE? WHEN MOTHER NATURE'S SILKEN HAND TICKLES ME WITH THE FEATHERS OF HYPOTHESIS? ... ROY ORBISON'S NECK.
HOW DOES A SACK OF PUDDING MAKE THAT SOUND?
Meet Eddie, the dolphin fish!
you know that dolphin
mate for life? It's
Good for you, Eddie...
society could learn a
thing a thing or two from your example!
YEAH! WELL, IT'S PAST TEN, SO–
DUTY CALLS US AWAY FROM THE BIG QUESTIONS, HM? VERY WELL.
WHAT'S THIS? A CAT-EYED INTERN WITH GOOD NEWS FROM THE LOONEY BIN?
YES SIR! MISS MASINA IS STILL THERE!
HOT DOG! WHEN CAN WE GET HER IN FOR SOME TESTS?
WELL, THEY'RE ADAMANT ABOUT NOT MOVING HER FROM HER ROOM ... SINCE SHE'S NOT UNDER POLICE JURISDICTION–
AM I ABOUT TO BE CHAGRINED, MERYL? WHY NOT CALL THEM BACK, AND LET THEM KNOW WHERE OUR FUNDING COMES FROM?
A LITTLE NASTY CAN GO A LONG WAY. REMEMBER THAT.
YES, SIR.

PETE AND I ARE GOING TO CYCLE THE TANK. GET US A COUPLE COFFEES, WOULD YA?

CAN I COME SEE IT *TOO*, DOCTOR??

SOMEONE DIE AND MAKE YOU *NOT* AN INTERN? COFFEE, PLEASE.

'A CANDY COLORED CLOWN, DABA-DA-BABA... TICKLES MY NECK PUDDING EVERY NIGHT...'

RESTRICTED

STILL, SHE'S NOT A BAD LOOKER, THAT *MERYL*! EH?

WHATVER YOU SAY, *DOC*. I'M JUST HERE FOR THE WORK! AND I *GOT* A GIRL ALREADY.

I UNDERSTAND, I SUPPOSE.

I NEVER THOUGHT I'D HAVE EYES FOR ANYTHING BUT ODONTOCETI AND ARCHITEUTHIS...

CLINK CLINK

BUT *LOOK* AT THAT! IT MAKES ME—*OH*, IT MAKES THE LITTLE SCIENTIST IN ME WANT TO *CRY!*

165

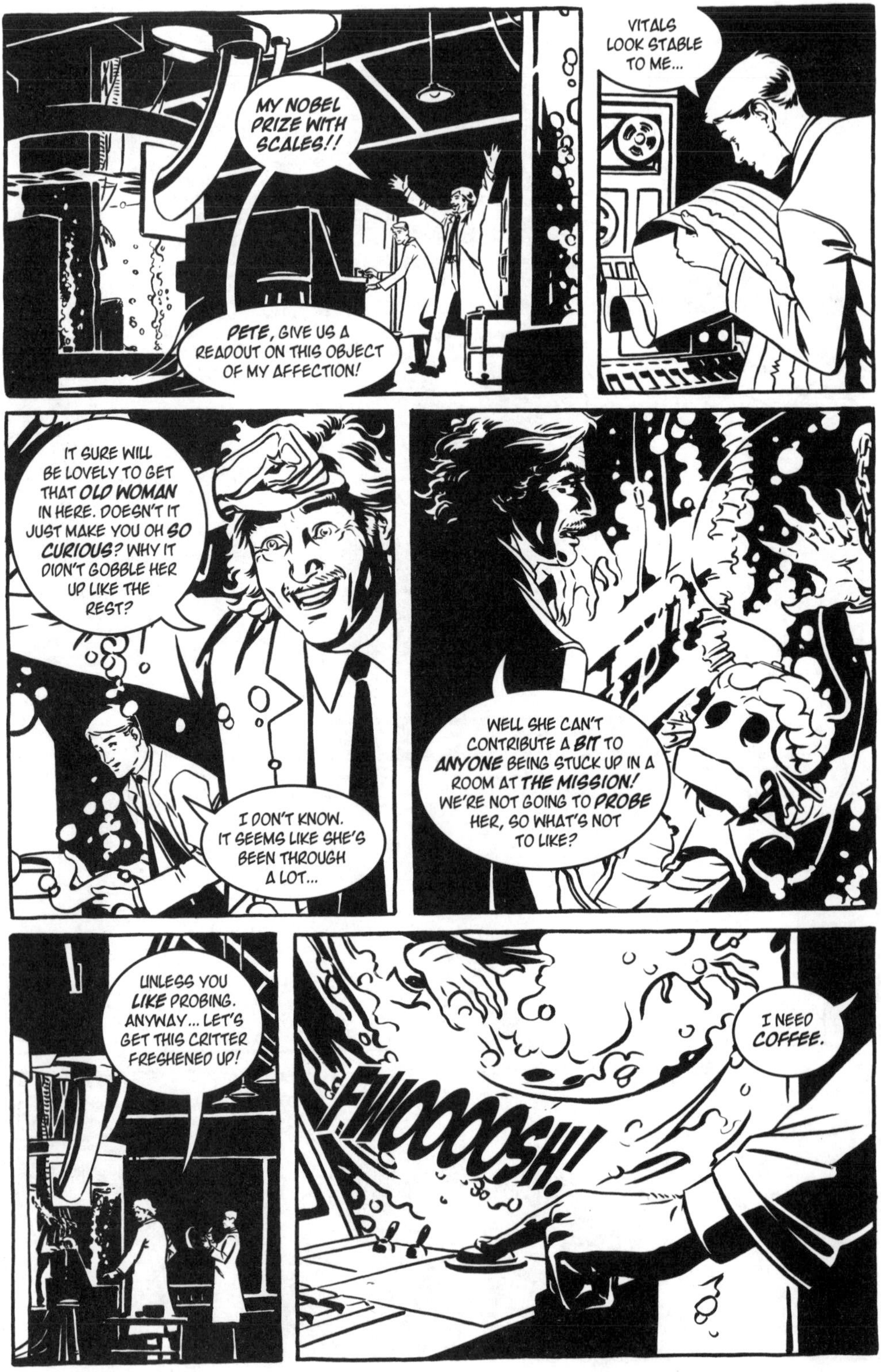
MY NOBEL PRIZE WITH SCALES!!
PETE, GIVE US A READOUT ON THIS OBJECT OF MY AFFECTION!
VITALS LOOK STABLE TO ME...
IT SURE WILL BE LOVELY TO GET THAT OLD WOMAN IN HERE. DOESN'T IT JUST MAKE YOU OH SO CURIOUS? WHY IT DIDN'T GOBBLE HER UP LIKE THE REST?
I DON'T KNOW. IT SEEMS LIKE SHE'S BEEN THROUGH A LOT...
WELL SHE CAN'T CONTRIBUTE A BIT TO ANYONE BEING STUCK UP IN A ROOM AT THE MISSION! WE'RE NOT GOING TO PROBE HER, SO WHAT'S NOT TO LIKE?
UNLESS YOU LIKE PROBING. ANYWAY... LET'S GET THIS CRITTER FRESHENED UP!
FWOOOOOSH!
I NEED COFFEE.

168

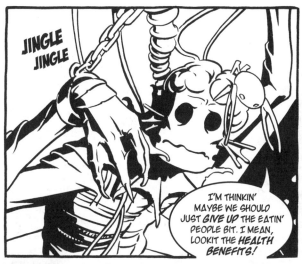

JINGLE
JINGLE

I'M THINKIN' MAYBE WE SHOULD JUST *GIVE UP* THE EATIN' PEOPLE BIT. I MEAN, LOOKIT THE *HEALTH BENEFITS!*

SLAM!

I CANNOT—LET THEM *BRING HER* HERE...I CAN'T—

WHSSSH

GIVE IT A REST, ALREADY! YER JUST GONNA HURT YERSELF!

YIPE!

MMMMF!

O, SCREW YE, CHAINS! I *HATE* THY *CHAINEY* GUTS!

YEAH! WELL SAID!

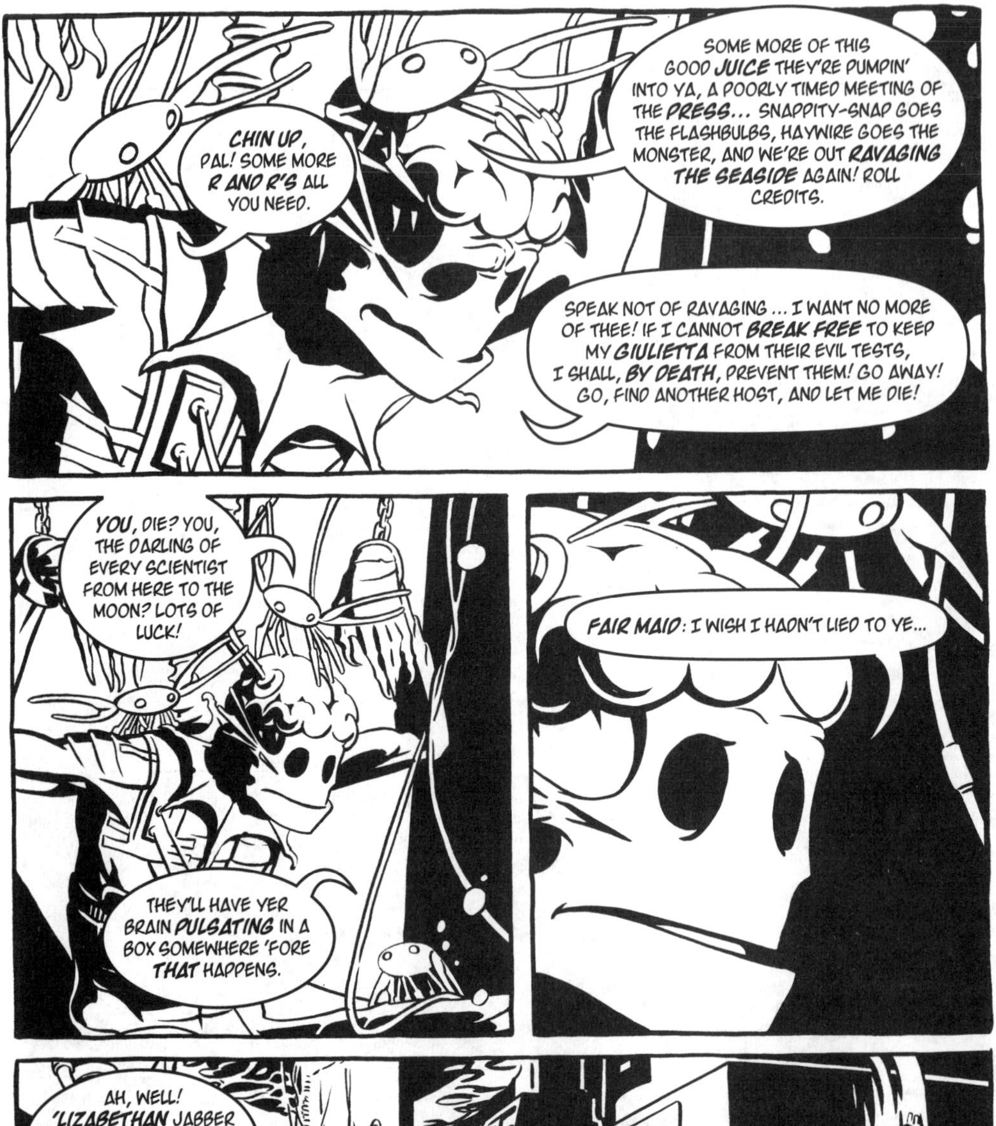
CHIN UP, PAL! SOME MORE R AND R'S ALL YOU NEED.
SOME MORE OF THIS GOOD JUICE THEY'RE PUMPIN' INTO YA, A POORLY TIMED MEETING OF THE PRESS... SNAPPITY-SNAP GOES THE FLASHBULBS, HAYWIRE GOES THE MONSTER, AND WE'RE OUT RAVAGING THE SEASIDE AGAIN! ROLL CREDITS.
SPEAK NOT OF RAVAGING ... I WANT NO MORE OF THEE! IF I CANNOT BREAK FREE TO KEEP MY GIULIETTA FROM THEIR EVIL TESTS, I SHALL, BY DEATH, PREVENT THEM! GO AWAY! GO, FIND ANOTHER HOST, AND LET ME DIE!
YOU, DIE? YOU, THE DARLING OF EVERY SCIENTIST FROM HERE TO THE MOON? LOTS OF LUCK!
THEY'LL HAVE YER BRAIN PULSATING IN A BOX SOMEWHERE 'FORE THAT HAPPENS.
FAIR MAID: I WISH I HADN'T LIED TO YE...
AH, WELL! 'LIZABETHAN JABBER AND ATOMIC TONGUES JUST WEREN'T MADE TA' MIX, THAT'S ALL!
CLUNK

JEEZ, NORMAN! WE'RE GONNA GET FIRED!

C'MON, THERE'S NOBODY HERE, ANYWAY...

WANNA SEE IT, OR NOT?

OH MY GAWSH—LOOK! IT'S WATCHING US... THAT'S SO CREEPY.

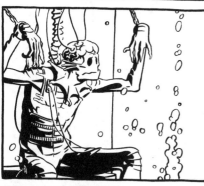

OH, WOW!

YEP, THERE HE IS: A FACE EVEN MOTHER NATURE COULDN'T LOVE! HEH-HYULK! GO AHEAD'N HAVE A LOOK. HE WON'T EAT MUCH.

IT REALLY KILLED ALL THOSE PEOPLE?

WOW!

EVERY ONE OF 'EM. THAT OLD CAP'N FIGURED IT WAS ALWAYS COUPLES, OUT ON A LATE-NIGHT TRYST—THEN BAM!

I WONDER WHAT THEY ALL THOUGHT WHEN IT WAS COMING AT 'EM ... I BET THEIR HEARTS JUST STOPPED DEAD, RIGHT THERE—

WOULDN'T THAT HAVE BEEN SOMETHIN' TO SEE!

<SNORT!>

YOU'RE A SICK GIRL, MERYL STEVENSON!

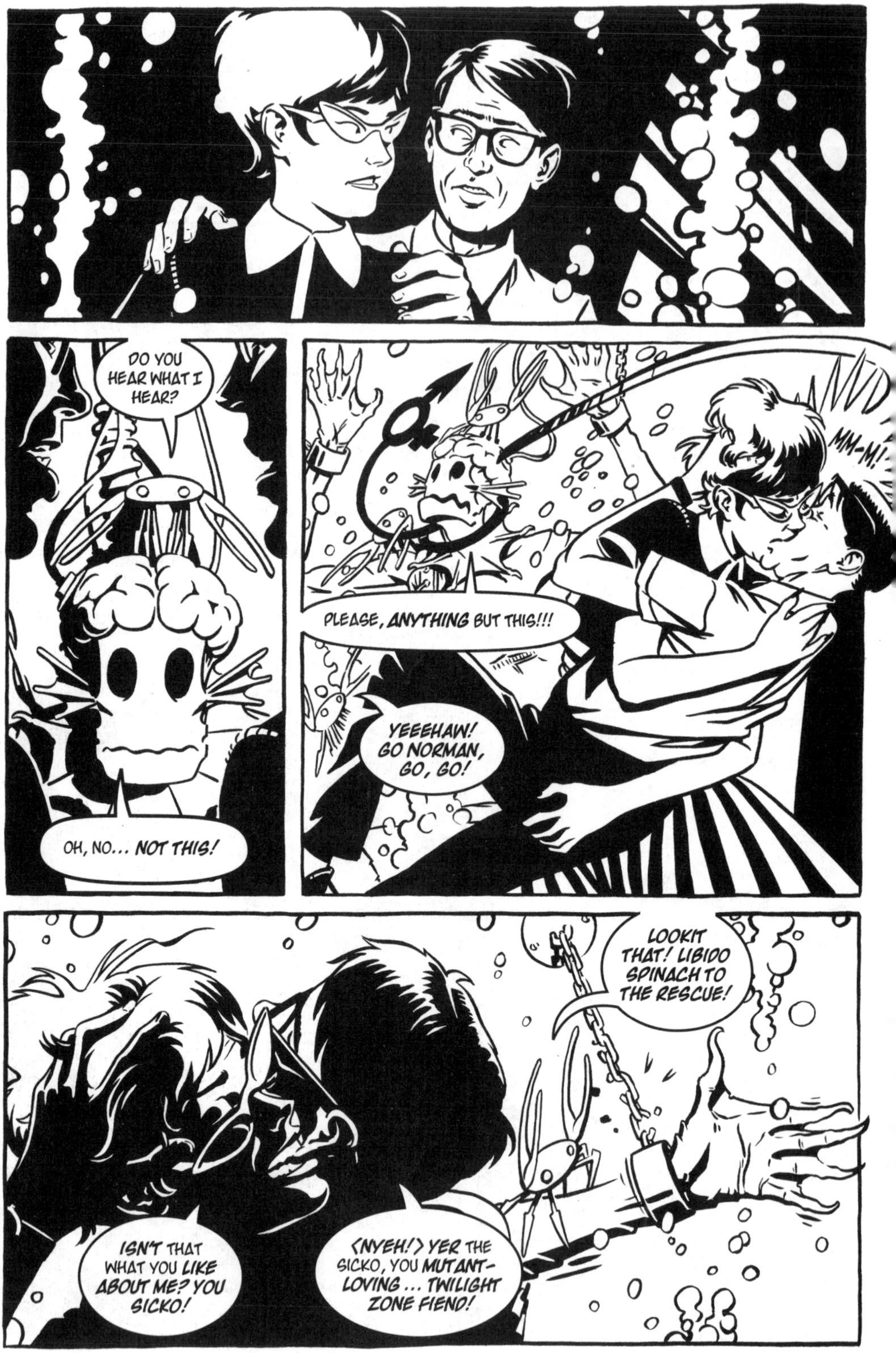
DO YOU HEAR WHAT I HEAR?
OH, NO... NOT THIS!
MM-M!
PLEASE, ANYTHING BUT THIS!!!
YEEEHAW! GO NORMAN, GO, GO!
LOOKIT THAT! LIBIDO SPINACH TO THE RESCUE!
ISN'T THAT WHAT YOU LIKE ABOUT ME? YOU SICKO!
<NYEH!> YER THE SICKO, YOU MUTANT-LOVING... TWILIGHT ZONE FIEND!

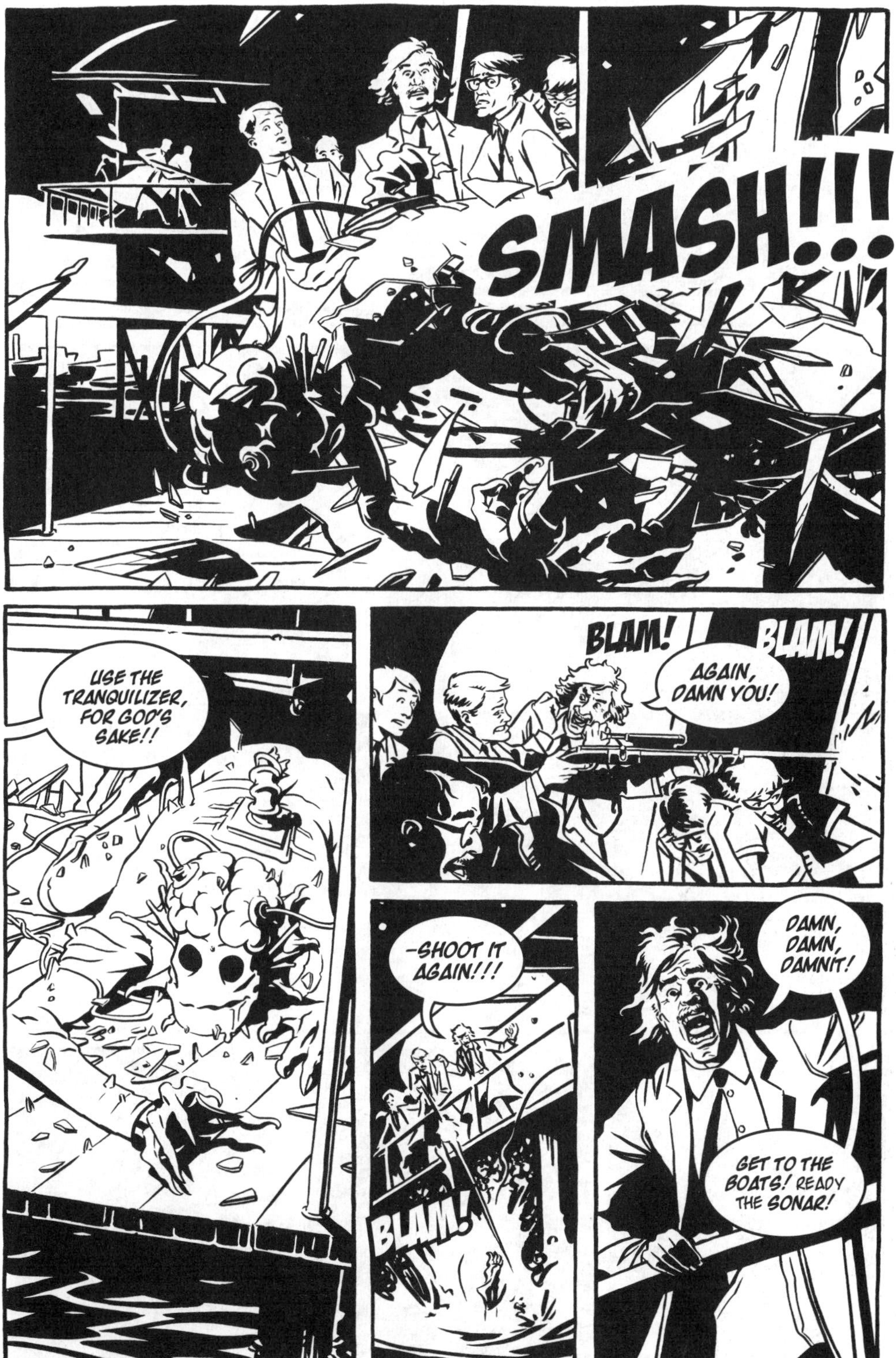
SMASH!!!...
USE THE TRANQUILIZER, FOR GOD'S SAKE!!
BLAM!
BLAM!
AGAIN, DAMN YOU!
–SHOOT IT AGAIN!!!
BLAM!
DAMN, DAMN, DAMNIT!
GET TO THE BOATS! READY THE SONAR!

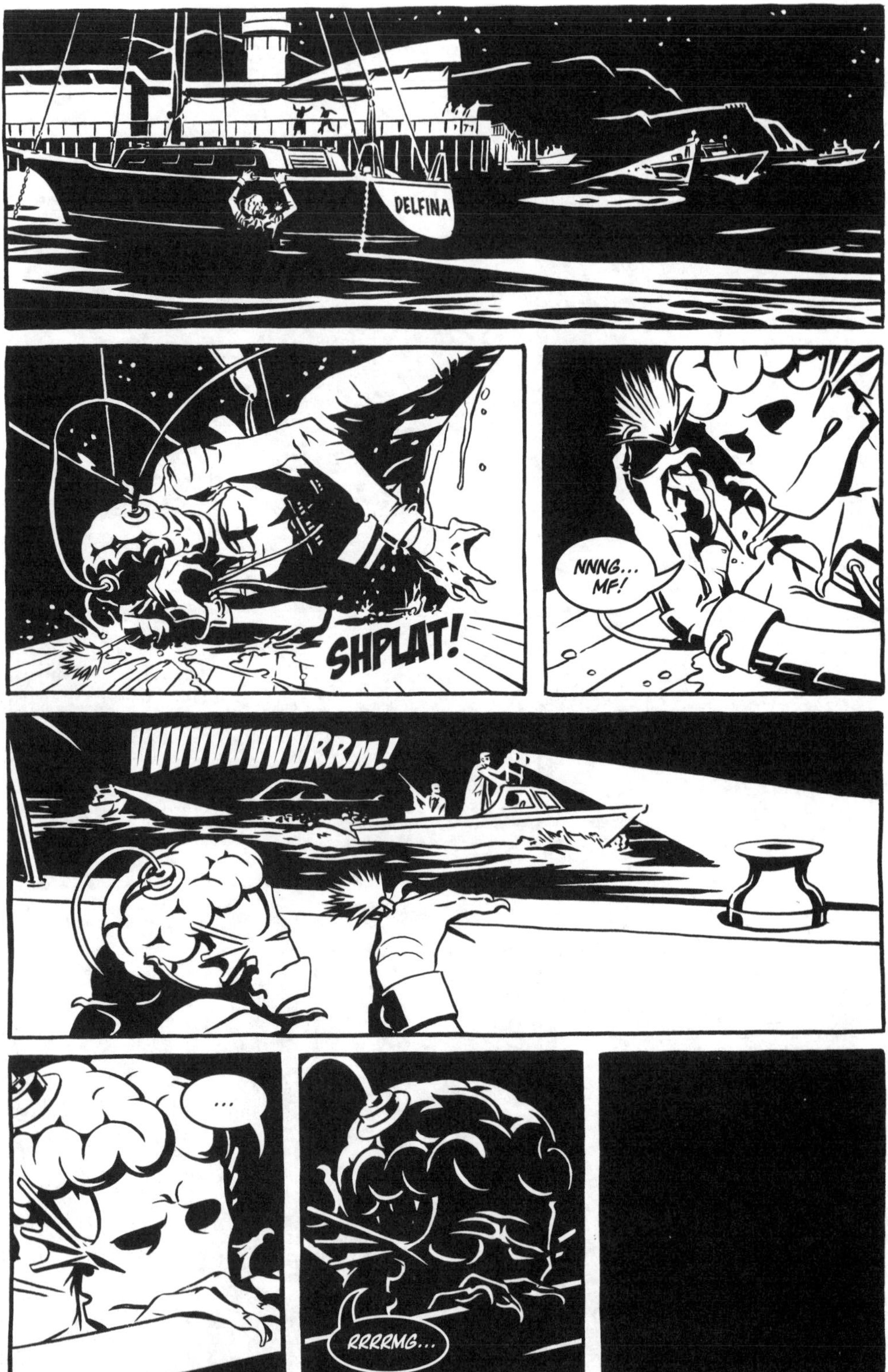
DELFINA
SHPLAT!
NNNG... MF!
VVVVVVVVVVRRM!
...
RRRRMG...

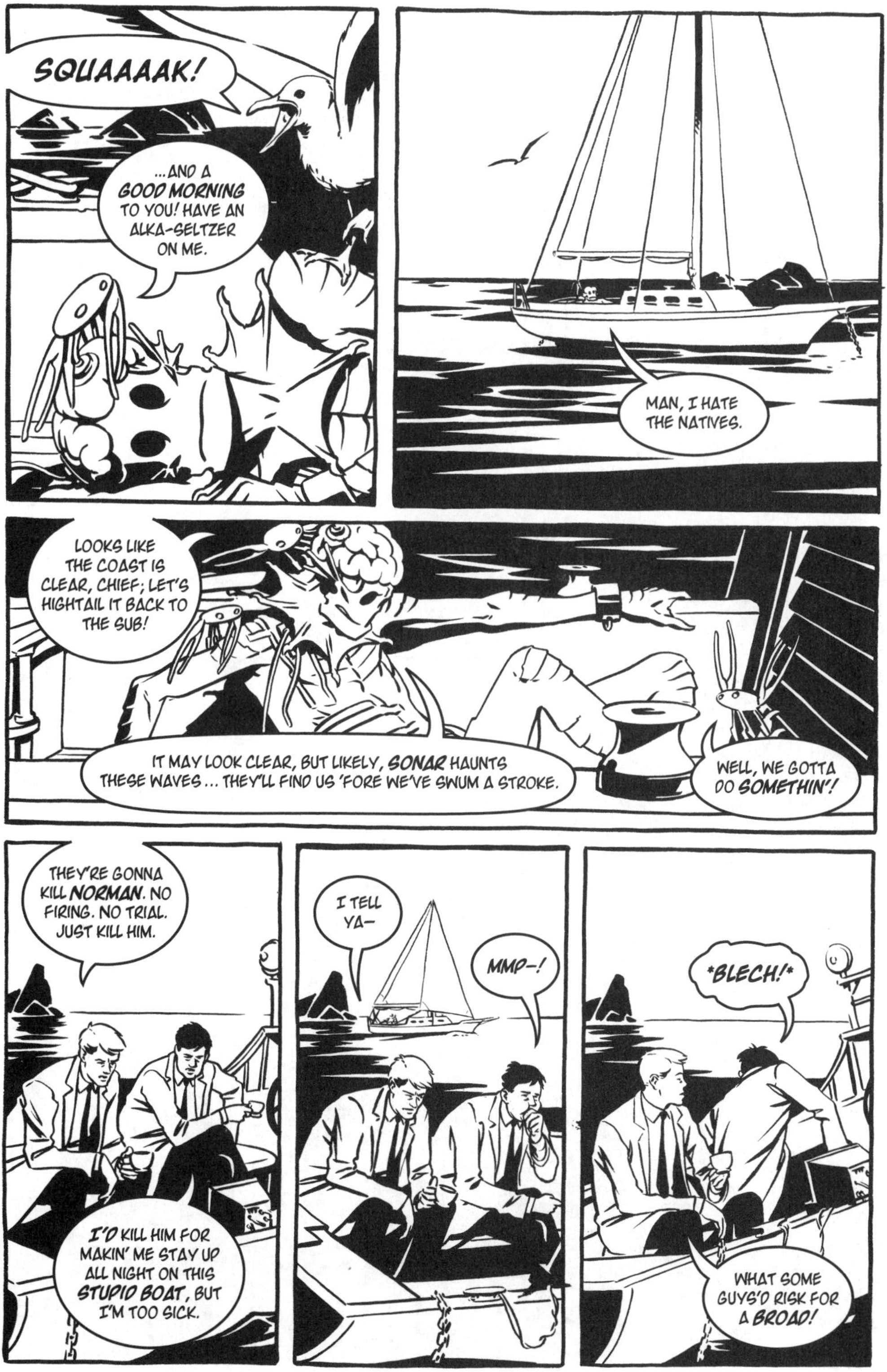
SQUAAAAK!
...AND A GOOD MORNING TO YOU! HAVE AN ALKA-SELTZER ON ME.
MAN, I HATE THE NATIVES.
LOOKS LIKE THE COAST IS CLEAR, CHIEF; LET'S HIGHTAIL IT BACK TO THE SUB!
IT MAY LOOK CLEAR, BUT LIKELY, SONAR HAUNTS THESE WAVES ... THEY'LL FIND US 'FORE WE'VE SWUM A STROKE.
WELL, WE GOTTA DO SOMETHIN'!
THEY'RE GONNA KILL NORMAN. NO FIRING. NO TRIAL. JUST KILL HIM.
I'D KILL HIM FOR MAKIN' ME STAY UP ALL NIGHT ON THIS STUPID BOAT, BUT I'M TOO SICK.
I TELL YA—
MMP—!
BLECH!
WHAT SOME GUYS'D RISK FOR A BROAD!

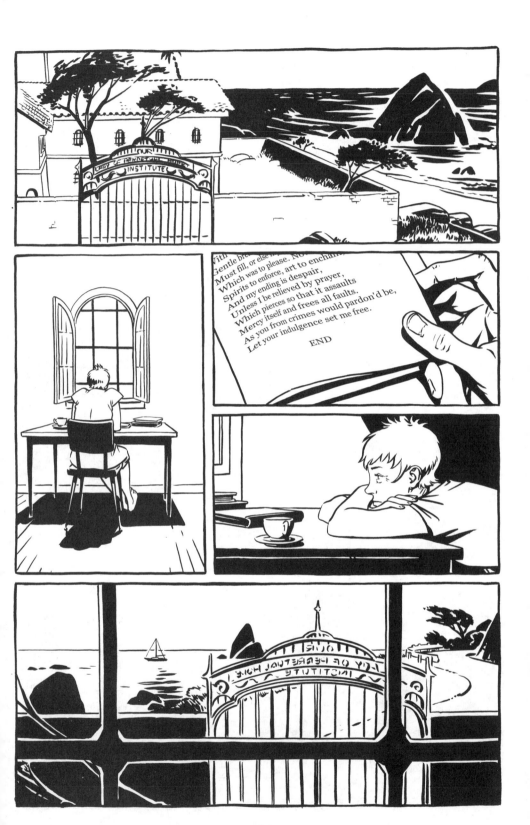

TO CALL *OUR LADY* BEAUTIFUL IS TRITE. NO WORD CAN SUM HER; I INDEED HAVE TRIED!

HELLO, *FAIR ORGANISM.* FRET YE NOT—YOUR NEPHEW'S SAFE, AND I AM... DISINCLINED TO FURTHER *MISCHIEF!* I COME NOT TO SEEK FORGIVENESS, BUT TO SEE THAT YE BE WELL.

YOU'RE HURT!

A LADY EVER, *GIULIETTA!* CARE NOT FOR ME... I AM A MONSTER, AS YE SAID. BUT HOW FARE YE, MY LITTLE CRAZY ONE?

...*ZOLA* TOLD ME THE *CAPTAIN* HAD KILLED YOU!

OH, *GIULIETTA*—SAY SHE'LL COME AT ONCE, AND LET YE LOOSE, SINCE ALL YOUR SCHOOL'S ABSOLVED! I CANNOT REST WITH YE BEHIND THESE BARS—

SHE KNOWS WHAT HAPPENED BETWEEN US—

SHE'S LEFT.

O, LOVE...!

...I'VE CURSED YE *MORE*—I AM UNDONE!

179

180

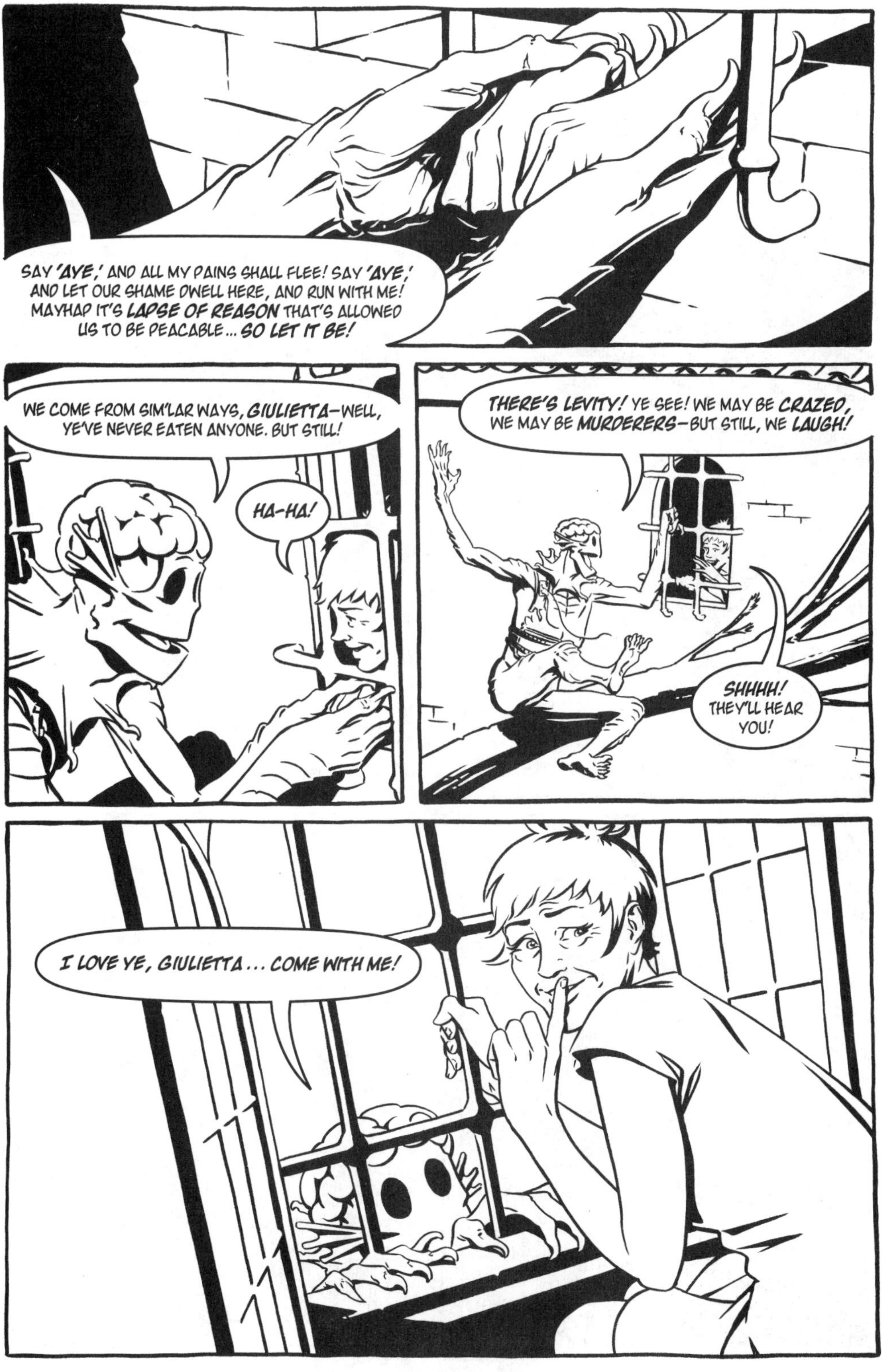
SAY 'AYE,' AND ALL MY PAINS SHALL FLEE! SAY 'AYE,' AND LET OUR SHAME DWELL HERE, AND RUN WITH ME! MAYHAP IT'S LAPSE OF REASON THAT'S ALLOWED US TO BE PEACABLE... SO LET IT BE!
WE COME FROM SIM'LAR WAYS, GIULIETTA—WELL, YE'VE NEVER EATEN ANYONE. BUT STILL!
HA-HA!
THERE'S LEVITY! YE SEE! WE MAY BE CRAZED, WE MAY BE MURDERERS—BUT STILL, WE LAUGH!
SHHHH! THEY'LL HEAR YOU!
I LOVE YE, GIULIETTA... COME WITH ME!

AVAUNT, FAIR WINDS, AND SPEED US TO NEW DAYS!

SEA MUTANT'S **SECRET**, CRAB... NOW **LEAVE ME BE!**

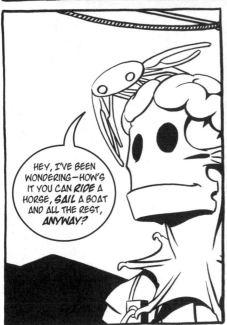

HEY, I'VE BEEN WONDERING—HOW'S IT YOU CAN **RIDE** A HORSE, **SAIL** A BOAT AND ALL THE REST, **ANYWAY?**

OH, **WAIT**, YOU WANT US TO **LEAVE?** ...WHY DIDN'T YOU **SAY** SOMETHING?

HAR-HAR. THAT'S PRETTY GOOD, I MUST ADMIT. BUT LET ME **DREAM!** A MONSTER NEEDS A DREAM.

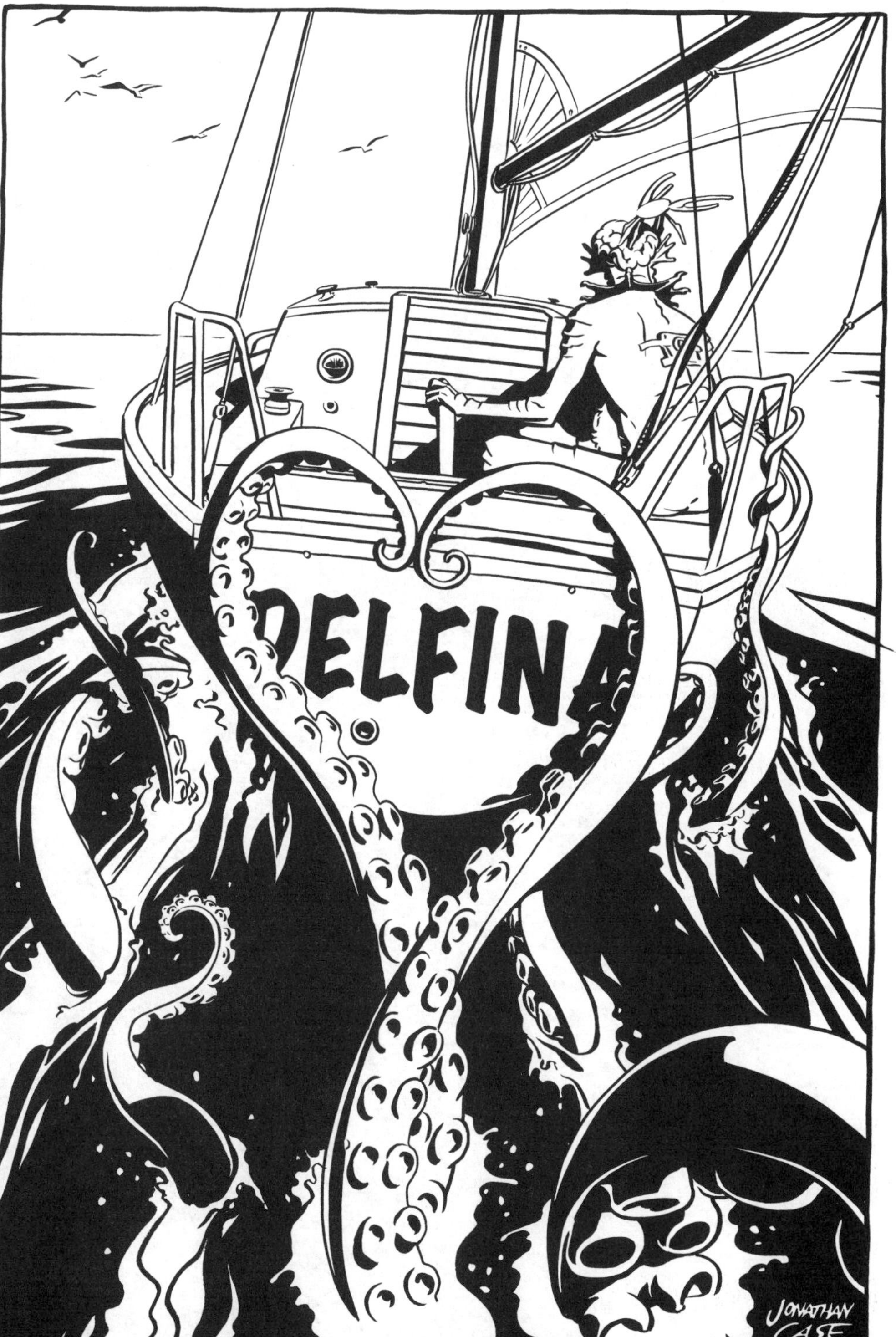
DELFINA
JONATHAN CASE

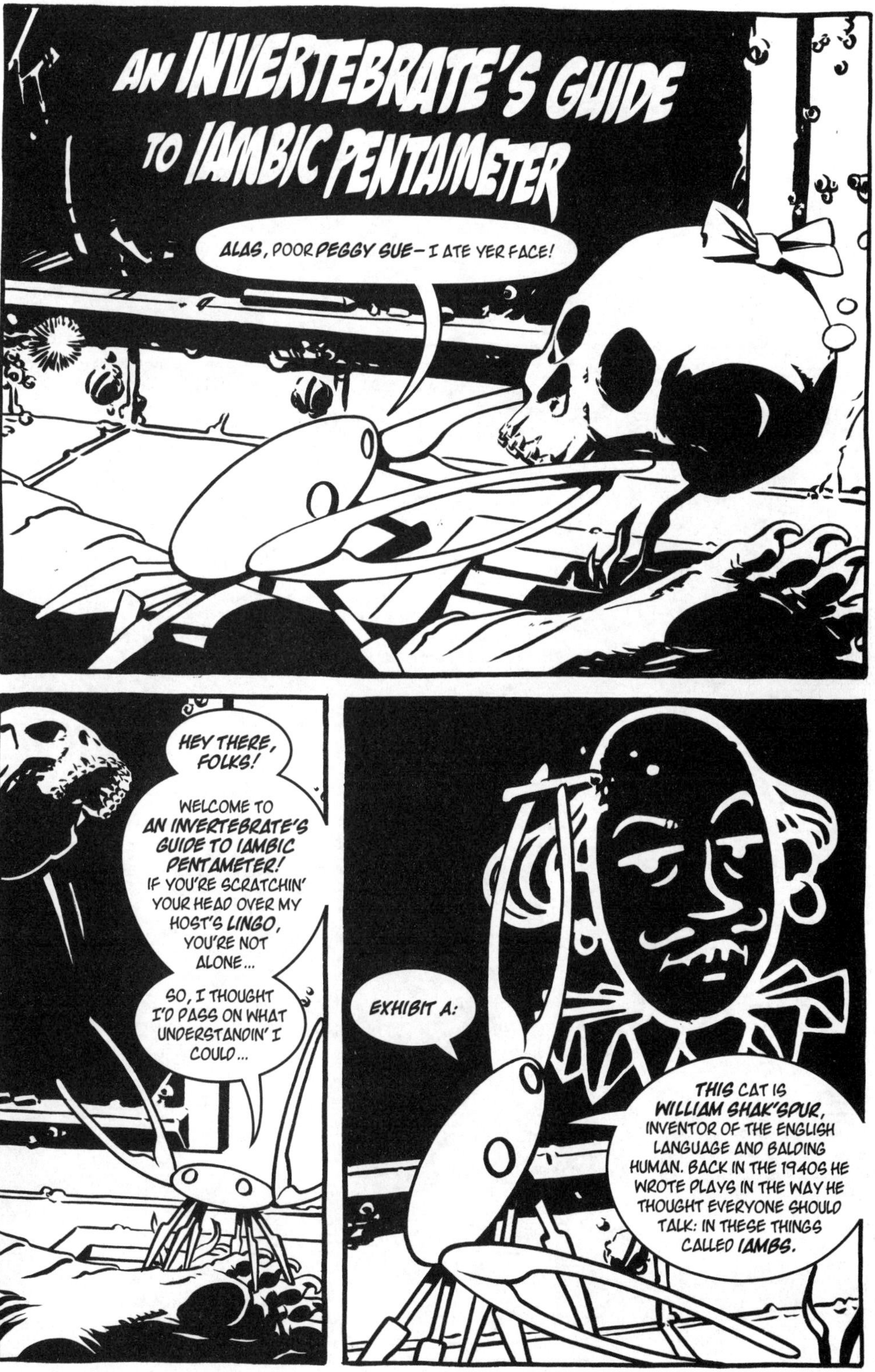
AN INVERTEBRATE'S GUIDE TO IAMBIC PENTAMETER
ALAS, POOR PEGGY SUE— I ATE YER FACE!
HEY THERE, FOLKS!
WELCOME TO AN INVERTEBRATE'S GUIDE TO IAMBIC PENTAMETER! IF YOU'RE SCRATCHIN' YOUR HEAD OVER MY HOST'S LINGO, YOU'RE NOT ALONE...
SO, I THOUGHT I'D PASS ON WHAT UNDERSTANDIN' I COULD...
EXHIBIT A:
THIS CAT IS WILLIAM SHAK'SPUR, INVENTOR OF THE ENGLISH LANGUAGE AND BALDING HUMAN. BACK IN THE 1940S HE WROTE PLAYS IN THE WAY HE THOUGHT EVERYONE SHOULD TALK: IN THESE THINGS CALLED IAMBS.

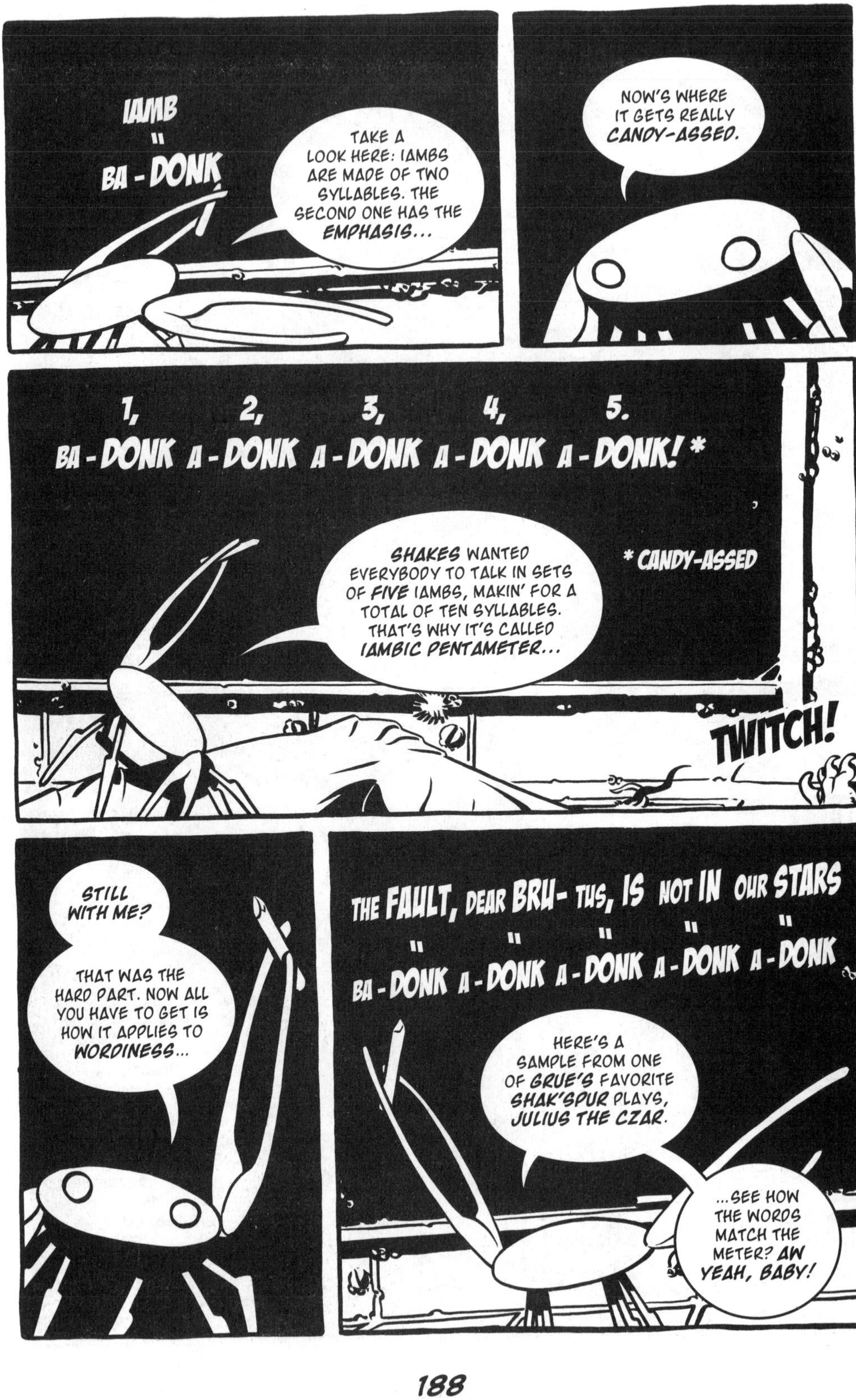
IAMB
"
BA-DONK
TAKE A LOOK HERE: IAMBS ARE MADE OF TWO SYLLABLES. THE SECOND ONE HAS THE EMPHASIS...
NOW'S WHERE IT GETS REALLY CANDY-ASSED.
1, 2, 3, 4, 5.
BA-DONK A-DONK A-DONK A-DONK A-DONK! *
SHAKES WANTED EVERYBODY TO TALK IN SETS OF FIVE IAMBS, MAKIN' FOR A TOTAL OF TEN SYLLABLES. THAT'S WHY IT'S CALLED IAMBIC PENTAMETER...
* CANDY-ASSED
TWITCH!
STILL WITH ME?
THAT WAS THE HARD PART. NOW ALL YOU HAVE TO GET IS HOW IT APPLIES TO WORDINESS...
THE FAULT, DEAR BRU- TUS, IS NOT IN OUR STARS
" " " " "
BA-DONK A-DONK A-DONK A-DONK A-DONK
HERE'S A SAMPLE FROM ONE OF GRUE'S FAVORITE SHAK'SPUR PLAYS, JULIUS THE CZAR.
...SEE HOW THE WORDS MATCH THE METER? AW YEAH, BABY!

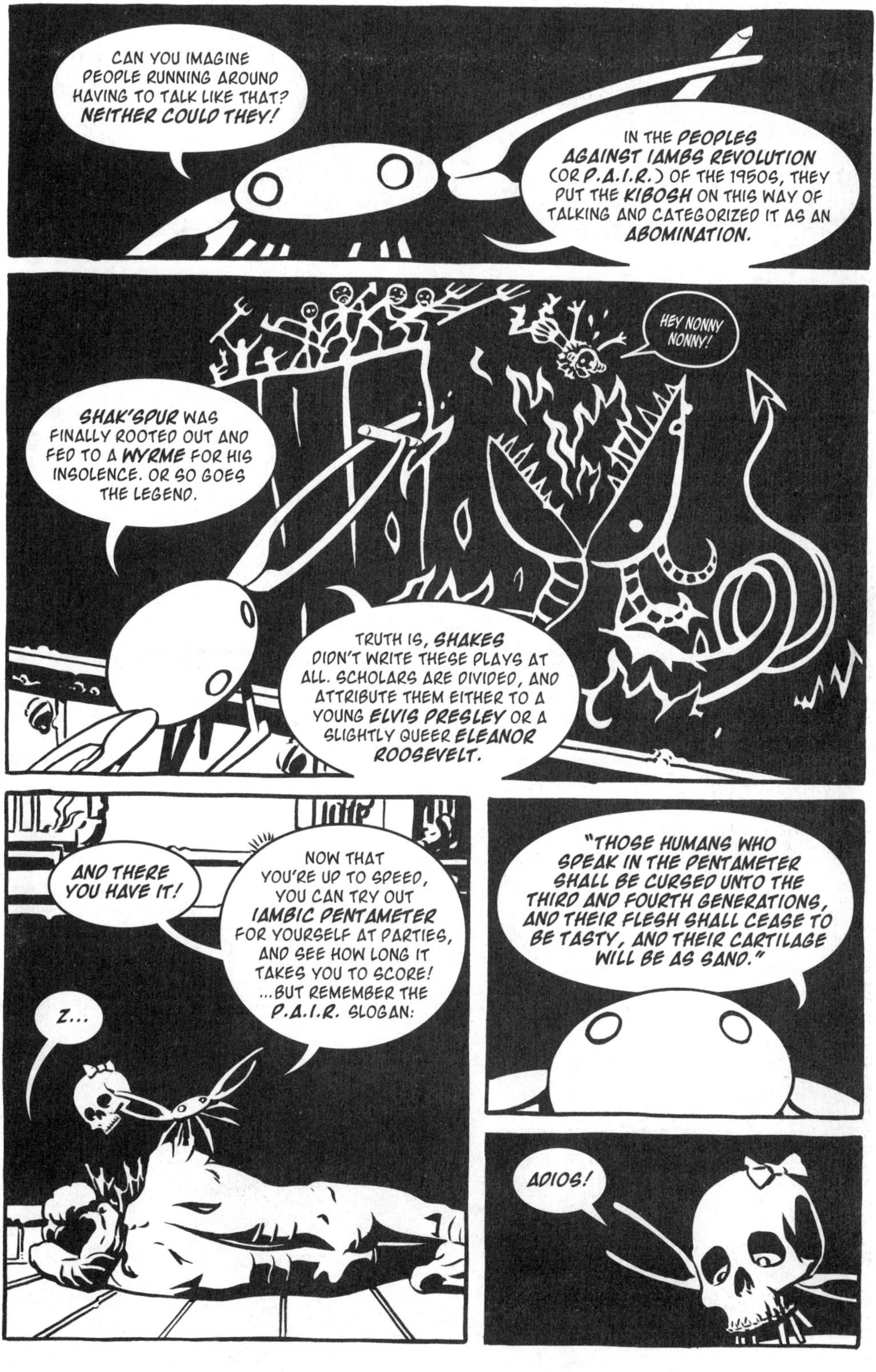
CAN YOU IMAGINE PEOPLE RUNNING AROUND HAVING TO TALK LIKE THAT? NEITHER COULD THEY!
IN THE PEOPLES AGAINST IAMBS REVOLUTION (OR P.A.I.R.) OF THE 1950S, THEY PUT THE KIBOSH ON THIS WAY OF TALKING AND CATEGORIZED IT AS AN ABOMINATION.
HEY NONNY NONNY!
SHAK'SPUR WAS FINALLY ROOTED OUT AND FED TO A WYRME FOR HIS INSOLENCE. OR SO GOES THE LEGEND.
TRUTH IS, SHAKES DIDN'T WRITE THESE PLAYS AT ALL. SCHOLARS ARE DIVIDED, AND ATTRIBUTE THEM EITHER TO A YOUNG ELVIS PRESLEY OR A SLIGHTLY QUEER ELEANOR ROOSEVELT.
AND THERE YOU HAVE IT!
NOW THAT YOU'RE UP TO SPEED, YOU CAN TRY OUT IAMBIC PENTAMETER FOR YOURSELF AT PARTIES, AND SEE HOW LONG IT TAKES YOU TO SCORE! ...BUT REMEMBER THE P.A.I.R. SLOGAN:
Z...
"THOSE HUMANS WHO SPEAK IN THE PENTAMETER SHALL BE CURSED UNTO THE THIRD AND FOURTH GENERATIONS, AND THEIR FLESH SHALL CEASE TO BE TASTY, AND THEIR CARTILAGE WILL BE AS SAND."
ADIOS!

Thanks:

Sarah Case
Alex Kamer
Team Kiki
Mom and Dad
Grandpa
Periscope Studio
Barbara Williams

and

Dave and Bonnie Zollner,
for giving me the best.